Foreword by **Iwan Baan**

CHINA DIALOGUES

Edited by **Vladimir Belogolovsky**

EDITIONS

**TONGJI
UNIVERSITY
PRESS**

ORO Editions
Publishers of Architecture, Art, and Design
Gordon Goff: Publisher

www.oroeditions.com
info@oroeditions.com

Published by ORO Editions

Author: Vladimir Belogolovsky
Foreword: Iwan Baan
Editor: Charles Linn
Book Design: Ahankara Art
Coordinator: Jialin (Crisie) Yuan
Managing Editor: Jake Anderson
10 9 8 7 6 5 4 3 2 1 First Edition

ISBN: 978-1-951541-62-0

Color Separations and Printing: ORO Group Ltd.

Printed in China.

ORO Editions makes a continuous effort to minimize the overall carbon footprint of its publications. As part of this goal, ORO Editions, in association with Global ReLeaf, arranges to plant trees to replace those used in the manufacturing of the paper produced for its books. Global ReLeaf is an international campaign run by American Forests, one of the world's oldest nonprofit conservation organizations. Global ReLeaf is American Forests' education and action program that helps individuals, organizations, agencies, and corporations improve the local and global environment by planting and caring for trees.

Cover Photo: UCCA Dune Art Museum, Aranya, Qinhuangdao, Hebei Province, 2018. Photo by Wu Qingshan
© OPEN Architecture

Foreword

BY IWAN BAAN

My introduction to China occurred in 2005, when I first flew to Beijing with Rem Koolhaas to start documenting the construction of his CCTV complex [001]. It was just about to go into construction then, and I proposed to Rem that I would document the whole process from start to finish. I felt that there was an interesting story to tell, which related to how Beijing was changing, how this massive project would impact the city. It was an interesting time for China, and I am glad I was there to record it. My background is in documentary photography and I had only started working documenting Rem's work in Europe and the U.S. one year before. We have similar interests in cities and public spaces. What I like most is depicting how people live. Photography is an amazing tool

that allows me to step into very different worlds to capture the life within. I am particularly fascinated with people's adaptability to different circumstances and their endless creativity in creating their own, unique environments. I am interested in documenting a whole spectrum of lifestyles–from within sleek and sophisticated structures and vernacular and humble places. I think the most interesting part starts when the architect has left, and people start to take over and explore the place how they see fit. I like to capture these moments. I like to discover things that are unforeseen and serendipitous.

What was particularly striking about building CCTV was the construction site itself, documenting how migrant workers from all over rural China lived

001 **OMA, CCTV Headquarters, Beijing, 2002-12** © Iwan Baan (2007)

right there by the thousands. There were at times 10,000 of them working and living on the site. They were building this grand, technologically advanced building, but the way they did it was largely by hand, using basic materials and techniques. The whole thing felt often so primitive, crude, and somewhat medieval. It was a community of people living on the construction site around the clock–working, resting, eating, conversing, watching TV, working again, and so on. That's what I was trying to capture. Every six to eight weeks I would go back, and that went on for a few years.

It was an incredible time to be able to experience Chinese cities' transformation on an epic scale, and because I was going to Beijing so frequently, I approached Jacques Herzog and Pierre de Meuron to document their Olympic Stadium, the Bird's Nest [002]. I also met Steven Holl and started working with him on the Linked Hybrid residential complex in Beijing [003] and his other projects in Shenzhen, Nanjing, and Chengdu. I eventually photographed all Zaha Hadid's buildings in China–in Beijing, Shanghai, and Guangzhou. I was fortunate to experience up close how these Western architects were making a great impact, as I went to China with them on multiple occasions. I always had my own space and time to explore these sites. Critics may complain that some of these buildings were not perfectly executed. But we need to stand back and realize where

5

002 Herzog & de Meuron, National Olympic Stadium (Bird's Nest), Beijing, 2003-08 © Iwan Baan

003 Steven Holl Architects, Linked Hybrid Housing, Beijing, 2003-09
© Iwan Baan

they were built, under what circumstances, on what scale, and of what complexity.

Given that, I think these buildings were a great success for China. These architects realized their lofty dreams in China. At that time, they could not have done such projects anywhere else in the world on that scale. That in itself is an incredible achievement.

On these trips I also started noticing very different kind of projects being built by local architects. They were the works by the very architects that Vladimir Belogolovsky met and interviewed for this book, *China Dialogues*. First, I met Wang Shu and his wife Lu Wenyu. At the time he did not speak English and we communicated mostly through Wenyu. I was fascinated by his architecture because it was so different from what I was used to see in China. Unlike many of the new construction projects in Chinese cities that follow the same strategy of building from scratch, here was this local architect who resisted that tendency and tried to do his architecture differently.

Or, for instance the Jinhua Architecture Park in Jinhua near Hangzhou, a micro city of 17 pavilions scattered along the banks of the river Wu [004]. They were

designed both by architects from China and around the world. They were all brought together by Ai Weiwei. Apart from Wang Shu there were such locals as Liu Jiakun and Xu Tiantian. Throughout my travels in China, I met other architects like Zhu Pei, Zhang Lei of AZL Architects, URBANUS, and Ma Yansong of MAD Architects. I worked with Ma Yansong on many of his projects and I documented the construction of Harbin Opera House [106].

But working with Wang Shu remains my closest collaboration in China. Over the years, I documented all

004 Fernando Romero, Bridging Teahouse, Jinhua Architecture Park, Jinhua, Zhejiang Province, 2014 © Iwan Baan

his buildings there, and we worked on many publications and his only monograph (Lars Müller, 2017). I find his work incredibly refreshing, particularly the way he combines his knowledge of Chinese culture, building materials, and techniques and incorporates them in very original and contemporary ways. Shu understands the difficulties of building in China. He is very selective about focusing on what he wants to articulate, understanding that certain details or finishes can't be achieved. He brings a traditional understanding of Chinese architecture to the new era.

One of my favorite projects is his Academy of Art, Xiangshan Campus in Hangzhou [005-008], because he has been working there for so many years. These buildings are completely embraced by the students. They are great for working and studying. There is nothing polished or pristine about them. These spaces are sometimes rough and can be beat up by art students, and the whole campus feels like a small city. The buildings are not just singular freestanding structures, but are experienced as a single organism of interconnected creatures. They are intertwined with each other and the landscape all around. Now

005 Xiangshan Campus, China Academy of Art, Hangzhou, Phase II, 2004-07 © Iwan Baan

he is working on many projects throughout China and the quality is getting better and better. He is able to push clients into his direction and buildings are becoming more complex. He keeps exploring his idea that every project is a little village where every nook and cranny is completely different. All of his buildings are independent, confident, and surprising.

What is especially rewarding about traveling in China is exploring the country's rich and very diverse history. There is such an incredible variety of vernacular architecture in terms of building materials, methods, and understandings of space. There are many building techniques based on local materials,

traditions, culture, topography, and so on. Every place is a discovery. But much of that is now being lost due to the breakneck speed of development. It is the disappearance of such rich culture that gives me pressure to document it as much as I can every time I go to China.

The historic Tulou Housing in Yongding in Fujian Province [009] is among the most memorable places that I had a chance to visit. This is where the Hakka people live in round multi-family fortress-like buildings that are made of stone, earth, and timber. Some of them were given World Heritage listings. Then there are underground houses in the north that are called yaodong, which means a house cave, an earth

006 Xiangshan Campus, China Academy of Art, Hangzhou, Phase II 2004-07 © Iwan Baan

007 Xiangshan Campus, China Academy of Art, Hangzhou, Phase II 2004-07 © Iwan Baan

008 Wang Shu of Amateur Architecture Studio, Xiangshan Campus, China Academy of Art, Hangzhou, Phases I & II, III 2002-13 © Iwan Baan

009 Tulou Housing, Yongding, Fujian Province © Iwan Baan

010 Underground dwellings, Sanmenxia, Henan Province © Iwan Baan

011 Underground dwellings, Sanmenxia, Henan Province © Iwan Baan

shelter dwelling [010-012]. These houses are excavated horizontally from a sunken courtyard in the center. Other buildings I came across on the East Coast of Shandong province are distinguished by high-pitched roofs, all covered in dry plants. They are called seaweed bungalows and are designed to keep the interior warm in winter and cool in summer. Then there are incredible mud houses in Xinjiang province in the west part of the country. Each province presents very different thinking about architecture.

Unfortunately, many of these unique structures are disappearing. Demolition is occurring all over China–from hutongs in Beijing to ancient housing projects on the outskirts of many provincial cities. Structures that are preserved often become tourist hot spots and tend to lose their authentic character. For a long time, I tried to go to Ürümqi, the capital of Xinjiang Uyghur Autonomous Region. There used to be an incredible citadel entirely built out of mud. Finally, when I was able to go there, I discovered that it was entirely razed and parts of it were being rebuilt

012 Underground dwellings, Sanmenxia, Henan Province © Iwan Baan

as a replica. Such demolition is reasoned as the only way to protect these fragile, and therefore unsafe, structures.

So often these unique buildings are being bull-dozed and reconstructed as fake concrete versions. Authenticity is being lost. It is heartbreaking to see that kind of destruction. Very little real history is being preserved. Recently, this attitude is beginning to change, but for so many places it is too late. What's fascinating about all these buildings is that they are built by hand, all from the most local materials, with great knowledge of what you can do with very specif-ic materials right from the site. Nothing is mass-pro-duced, but, of course, these structures need to be repaired by hand, by people who understand the traditional building techniques, something which is vanishing quickly. There is an incredible beauty in these spaces, which is being lost. Naturally, I have a sense of urgency, a mission of sort, to document these unique places as much as possible.

In the '90s,
We All Became Free
AN INTRODUCTION BY VLADIMIR BELOGOLOVSKY

EVEN WITHOUT FLOWERS AND TREES
IT WOULD STILL MAKE A GARDEN

TONG Jun (TUNG Chuin, 1900-83)
Glimpses of Gardens in Eastern China

TO ME, ANY TYPE OF ARCHITECTURE,
NO MATTER WHAT ITS FUNCTION,
IS A HOUSE.

WANG Shu
Imagining the House

I first went to China in 2002, a year after the International Olympic Committee awarded the 2008 Summer Games to Beijing. That initial trip was about exploring nature, cuisine, ancient temples, archeological sites, and, in general, experiencing lifestyles in China, mainly outside of its major cities. I was motivated by the pure curiosity of a Western tourist driven to an Eastern country in search of the old world, the exotic, hoping to catch a glimpse of a rich traditional culture on the cusp of its inevitable radical transformation. At the time, there was no modern, or rather contemporary, architecture in China to speak of. There were only the promising first hints of the development of a potentially new architectural language being undertaken by just a handful of independent architects almost entirely under radar at that time.

Speaking of modern architecture in China, virtually all buildings built there during the 20th century, no matter how distinctive and compelling, were derivative one way or another. No architectural masterpieces were created in China in the entire 20th century either by local or foreign masters. It was a combination of factors, including the weight of millennia-old Chinese history, the Chinese Civil War (1927-49), wars with Japan, the Cultural Revolution, and the country's prolonged isolation from much of the world that held its architecture from the eventual entry into the modern period for so long.

When China finally ascended onto the world's stage it did so with a bang [013]. And it was architecture that gave its many achievements a tangible substance. The Beijing Olympics in 2008 and Shanghai Expo in 2010 came off spectacularly. One ambitious development followed another, encouraging hundreds of millions of Chinese to relocate from sleepy villages to roaring cities. We now no longer seem to be surprised by the sheer scale and complexity of the kinds of engineering and architectural projects that today are more likely to take place in China than anywhere else on the planet.

We have become accustomed to the spectacular buildings and infrastructure being built there: CCTV

013 **CBD Under Construction, Beijing, 2017. Photo by Vladimir Belogolovsky**

by Rem Koolhaas (2002-12), the Bird's Nest Olympic Stadium by Herzog & de Meuron (2002-08), the Linked Hybrid residential complex in Beijing (2003-09) and Vanke Center in Shenzhen (2006-09) both by Steven Holl, Raffles City in Chongqing (2013-20) by Moshe Safdie, and the National Centre for the Performing Arts by Paul Andreu in Beijing (1999-2007). And there are the transportation projects: airports in Beijing by Zaha Hadid (2014-19) and Norman Foster (2003-08), and train stations by Terry Farrell in Beijing (2005-08) and Guangzhou (2007-10), and by GMP in Hangzhou (2011-18) and Tianjin (2007-11). These are remarkable achievements.

Numerous other eye-catching buildings have been implanted into cities we never even heard of until very recently. For over a decade now China has served as a fantastic playground for world's top architects, particularly from Western Europe and the United States. These projects are all significant milestones for global architecture. Yet, something else has occurred since the turn of the century, notably over the last decade: China, not only embraced cutting-edge architecture by welcoming and commissioning starchitects, it succeeded in forming its own architectural identity in the process. In the span of the last two decades it has produced a whole new constellation of local architects who have accumulated diverse

portfolios and developed their highly original voices. More so, it is quite clear now that the most thoughtful, relevant, and original architecture in China today is being produced by the local architects.

These changes were enabled by the aggressive and transformative learning curve that the architectural profession in China went through. It is critical to realize that all the aforementioned and other outstanding projects designed by foreign designers were actually drawn by architects at the state-run Local Design Institutes (LDIs). They collaborated intently, while receiving invaluable first-hand experience directly under the stewardship of world's most accomplished masters. Paralleling that, many Chinese architects had a chance to acquire first-rate educations at the leading American and European universities. Once they apprenticed in the West, they rushed back to start their own independent practices.

The cumulative work they produced since the turn of the century can now be identified as distinctly Chinese architecture, not vernacular, but uncompromisingly rooted in Modernist traditions. This book puts together a collection of my interviews with founders of 21 of China's leading architectural studios. They were selected out of more than 30 interviews that I conducted over the last several years. I had a chance to meet with these pioneers—with some multiple times–to discuss their intentions, preferences, anxieties, and visions. But before turning to these intimate conversations, let us go over some of the origins of China's modern architecture and identify the most influential contemporary highpoints– both in terms of events and buildings.

MODERN ORIGINS

Surely, the first modern building in the country should be identified as the Sun Yat-sen Mausoleum in Nanjing [014]. Finished in 1929, this enormous complex, reclining at the foot of the second peak of Purple Mountain, memorializes the nation's father. Somewhat a nod to Mayan pyramids, the memorial was designed by Shanghai-based architect LÜ Yanzhi (1894–1929). Lü was trained at Cornell University, apprenticed in America, and established the first Chinese-owned architectural practice. His Mausoleum won an open international competition that specifically asked participants to design their anonymous proposals in "traditional Chinese style that would also evoke a modern design with special memorial substance."

The architect who is referred to as the Father of Modern Chinese architecture is LIANG Sicheng (1901-72). Trained at the University of Pennsylvania under Paul Cret, Liang is known for his restoration projects on cultural heritage sites and his active role in advocating for preserving much of the old Beijing, including a half-a-millennium-old inner-city wall, now demolished, that he envisioned as an elevated linear park. In his new designs, he tried to develop a national style of architecture. Together with his wife LIN Huiyin (Phyllis LIN, 1904-55), the first female architect in modern China, who was also a poet, he surveyed many important ancient buildings that led to discovering what they called the "Grammar of Chinese Architecture." Liang was the author of *Chinese Architecture, A Pictorial History*, which he wrote in English for a Western audience. He was also the founder of Architecture Departments at Northeastern University in Shenyang (1929) and Tsinghua University in Beijing (1946).

It is apt to mention here that historically, China did not have architects as in the West. There wasn't

014 Lü Yanzhi, Sun Yat-sen Mausoleum, Nanjing, 1929
Photo by Alex Ystanov

even a word for "architect" in classical Chinese language. Buildings were designed and built by craftsmen-builders. Scholars such as poets, painters, philosophers, or court officials did not mix with carpenters and masons who were often uneducated, and their work was almost always anonymous. They diligently guarded their building techniques and passed the acquired skills directly to their apprentices. It was an effective way to keep the accumulated knowledge inside each community.

Architectural education in China started only in the 1920s. Lü, Liang, and Lin belong to the very first generation of Chinese architects. All these architects were educated in the United States, most at the University of Pennsylvania, at a time when American education followed the Beaux Arts principles developed in France. Meanwhile, Europe was already moving far ahead, particularly following the example of the Bauhaus in Germany led by the groundbreaking theories and projects of Le Corbusier, Walter Gropius, and Mies van der Rohe. But it was the Beaux Arts tradition that was taught to the Chinese students and that's the model that became widely imitated by Chinese universities with their focus on exploring and finding ways of combining "modern" and "Chinese" elements of architecture. By early 1950s, there were fewer than a dozen universities offering architectural degrees. There are now more than 300.

The campus of Tsinghua University is home to a number of modern buildings that illustrate well various references for Chinese architects throughout the 1900s. The Old Gate followed a Palladian prototype (originally built in 1909, it fell victim to the Cultural Revolution and was rebuilt in 1991). The Grand Auditorium of 1917 was designed as a version of Jeffersonian architecture. Mid-century facilities and residential blocks are distinguished by a mixture of features, from classical and traditional Chinese motifs to Stalin-era décor. The Main Building (1968), a symmetrical composition of interconnected administrative blocks, is a flattened and stripped-down version of the Moscow State University building of 1953.

Examples of important modern architecture can be found throughout China. Apart from Shanghai and Beijing they were also built in Nanjing, Tianjin, Guangzhou, Shenyang, and Chongqing, but let's focus on the two major cities. The Bund, a stretch of embanked riverfront along the Huangpu River in Shanghai, is widely known for two dozen magnificent buildings–banks, trading houses, clubs, insurance and petroleum companies, and hotels built in from the 1850s through the 1930s by reputable commercial corporations headquartered in the United Kingdom, France, Russia, Italy, Germany, the Netherlands, Japan, and the United States.

These opulent structures were proudly designed in a variety of European styles–from Renaissance and Baroque Revival to Beaux Arts and Art Deco–by international architectural practices, typically led by British or American architects. The most famous of these firms, Hong Kong-based Palmer & Turner, which was the architect of the iconic Peace Hotel (the former Sassoon House, 1929), is still in operation. Other prominent foreign practices included Lester, Johnson & Morriss, Hazzard & Phillips, and famous Hungarian-Slovak architect László Hudec (1893-1958) whose Park Hotel Shanghai (1934) is among the city's most iconic Art Deco structures. Inspired by the American Radiator Building (1924) in New York this dark, 22-story tower remained the tallest building in Asia until the mid-1960s.

When dozens of freshly trained and patriotically-minded Chinese architects started coming back home in the late 1920s and throughout the 1930s, the dominance of foreign architects based in Shanghai and other cities was about to end. These architects were ready to play a major role in building the new nation and developing a new kind of architecture that would aim at expressing both national identity and new modern sensitivities. The Bank of China Building (1937), on the Bund right next to the Peace Hotel, is an important example of the so-called Chinese Art Deco style, a rare mixture of Western and Asian features [015]. The building was designed by Palmer & Turner in collaboration with Hong Kong-born architect Luke Him Sau (Lu Qianshou). Walking in front of this high-rise may not reveal much of a difference from its neighboring European buildings, but a glance from across the street shows a striking contrast. It is one of the earliest examples of a traditional Chinese roof being placed over what is essentially a modern building. The result is quite disingenuous: it disregards the most fundamental construction principles of traditional Chinese architecture.

Attempts to combine Western buildings and Chinese roofs had been undertaken before, but they were done on a much smaller scale with more thoughtful and sensitive results. The issue here is that Chinese architecture is based on a post-and-beam scaffolding system. That's the structure that holds the roof, while walls below are independently erected. The idea of non-load bearing facades and freestanding interior partitions, at least on the scale of tall buildings, was only introduced in the West in late 1800s, when skeleton frame office buildings began to be constructed in Chicago, making load-bearing walls unnecessary. Simply placing Chinese roofs on top of Western buildings, ignoring the intricate wood-frame building technique and hiding the structure behind curtainwall facades, clashes conceptually, culturally, and aesthetically. That kind of unnatural juxtaposition can only produce very superficial buildings that project purely decorative symbols, wrongly proportioned, and grossly oversimplified.

Architecture rarely follows a single ideology. Even individual careers go through multiple turns, twists, and U-turns. In the interwar period Shanghai became the stage for all kinds of architectural tastes and fashions. There were those who searched for new ways to express China's national character. Others continued following long-established traditional canons. And then there were those who explored modernity inspired by new ideas coming from Europe, especially since there were tens of thousands of European refugees escaping Bolshevism and Nazism. The city was also flooded with many thousands of Chinese refugees fleeing the Civil War and the Japanese invasion. Shanghai was a booming city, turning rapidly into a modern metropolis. Its new buildings–apartment blocks, nightclubs, cinemas, and villas – expressed streamlined Modernist forms underlined by chic curved lines. And numerous office buildings, banks, hotels, and department stores graced the city with their towering silhouettes of multiple setbacks, evoking their American prototypes.

The most prolific architectural firms started by the returned Chinese students included Zhuang Jun Architects, Doon Da Yu Architects, Fan Wenzhao Architects, and the Allied Architects. Zhuang Jun and Doon Da Yu were elected as presidents of the Chinese Institute of Architects in the 1920s and '30s, and after 1949, when the Chinese Communist Party came to power, they, as well as other owners of independent practices, were employed by the newly formed, government-run Local Design Institutes (LDIs). In contrast, Fan Wenzhao fled the country for Hong Kong where he continued practicing.

The next important architectural milestone became a group of so-called Ten Great Buildings completed in Beijing in 1959 to commemorate the tenth anniversary of the founding of the People's Republic of China. Among them are the Great Hall of the People and the Chinese Revolution and History Museum (today the National Museum of China) that face each other in Tiananmen Square, the Chinese People's Revolutionary Military Museum, Beijing Railways Station, and Gongti Stadium or Workers' Stadium (demolished in 2020 and currently being rebuilt to host the 2023 Asian Football Confederation Asian Cup). All these stately edifices that marked the ambition of building a new, modern capital were designed by Beijing Institute of Architectural Design (BIAD, est. 1949). They were closely modeled on the

015 Palmer & Turner with Luke Him Sau, Bank of China Building, Shanghai, 1937. Photo by Zhang Xuefei

Soviet Socialist Realism style, although their décor is somewhat restrained due to limited resources available at the time.

Another politically and architecturally significant structure, is the Mausoleum of Mao Zedong (1977), the final resting place of Chairman Mao. The building is a fundamentally modern structure situated in the middle of Tiananmen Square. Symbolically, it is constructed out of a range of materials brought from all over China, including water and sand from the Taiwan Straits, and distinguished by its double-eaved flat roof. Its design is much closer in spirit to sleek mid-Century modern American examples than to the previously popular Soviet prototypes. The shift followed President Richard Nixon's 1972 visit to China and was a reflection of the times when

016 I.M. Pei, Fragrant Hill Hotel, Beijing, 1982 © C.C.Pei

the United States and China began moving closer to one another politically, economically, and culturally. The building's design aspirations can be traced particularly to one of the most representative works by American architect Edward Durell Stone, the John F. Kennedy Center for the Performing Arts in Washington, D.C. (1962).

One influential structure, without which this rather brief list of modern-era Chinese buildings would surely be incomplete, is the Fragrant Hill Hotel (1982) designed by I.M. Pei and built on the outskirts of Beijing [016]. It was the first attempt in China to build a modern, exemplary structure following Deng Xiaoping's initiative to open up the country to foreign investment and the global market in 1978. The Chinese-American architect was initially asked to design a high-rise hotel in central Beijing. He retreated by taking a more cautionary approach, choosing a site in the vicinity of the Summer Palace, situated between the current 4th and 5th Ring Roads.

The building is a timid pursuit of trying to marry Chinese vernacular with modern architecture by bringing in references of traditional roof design and decorative stone facade patterns around generously spaced windows. The result—a simplified hybrid of a box-like modern building with a thin layer of folkloric décor topped by a coy version of a traditional Chinese roof—has little to do with modernity or the architect's own work either before or since. Pei's ambivalent exercise in post-modernist style was rather a watered-down version of some of the government complexes in Beijing of the 1950s, distinguished by prominently expressed Chinese roofs or "Chinese hats." These buildings were already viewed as exemplary by LDIs. The most characteristic of them is the Sanlihe Government Complex by Zhang Kaiji in Beijing of 1955 [017]. The building recalls an enlarged section of the Great Wall with watchtowers at its center and at each end. Once the world-famous American modernist Pei confirmed the validity of such projects there was little need to question the direction that by then had grown into a trend anyway.

Pei's compromised design called for a need to identify first what could embody the Chinese in architecture, before offering a potential alternative of a modern attitude. The nostalgic image of the Fragrant Hill Hotel did for China what Daniel Burnham's 1893 World's Colombian Exhibition in Chicago had done for America. In both cases sentimental-looking buildings diverted local architects' focus from their search

017 Zhang Kaiji, Sanlihe Government Complex, Beijing, 1955 © Nancy Steinhardt

for what could potentially become the modern project, freeing themselves from limitations of the symbolic past, similar to the way Western architects freed themselves from the pediments of the Classical period in the beginning of the 20th century. Thus, Pei's hotel became accepted as one of the mainstream prototypes for the next 20 years.

A year after Pei's building was completed, Chen Xitong (1930-2013) became Beijing's mayor. In the midst of the building boom that started in the late '80s, he issued an ordinance requiring all new structures to be capped with the Chinese roofs. These pseudo-traditional features were nicknamed "Xitong hats." The practice continued until mid-1990s when Chen Xitong was dismissed and sent to prison on charges of corruption. The buildings that sprouted in the capital during Chen's time in power still define his epoch.

Curiously, the construction of the aforementioned Bank of China Building in Shanghai was headed by Tsuyee Pei. He was then both the manager of the Head Office Overseas Department and the Shanghai Branch, and in the 1940s became the general manager of the Bank of China. He was also the father of I.M. Pei. The younger Pei eventually designed two

more buildings for the Bank of China, in Hong Kong (1990) and in Beijing (1999). Neither example ventured into the appropriation of traditional Chinese features and, instead, relied on Pei's own abstracted geometric language, confirming that his earlier Fragrant Hill Hotel was a compromise not worth repeating.

Finally, before the 20th century came to a close, there was one more attempt to find an appropriate solution for a modern Chinese building, again a tower. The 88-story Jin Mao Tower of 1999 was undertaken by an American architect, Adrian Smith, then with Skidmore, Owings & Merrill (SOM). The 420-meter-high building, China's tallest at the time, is in the Pudong New Area in Shanghai and was designed to evoke the forms of a Chinese pagoda. The building is a prominent example in a series of shots at creating an Asian cultural identity. A few years earlier, César Pelli's Petronas Towers in Kuala Lumpur, Malaysia (1996), was designed to resemble Islamic motifs. And a few years later Taipei 101, the world's tallest building when completed in 2004, was designed as another version of a pagoda by American-trained Taiwanese architect C.P. Wang of C.Y. Lee & Partners. However, unlike the Fragrant Hill Hotel, the Jin Mao

Tower did not attract much of a following in China and it has not become a prototype. The solution to the problem of what constitutes Chinese modern architecture was eventually found by the local architects themselves who realized that the answer would have to be indirect and subtle, in other words, not form-driven.

018 Wang Shu of Amateur Architecture Studio, Library of Wenzheng College, Suzhou University, 2000. Photo by Lu Wenyu
Courtesy of Amateur Architecture Studio

THE CONTEMPORARY PERIOD;
THE PIONEERS

The earliest deliberate attempts to create uncompromisingly modern works of architecture in China were undertaken by the Hangzhou-based architect WANG Shu (b. 1963). He experimented with small-scale projects for about a decade, between 1988, when he graduated from Nanjing Institute of Technology, and 1997, when he opened an independent practice, Amateur Architecture Studio with his wife LU Wenyu (b. 1967). Those projects reflected Wang's interests in deconstructivist architecture, which can still be felt in his contorted and disjunctive forms, cavities, and erratically juxtaposed materials. His Library of Wenzheng College at Suzhou University of 2000 is thoroughly modern, a poetic pavilion-like

contemplative structure on a lake [018]. It is arguably the first pure modernist or rather neo-modernist project in China, although, in our interview Wang emphasized that he sees this project as post-modernist. Its references are multiple–from Aldo Rossi and Richard Meier to Alvaro Siza and Tadao Ando, and to Chinese traditional gardens and pavilions. Yet, none are explicit or literal. The building is the first major independent architectural statement by any Chinese architect that does not rely on direct historical prototypes. In our interview, Wang discussed his transition from what the architect calls his white period–when he followed abstracted Western models–to a black or rather dark period, referring to the natural colors of the traditional materials utilized in his buildings–soil, bricks, pottery plates, and tiles.

Wang's dark period is best represented by three key projects. The first is the regeneration of Wencun Village in Zhejiang province (2012-16), a strategic design of public squares, bridges, and insertions of two dozen houses and small inns into the village's historical fabric [019,034]. The second is the Xiangshan Campus at the China Academy of Art in Hangzhou, a collection of 30 academic buildings completed between 2004 and 2013 [005-008]. And the third, the Ningbo History Museum, built in 2008 [020].

Out of these three large public works it is the Museum that expresses its design most clearly as a manifesto, a personal stance. It is at once a manifestation of strong aesthetics and ethics. The building's enigmatic form evokes a medieval fortress surrounded by a moat. But its greatest impact is on its multifaceted surface, largely covered by a mosaic of beautifully arranged gray, brown, and red bricks and tiles salvaged from dozens of old villages that were demolished in the area, now occupied by the Museum. Wang clarified his intent, "I want to build a small town with its own life, which could once again, wake up the latent memory of the city." Not only is the result a stunning work of art, it communicates a very strong message to opportunistic developers: Stop demolishing our heritage! Look how beautiful it is! Among the Museum's visitors are those displaced villagers who come here to reconnect with their past both spiritually and literally.

019 Regeneration of Wencun Village, Zhejiang Province, 2012-16. Photo by Lu Wenyu © Amateur Architecture Studio

Using architecture as a tool of resistance (his term) on such grand scale and with such compelling prowess, the Ningbo History Museum, completed the same year as the Olympic venues, designed by the starchitects, has become the embodiment of an alternative way for many local architects. In fact, it is their most dominating reference, a spiritual anchor of contemporary Chinese architecture. Over the last decade, working with either salvaged or brand-new traditional materials in contemporary ways has turned into the single most recurring theme in the work of many Chinese architects. In fact, it is the use of traditional materials, most apparently in the countryside, that now constitutes contemporary Chinese architecture's identity. Wang's contribution here is twofold. On the one hand, he reinstated the value of everything traditional, and on the other, his ingenious imagination unleashed boundless creative exploration for spatial, structural, and material originality.

The architect's Wa Shan Guesthouse for the Xiangshan Campus at China Academy of Art in Hangzhou (2013), is a case in point [030-033]. A

020 Ningbo History Museum, Ningbo, 2008 © Iwan Baan

021 Atelier FCJZ, Split House, Beijing, 2002 © Fu Xing

social-cum-conference center, hotel, and dining hall, this labyrinthian, creature-like building is covered by a single, multifold roof, turned into an adventurous attraction for viewing by means of an idiosyncratic system of zigzagging ramps, stairs, landing platforms, and bridges. The building enables these chaotic passages and links to carry visitors both under and above the roof with seemingly just one purpose–to showcase itself. Everything here is an invention. There is a cloud of geodesic dome-like wooden struts that sprawl in every direction in a noble effort to hold up the roof, but in reality, it is held up by a disguised framework of reinforced concrete and steel supports. Still, this seemingly redundant wood structure creates a series of wonderfully baroque, Piranesian spaces. The whole building provides an entirely original and emotionally charged experience, evoking some of the best works by such inventive and self-referential European architects as Carlo Scarpa and Enric Miralles.

Another early critical project is the "Commune by the Wall" development, a boutique resort originally made up of 12 villas built in 2002, next to popular Badaling section of the Great Wall. It was eventually expanded to 40 villas (regrettably, these additional houses were poorly built clones of the original 12) and other public buildings. The project came from the initiative of Zhang Xin and Pan Shiyi, the developer and property-tycoon couple behind SOHO China, the largest developer in the country, who also have prime commercial and office assets in Beijing and Shanghai. As an active architectural patron, Zhang has been a key force behind the hiring of celebrity architects, most notably Zaha Hadid, for many of the company's subsequent commercial developments, in particular office buildings and shopping malls.

For the Commune, Zhang originally invited 12 up-and-coming Asian architects from China, Hong Kong, Taiwan, Japan, South Korea, Thailand, and Singapore to each design a villa with a one-million dollar budget. The innovative houses, designed by the likes

26

public wing

private wing

022 Split House, Beijing, 2002. 1st Floor Plan. Courtesy of Atelier FCJZ

of Shigeru Ban, Kengo Kuma, and Gary Chang, were built to test whether progressive architecture could be used as a marketing tool. Needless to say, that the model proved to be highly effective.

One of the original 12 villas, the "Split House" [021-023] was designed by a local architect Yung Ho CHANG (b. 1956). The house is an uncompromisingly modern and concept-driven structure. Entirely stripped of typical traditional Chinese formal references and décor, the Split House is among the first self-confident works that refused to follow the expected nationalistic model that the Chinese architects were pursuing so diligently for a good part of the 20th century. During our interview at the architect's Beijing studio, Chang told me, "I don't think the world of architecture should be divided into East and West. I want to think of it as divided into north and south climatically, not culturally." The house is a conceptual work. The title comes from a physical rending that splits its volume into two halves, forming an open courtyard to save the existing trees

023 Atelier FCJZ, Split House, Beijing, 2002 © Asakawa Satoshi

27

and bring nature within, quite literally: the glass floor at the entry area hovers right over the creek [023]. The house is conceived as a variation of a flexible prototype, which surely was the architect's response to the client's vision of eventually building additional copies of the original villas.

Chang's ingenious idea anticipated different angles between the two halves to be adjusted to a particular topography. The house is envisioned in at least nine distinct designs–a single volume house (with no split), a house with two parallel bars, one with two bars at an angle, a right-angle house, a single volume back-to-back house, and so on. Yet, only the original version of the house was built. Perhaps the whole point of Chang's elaborate site-specific exercise was undertaken to make sure that no two Split Houses would be exactly the same. To complete the architect's elegant concept, the house serves as an environmental model: it is built out of rammed earth walls and timber framing, and can be quickly taken apart or, if abandoned, eventually will disintegrate and disappear back into nature.

Yung Ho Chang's work is discussed in greater detail in this book. He is rightfully referred to as the father of contemporary architecture in China. His independent practice Atelier FCJZ, which he started with his wife Lijia LU (b. 1960) in 1993, is modern China's first independent architectural studio. It laid the foundation for contemporary practice in the country. Chang spent years of teaching at the leading universities in China where he founded and headed the architecture program at Peking University. He was a professor at Harvard's GSD and headed the MIT School of Architecture from 2005 to 2010. In 2012, the architect was invited to join the Pritzker Prize Jury. He was instrumental in awarding that year's Prize to Wang Shu who became the first, and so far, the only Chinese citizen to win the profession's highest honor.

Another important independent architect and educator, Qingyun MA (b. 1965) founded his practice, MADA s.p.a.m., in New York in 1996 and moved to Shanghai in 1999. He also taught in China, Europe, and the U.S. at the time and was the dean at the University of Southern California School of

024 Qingyun Ma, Father's House, Lantian County, 1992-2002. Photo by Qingyun Ma

Architecture from 2007 to 2017. Ma's earliest and most palpable project is his Father's House in Lantian County on the outskirts of Xi'an [024]. Completed in 2002, it is the result of a decade-long design and construction process. This introspective structure, tucked into a gentle slope of a green valley, is an intense hybrid of an unadorned modern reinforced-concrete frame, vernacular looking floor-to-ceiling timber shutter panels, and smooth pebbles from a nearby river. The result achieves an appealing visual coherence. It is reminiscent of Herzog & de Meuron's Stone House (1982-88, Tavole, Italy) where the architects in-filled the exposed, reinforced-concrete frame with dry stones, leaving part of it open to accentuate the abstract nature of the structural grid. The Xi'an version is more compact and closed off building, like a secluded monastery. Even a single-lane lap pool is inscribed tightly into a rectangular courtyard with tall stone walls on all sides. Unfortunately, I was not able to discuss Ma's intentions in person.

Chengdu architect LIU Jiakun (b. 1956) is a pioneering master who dedicated his practice to the revival of traditional materials and skills. Liu's much celebrated Rebirth Brick project, initiated after the 2008 Sichuan earthquake, was based on producing bricks and cement blocks from the rubble of damaged buildings to facilitate "rebirth" of culture and place [091]. The project earned him a reputation as the "architect of memory." Another one of his important projects is an attempt to reverse the erosion of public spaces in China by rethinking the urban residential block. His West Village development, realized at the architect's hometown in 2015, is an inventive solution that has the potential to become a new urban prototype, perhaps even for cities beyond China [093-095]. This six-story residential, cultural, commercial, and sports complex, with a publicly accessible bicycle and pedestrian rooftop promenade along its perimeter, is a dense development that revives the healthy sense of a vibrant community.

Speaking of his fellow Chinese architects, Liu told me, "I think what we all have in common is a certain hunger for learning and opening up to many ideas that were out of reach before. And most of these architects were exposed to living and studying abroad for many years before coming back, so their work was infused by what they have learned overseas. And there was a kind of urgency to innovate and build after a long period of official government-approved style. Then in the '90s, we all became free."

Another of Liu's passages describes China's rush for modernization, which has taken its cities by storm, as his and all Chinese architects' personal challenge. "The city grows madly, memories are vanishing, public space has been slowly eroded, as are the genius loci and conventional lifestyles. Is it possible to transfer the all-consuming nature of capitalism into a win-win case of sharing, and thriving on the gathering of the often-overlooked contents of daily life? To regain the initiative of today's vulnerable public spaces? To keep up the traditional cultural genes in contemporary cities? To turn the marketplace into art? This is our challenge."

To put into perspective on how maddening China's development has become, here are some extremely sobering statistics. According to historian Vaclav Smil's book *Making the Modern World: Materials and Dematerialization*, China used one and a half times more cement in three years between 2011 and 2013 than the U.S. in the entire 20th century. Of course, that was the American century, when the United States built its Interstate Highway System, bridges, Hoover Dam, and a forest of skyscrapers. China produces and consumes about 60 percent of the world's cement and erects more than 60 percent of all skyscrapers, six times more than its nearest rival, the United States.

This unprecedented development has a price. According to Tianjin University research, in the first decade of this century, the number of traditional villages in the country was reduced from 3.7 million to 2.6 million–a destruction of more than 300 villages a day. The urgency of this situation brought many Chinese architects to the countryside. In 2018, the Chinese Pavilion at the 16th Venice Architecture Biennale presented an ambitious show called *Building a Future Countryside*. It was organized by the Ministry of Culture and Tourism of the People's Republic of China, and curated by Li Xiangning, dean and professor at Tongji University.

At this exhibit the professional world was suddenly confronted with how much original architecture was built by Chinese architects in just a few years. What was impressive is not just the quantity but the quality. Many of these projects share the inventive use of traditional construction techniques, materials, and community-oriented programs. But by and large, these projects are not used by architects to express their personal styles. As a result, we can already see a strong common typology of these projects, in a way, shaped by collective, regional forces. They share an identity of their own. Some of the reasons for this development and the role of collectiveness versus individuality were discussed in my interview with Li Xiaodong (b. 1963). He said, "We need to be more confident about our culture collectively before we can pursue our ideas individually."

In addition to Wang Shu, Yung Ho Chang, Liu Jiakun, and Li Xiaodong, other first-generation independent architects who I included in this book are ZHU Pei (b. 1962), ZHANG Lei (b. 1964), and WANG Hui (b. 1967).

Together with Wang Hui, Zhu Pei and two other partners, LIU Xiaodu (b. 1962) and MENG Yan (b. 1965), founded URBANUS in Shenzhen in 1999. It is now among the biggest and most successful independent practices in China with its second office in Beijing headed by Wang Hui. In my interview with Wang we discussed the speed and scale of urban development in China. The architect said, "Our generation enjoyed so much development...We simply had to make a choice between working on either good projects or bad projects. But my students will live in the world without the pressure to keep adding more and more buildings...What I want to teach them is how to propose projects that could address social issues and present useful, interesting, and valuable typologies to resolve them."

Zhu Pei left URBANUS in 2004 to start his own practice, Studio Zhu-Pei in Beijing the following year. The new practice attracted a lot of international attention with its diverse and impressive body of work, in particular its art museums, which are built all over the country. In 2011, the *Huffington Post* named Zhu one of "the five greatest architects under 50."

Li Xiaodong refers to himself as a reflexive regionalist. He spent 15 years outside of China pursuing his PhD at the Delft University of Technology in the Netherlands, and teaching both in Delft and Singapore. In 1997, he returned to his homeland to establish Li Xiaodong Atelier. Unlike many of his fellow independent architects, Li works alone, occasionally relying on the help of his students at Tsinghua University. The architect's production is predominantly focused on small-scale educational projects that he rigorously labors on one at a time. His Li Yuan Library near Beijing (2011) is among the tiniest but most alluring buildings in China, proof that great architecture can reside in a variety of scales [100-103].

Apart from my interview with Li, his influence in China is also discussed in my conversation with ZHANG Li (b. 1970) with whom I had an enlightening discussion about how architects "try to mix the line of ethics with the line of aesthetics." But, he concluded, "Great architecture is always about this line of aesthetics. No matter how moral, how ethical, how correct you are, if you can't do beautiful things you are doomed."

THE SECOND GENERATION

Looking at the current architectural production by the Chinese architects, it is now clear that the most prolific of them are those who were born in the late 1960s and in 1970s. Now is the time of this second generation of China's contemporary architects, all of whom are based in Beijing and Shanghai. In addition to just mentioned Zhang Li, they are TONG Ming (b. 1968), LI Xinggang (b. 1969), LIU Yichun (b. 1969) and CHEN Yifeng (b. 1972) of Atelier Deshaus, ZHANG Ke (1970), DONG Gong (b. 1972), HUA Li (b. 1972), Philip F. YUAN (b. 1971), XU Tiantian (b. 1975), MA Yansong (b. 1975), and three husband-and-wife teams–Lyndon NERI (b. 1965) and Rossana HU (b. 1968) of Neri&Hu, LI Hu (b. 1973) and HUANG Wenjing (b. 1973) of Open Architecture, and Binke Lenhardt (b. 1971) and DONG Hao (b. 1973) of Crossboundaries.

The Long Museum on the West Bund in Shanghai (2014) is one of the most important new buildings students of Chinese architecture should be aware of [045-047]. It was designed by Liu Yichun and Chen Yifeng of Shanghai-based Atelier Deshaus. The firm has built several major art museums in their hometown. This fact alone makes Atelier Deshaus the most visible independent architectural practice in China. As in the case of their other museums here, the Long Museum is a renovation and transformation. The new building is placed on two sides of the 1950s-era ruin of a coal-hopper unloading bridge, and on top of an underground garage built in recent years. The ingenious design is based on a repetition of a tree-like structural module cast in finely polished concrete. Assembled in a variety of scales and arranged either parallel or perpendicular to each other, these large sections of straight walls, curving overhead, make up a matrix of interior spaces, a series of free-flowing unenclosed and uninterrupted galleries without any directional sequence. The plan evokes Theo van Doesburg's 1918 painting *Rhythm of a Russian Dance*. It achieves a surprising dynamism without a single diagonal or curved line.

025 Ma Yansong of MAD Architects, Harbin Opera House, Harbin, 2015. Photo by Vladimir Belogolovsky

If the original metaphor may suggest a forest, the final result is much more evocative of great architecture—from ancient Rome and Constantinople to the timeless vaulted volumes of Louis Kahn. If the building's facades appear rather understated, even uninterestingly flat, and forming dangerously sharp corners, nearly all parts of the interiors are among the most memorable and delightfully modern spaces anywhere.

What's fascinating about China is how quickly immensely talented young architects have appeared. In the 1990s and even early 2000s there were just a handful of practices capable of producing good work. Most of the architects in this book were still at school then. But China was getting ready for them. In 2006, Ma Yansong of MAD Architects, who trained at Yale and interned at such firms as Eisenman Architects in New York and Zaha Hadid Architects in London, won a competition to design the Absolute Towers in Mississauga, near Toronto, built in 2012. It was the first major international competition won by a Chinese architect. Since then the architect's practice has picked up one enviable commission after another. Apart from its headquarters in Beijing, the firm, now the largest and most active independent architectural practice in China, maintains three other offices—in Los Angeles, Rome, and Jiaxing in Zhejiang Province with the total of 130 employees.

Ma's Harbin Opera House (2015) is considered by some critics as the most beautiful modern building in China [106-110]. Its mountain-like formation appears to be sculpted naturally by wind and rain. A popular public path entices visitors to ascend to the peak-level observation area even during the off-hours. While the building serves as a sleek backdrop for brides and grooms [025], the locals turned a generous plaza all around it into their favorite spot for flying kites. Another high-profile commission that Ma won in an international competition is the appropriately futuristic-looking Lucas Museum of Narrative Art, which is expected to be completed in Los Angeles by 2021. These and other prestigious projects made Ma China's first celebrity architect.

Another Beijing-based architect, Dong Gong of Vector Architects, built his solid reputation on completing a number of projects that resonate enormously with students and architects around the world. His Yangshuo Sugar House Hotel of 2017, a resort complex on the Li River, surrounded by pointy karst peaks near Guilin, is an excellent case study on how to deal with preexisting context in the most alluring and convincing ways [026, 175-177]. The new complex, a renovation and addition to the late-1960s sugar mill, is one of the most seductively beautiful human-made places in China. As I spent a very comfortable weekend here, I could not help noticing a non-stop stream of visitors eagerly examining every

026 Vector Architects, Yangshuo Sugar House Hotel on the Li River near Guilin, 2017 © Chen Hao

hollow concrete block, brick, and concrete surface with a genuine admiration and out of control delight.

Still, to my taste, I felt the complex was a bit too "sweet" and ambiguous, as the architect purposefully avoided articulating clear distinctions between the old and the new layers of history. In fact, when I mentioned to one of the guests that the resort only opened a year before and that most of it was new construction, my remark was met with suspicion because the place felt as if it was always there. Dong and I discussed the project in our interview and I really liked his response. The architect said he tried to achieve "an atmospheric harmony" in his hotel. I think my initial resistance to embrace it fully has to do with the fact that this resort is primarily an image-driven and people-centric project. When I was there, I felt intellectually unchallenged without realizing an important point: this project, as well as many other buildings featured in this book, was created for people's pure enjoyment. That alone makes the hotel

project so persuading; it is sort of beyond criticism. What I can attest is that the time I spent there mellowed me as a critic.

Beijing-based architect Xu Tiantian heads her small but prolific practice DnA_Design and Architecture. Xu's studio is one of very few female-led in China, the only one in this book. She has built an extraordinary body of work by successfully collaborating with municipal government officials, residents, and craftspeople in Songyang County in Zhejiang, the same province where Wang Shu revitalized his Wencun Village restoration project from 2012 to 2016. Songyang County is a picturesque mountainous region of lush green valleys and terraces hugging the sides of Songyin River. The region is home to more than 400 villages and about a quarter of a million inhabitants. Since 2014, Xu has been surveying this depopulated area, abandoned by the villagers who took advantage of China's urban expansion and rushed to major cities in search of better jobs.

So far, the architect has completed around 30 small-scale projects here, both new and restorations, including museums, teahouses, galleries, community centers, factory demonstration workshops, performance pavilions, a bridge, and other buildings for hospitality use. She calls these interventions "architectural acupuncture." The strategy identifies what the most urgent needs are to determine what kind of functions and structures would be most appropriate in revitalizing this region by motivating investments and generating local jobs and revenues. In my interview with Xu, she discussed her intentions behind some of the most original of these structures including Pingtian Village Centre (2015), Brown Sugar Factory (2016), Tofu Factory (2018), and Shimen Bridge (2018).

The restored Shimen Bridge is particularly symbolic: it reconnects two villages, which were previously separated by the Songyin River [085]. Xu's project restored and reopened this previously abandoned link between the two communities, and by adding a wooden roof, benches, and trees, encourages villagers to socialize here and, on occasions, to turn the bridge into a lively market "square," a modern adaptation of the Rialto Bridge in Venice. Of course, there are also domestic prototypes for covered bridges, such as the Chengyang Wind and Rain Bridge in Guangxi (1912), a combination of bridge, corridor, veranda, and Chinese pavilion, also linking two villages. The other source is situated in Zhejiang, the same province where Shimen Bridge stands; the Xijwechatin Bridge (1718) is a much larger structure. Xu's strategic work across Songyang County is seen as an exemplary alternative to the common practice of widespread demolition of traditional villages that are commonly replaced with densely erected, insensitive cookie-cutter, developments of towers that bring comfort to the villagers, but uproot them from their land and eradicate local culture.

The work of Philip F. Yuan of Archi-Union Architects in Shanghai stands out for two reasons. The architect employs the latest pioneering digital techniques in his parametric designs to explore the poetics of architectural surfaces, and because his work in the countryside employs villagers in the building production process. A case in point is his cultural exchange center, "In Bamboo" in Daoming, a rural village in Sichuan province near Chengdu [041-043]. Built in 2018, this pavilion's dynamic form is based on a number eight-shaped Möbius strip superimposed on the footprints of two preexisting houses. While the new structure's roof is clad in gray ceramic tile to give it local context, the woven bamboo-cane panels that wrap its walls pay tribute to bamboo weaving, a specialty craft, for which Daoming is well regarded regionally.

In Bamboo has become a sort of Trojan Horse for Yuan, leading to commissions to design and build additional social projects in the same village. They include water infrastructure pavilions, education and internet centers, a package-delivery station, hotel, children's summer camp, and public restrooms. The key component of this project's success is that in addition to establishing a productive relationship with the local government, the architect set up his factory, equipped with advanced robots, to produce all the building components onsite in Daoming. The facility will be used to transform this entire village and, if necessary, other nearby villages across the region. The social impact of Yuan's architecture is in employing the villagers, both in building these facilities and their operation. Many of these locals are middle-aged and elderly women who stayed home, while their husbands and children migrated to the cities. The architect sees his projects in Daoming as a prototype that could be replicated all over China. "Imagine if every city in China will have a robotic factory like the one we set up in Daoming!" Exclaimed the architect in our detailed interview.

Zhang Ke of the Beijing practice ZAO/standardarchitecture is another prominent architect who has taken advantage of government-led initiatives to invest in the tourism industry across China. Zhang has built several distinctive structures in the Linzhi area, which is on the banks of Niyang and Yarluntzangbu rivers in southeastern Tibet in the Himalayan mountains. These very robust buildings—small boat terminals, visitor centers, and an art center—are built as if they were inseparable from the surrounding rugged landscape. They are quite literally embedded into the land as landscape and building become one. Their abstracted forms seem to be devoid of any scale and when viewed from a distance, they may be mistaken for boulders, scattered across the mountainside, according to the architect. These buildings are built of reinforced concrete walls acting as a substructure for local rubble stone cladding. They appear at once vernacular, even prehistoric, and yet modern due to the deep and wide recessed wall openings. All of the fundamental elements that we associate with architecture are rethought here. Roofs are replaced with flat viewing platforms, windows are abstracted as large, frameless glazed openings. Facades, parapets, steps, and pavement all blend into one seamless mass [182].

If Zhang's works in the countryside attract interest for their materiality, his urban projects–hutong restorations in the historical center of Beijing–are distinctive for their spatial originality. These kindergartens, artist residences, and other similar projects are playful spatial inventions achieved through techniques such as fragmentation of larger volumes and spaces into smaller ones, projecting windows, doors, and rooms or parts of rooms out and in and at various angles. They juxtapose different scales and pair such materials as glass and stone, concrete and wood, and metal and wood in stark contrast to each other [186, 187]. The architect's work expresses his protest against the way Chinese cities are being developed. As in the case of other local architects his work is a self-search for an alternative model against, as he told me, "so much copying and imitating, while a whole layer of the original, historical architecture was being erased." Zhang's architecture expresses his own ideas, while preserving history, materiality, and culture.

The next project is unique for bringing together several of the second generation practitioners. Aranya is both a place and a resort brand name. Similarly, to SOHO China, Vanke, Modern Green Development Co., and some other real estate developers, the company invests in world-class architecture as part of its business strategy to bring originality, sophistication, and prestige to its projects. Aranya, located on the Golden Beach in Beidaihe District near Qinhuangdao in Hebei Province, is an innovative private resort focusing on second-home market for China's growing urban middle class.

It was conceived and developed by businessman MA Yin. Due to the resort's proximity to the capital–it is now just two-hour high-speed train ride away–and its desirable location on the Bohai Sea coast, Beidaihe has been the site of many important official conferences and is a popular summer retreat for the Party's elite and home to resorts and camps for distinguished workers and their families.

The Aranya development features Mediterranean-style beach houses and high-rise apartments for sale, as well as a range of vacation-style hotel accommodations. What's unusual here is that apart from fresh air and shallow waters of typically calm sea, the resort offers top-notch architecture and cultural programs. Envisioned to create a town-like community, Ma, inspired by such world-class contemporary masters as Tadao Ando and Peter Zumthor, commissioned China's most creative architects to bring to his development the emotional value of small-scale poetic architecture–art galleries, restaurants, bookstores, a food market, a library, a chapel, and various facilities for children. The businessman calls these architects' projects "spiritual creations." In fact, they are the ones that attract many of the visitors, a constant stream of press and social media coverage, and most importantly, record-breaking home sales.

Seven of these buildings are featured in this book and it is worth noting that while they appear in photos as standalone objects, many are situated within a short walk from one another. Surely the most popular of the Aranya attractions is a cluster of three modestlyscaled buildings designed by Dong Gong. Lined up along the beach are his Seashore Library (2015), Seashore Chapel (2015), and Seashore Restaurant (2018). The Library and Chapel, in particular, have become international sensations [173,174]. They have appeared in numerous online and print publications, and their videos have gathered millions of views on social media. These lyrical concrete structures are inspired, in part, by forms, textures, and quality of light found in graceful buildings by Le Corbusier.

Close to Dong's trio is the UCCA Dune Art Museum (2018) by Li Hu and Huang Wenjing, a sculptural group of interconnected, cavernous spaces partially

027 Wang Shuo of META-Project, House T/House by the Sea, Aranya, Qinghuangdao, Hebei Province, 2018. Courtesy of META-Project

buried in sand that overlook the sea [132,133]. Next to the Dune Art Museum is a construction site where Xu Tiantian's Music Studio/Theater by the Sea is being built with completion anticipated in late 2021. Other buildings of note include the Aranya Qixing Youth Camp (2016) by Zhang Li [154,155] and several eye-catching projects by Shanghai-based Wutopia Lab.

Then, there is the Aranya Art Center by Lyndon Neri and Rossana Hu [125-128]. This tidy block, with a bench-scape molded in textured concrete, owes itself to a number of modernist influences–from the rows and columns of Marcel Breuer-inspired recessed windows and opaque panels throughout its sturdy facade to Wright's Guggenheim-like ramp, which is inserted into the hollowed-out core. All along the way to the roof terrace the spiraling ascent is accompanied by beautifully articulated balconies, viewing-wall apertures, ledges, handrails, and other sculptural fine details that bring to mind

Le Corbusier's best moments. The Center's soul is within its open-top conical courtyard and circular amphitheater at the bottom. This space is reserved for intimate concerts and art installations but is more impressive when entirely empty. Looking up from the very center of the gray disc here one can imagine the whole building spinning and floating above. Standing on that spot, I felt like I was inside the most magical room in all of China.

Before leaving Aranya, I would like to introduce one last, not-yet mentioned architect in this book, the 21st, to symbolize the 21st century. WANG Shuo (b. 1981) is the youngest in this cohort and the only one born in the 1980s. He designed a beach villa, House T or House by the Sea [027], just a stone's throw away from Dong's Chapel. A private dwelling is the true laboratory of architecture, and they are rare in China due to the fact that land can only be rented here, not owned. Designed as a single-family residence, House T isn't exactly that. It is used as a private club, shared by special guests. The title refers to the building's profile expressed by the T-shaped cast-in-concrete sleek wall that sits on a dark, layered rock plinth.

The reason I wanted to include Wang in the book is to contrast his design attitude as an indication of certain changes that already can be felt in the work of his generation. In our interview, he said, "There is something heroic about [these older architects'] urge to resurrect Chinese culture…It is not an issue for me. I have traveled the world and I see myself a part of it…I want to direct my attention to addressing various issues…I want to improve the situation and I have no idea what that is going to look like." He is talking about freeing his architecture from all pre-conceptions. Having worked for OMA in Rotterdam and Beijing his designs are based on observations of people's behavior, performance analysis, rethinking traditional programs, all-in-all driven by research and rational pragmatism.

Of course, there is never a clean cut between generations and similar thoughts were expressed in my conversation with Binke Lenhardt and Dong Hao. They said, "We are not just designing objects; we initiate discussions and interactions…style is not important. We don't want to limit ourselves to any particular materials or means of expression. We want to encourage a new kind of experience." The fact that Lenhardt is a German-born architect plays a role in their views. She told me, "[Our] work does not fit into the aesthetics, which are currently attributed to much of the contemporary 'Chinese architecture.' For me it is not about 'Chinese-ness,' but about practicing our beliefs in a certain context. And for us this context is China." Interestingly, those foreign architects who now live and practice in China stay away from employing even hints of Chinese semiology in their work altogether. In any case, the fact that local architects now feel entirely free in their creative choices is a positive development.

I see new interests in these approaches that reflect my own concerns about the current Chinese architects' production. Even though it seems to be quite vital at the moment, already I can feel that some of these architects have reached a certain rigidity. They feel satisfaction from their own work. Many follow a safe image-driven approach with preference for nostalgic imagery, a predictable range of materials, and an already conventional reliance on how to blend their architecture with landscape and ruins, as if there is a checklist for achieving the "right" look. What is clear, however, is that younger architects like Wang Shuo will continue to bring a healthy distraction and diversity into China's current architectural development to keep it dynamic and nonformulaic.

OBSERVATIONS ABOUT THE TWENTY-ONE

Looking at the group of the featured architects here, what immediately attracts attention is their young age. Whereas in the West many of the leading architects practicing today are well in their 60s, 70s, and some are even in their late 80s and 90s. In China, the oldest of the leading architects currently practicing are in their early and mid-60s. And the most active Chinese architects are in their 40s. The way these practitioners choose to name their firms is telling—only seven out of 21 used their own names. It is typical for them to appropriate coded meanings in English. Firms in this book include Amateur Architecture Studio, Archi-Union Architects, Atelier TeamMinus, Crossboundaries, DnA_Design and Architecture, META-Project, Open Architecture, URBANUS, Vector Architects, and ZAO/standardarchitecture. And beyond this book there are such names as Atelier Alter, Atelier Archmixing, Continual Architecture, Interval Architects, Naturabuild, Original Design Studio, People's Architecture Office, Regional Studio, Rural Urban Framework, Scenic Architecture, UFo (Un-Forbidden office), West-line Studio, and the already-mentioned Wutopia Lab. All these impersonal names attest to these architects' commitment to achieving a kind of architecture that goes beyond personal expression and has a certain collective identity. Notions of anonymity, the multiplicity of voices, and understated authorships were discussed in my interview with Wang Shu.

All the architects in the book share a close relationship with academia. Out of 25 individual architects of to 21 firms, 14 received their graduate degrees in the

U.S., one in Switzerland, and one in the Netherlands. Only nine did not study outside of China. Almost all of those nine are older architects. Apart from these architects' foreign architecture degrees it is critical to list the top domestic universities responsible for their educations. Here is the tally: 11 graduated from Tsinghua, five from Tongji, five from Southeast University in Nanjing (formerly the Nanjing Institute of Technology), two are from the Beijing University of Civil Engineering and Architecture, one from Tianjin University, and one from Chongqing Institute of Architecture and Engineering. Wang Shu and Tong Ming studied both at Southeast University and Tongji, and three foreign-born architects in this collection did not study architecture at Chinese universities at all.

All of the architects I interviewed teach, and many started their careers as university professors and only formed their practices later on. In fact, three of the featured architects are current deans and, as mentioned earlier, Yung Ho Chang was a head of architecture school in America. Wang Shu became dean of the Architecture School at the China Academy of Art in Hangzhou in 2007. Zhu Pei was named dean of the School of Architecture at the Central Academy of Fine Arts, CAFA in Beijing in 2018. And, Zhang Li became dean of the School of Architecture at Tsinghua University in 2020, after my interview with him. Other architects head their own departments such as Li Xiaodong at Tsinghua and Philip F. Yuan at Tongji. Tong Ming serves as the chief planner of Shanghai Tongji Urban Planning and Design Institute within Tongji University.

Out of the 21 practices in the book, not all are independent. Zhang Li's Atelier TeamMinus is a part of THAD, the Architectural Design & Research Institute of Tsinghua University. Li Xinggang's Atelier Li Xinggang operates within CADG, the China Architecture Design & Research Group. Some of the other architects also started their careers within LDIs, but eventually opened their own independent studios. The advantages, as well as drawbacks of working independently in China are discussed in my conversations with Li Xinggang, Zhang Lei, and Binke Lenhardt and Dong Hao.

The 21 featured studios are all based in Mainland China. I decided to exclude architects practicing in Hong Kong, Taiwan, and those who settled in the West to better present these architects as a group by focusing on their commonalities rather than distinctions. They practice out of five cities across China. Yet, two thirds of them–14 studios–work out of Beijing. Four offices are based in Shanghai, while Hangzhou, Nanjing, and Chengdu serve home to just one firm each. Three out of 25 architects were born outside of China. Binke Lenhardt was born in Germany and moved to China after meeting her husband Dong Hao during their studies in the U.S. They initially worked at the Beijing Institute of Architectural Design (BIAD) prior to opening their practice. Lyndon Neri and Rossana Hu are both overseas-born Chinese–she in Taiwan and he in the Philippines. Both immigrated to the U.S. during their teen years. They were educated in America and started their family there. The architects initially moved to China, while working for Michael Graves in Shanghai and decided to stay there to build their own practice.

For most architects in the book choosing architecture as a profession was an intuitive decision. Many heard what architects do for the first time when they were applying to university. Yet, two of the interviewees come from the families of prominent architects. Yung Ho Chang's father, Zhang Kaiji (1912-2006) was the chief architect of BIAD and the vice chairman of the Architectural Society of China. He designed the parade stands in front of the Forbidden City, the Chinese Revolution and History Museum in Tiananmen Square, the Beijing Planetarium, and Sanlihe Government Complex, mentioned above for its juxtaposition of traditional roof design onto modern buildings. Tong Ming's grandfather, Tong Jun (Tung Chuin, 1900-83), was one of China's first modern architects, a graduate of the University of Pennsylvania, and the author of the influential book *Glimpses of Gardens in Eastern China*, which was discussed in my interview with Tong. He published an updated Chinese version of the book in 2018, for which Wang Shu, the student of Tong Jun, wrote an introduction.

It is very unusual for Chinese architects to build outside of China. In fact, only Ma Yansong and

Neri&Hu are now regularly awarded foreign commissions. Interestingly, the work of these architects in China, particularly of Ma Yansong, can also be imagined elsewhere. What unites all 21 studios is their commitment to building in China's countryside. All find pleasure in working on small projects directly with builders, discovering and resurrecting traditional construction techniques and working with regional materials in new, unorthodox ways.

What is curiously revealing about these architects' characters is their self-awareness, competitiveness, and ambition that their work achieves recognition. When asked to name their favorite buildings in China, in most cases they spoke about their own projects, no matter how small or little known. This is something I have not encountered in my interviews in other parts of the world. On a personal note, I found all architects extremely generous, very accessible (much more so than in the West), and willing to discuss their work very openly and critically. On average, these dialogues lasted three hours each and the architects patiently allowed me to go through all my questions. They helped me arrange to visit their buildings and even willingly recommended and introduced me to other architects.

The following 21 interviews were conducted during my travels to China as a curator and lecturer. They were recorded in the span of three and a half years, starting with Ma Yansong at his Beijing studio in March 2017 and ending with Wang Shu and Lu Wenyu in October 2020 via a WeChat video call between New York and Hangzhou. In April 2017, I interviewed Li Xiaodong at his studio at Tsinghua University in Beijing. Our acquaintance led to a number of subsequent meetings. During one of them he abruptly asked me, "Do you want to teach here?" I stumbled for a second, responding, "I have never taught in my life." He did not waiver one bit, "There is always the first time. Yes or no?" He wanted me to make the decision right there. I liked that challenge and the following year I spent four months living and teaching on campus. I used that time to meet many architects, more than I was able to include in this book and traveled throughout the country to see numerous works described here.

One of my Tsinghua students, Chengdu-born and Singapore-based Weili Zhang helped me with arranging and translating for six interviews that were conducted via WeChat video calls from New York during the COVID-19 pandemic in 2020. All other interviews were done in person. The interviews gathered in this book were originally published in other media—my columns on *ArchDaily* and *STIR*, and in such magazines as *AV*, *SPEECH*, and *Metropolis*—although as much shorter versions. Therefore, all of the interviews in this book are presented in full for the first time. They are accompanied by drawings and photos of built projects only. I selected them not to explain these buildings but to convey their imagination, sense of belonging, and most importantly, their beauty.

Certainly, the works of the architects presented in this book constitute a subculture. All of them found their opportunities in the countryside and, for the most part, have built their best work there. This fact makes these buildings challenging to visit, as it may take many hours of driving even from the closest airports. In short, these works need to be discovered. And even when built in major cities, with a few exceptions, they are hidden from the typical tourist attractions.

The creative path that Chinese architecture has been navigating since the turn of the millennium is nothing short of extraordinary and should be celebrated, especially since the featured architects' efforts to repair the historical fabric in the villages contribute greatly to their survival, and help form new attitudes that elevate their cultural value to a deservedly high place. Of course, while these architects focus on small scale projects in the countryside, it is the powerful LDIs that influence major urban regeneration projects and continue shaping Chinese cities. Still, the images gathered here illustrate just a tip of the iceberg and a mere hint of the creative potential of the Chinese architects and where China is headed next. To become more relevant is their biggest challenge.

Interviews

BY VLADIMIR BELOGOLOVSKY

WANG Shu & LU Wenyu
AMATEUR ARCHITECTURE STUDIO

WANG Shu (b. 1963, Ürümqi, Xinjiang) and his wife LU Wenyu (b. 1967, Shanghai) met during their studies at Nanjing Institute of Technology, now Southeast University. He graduated from Nanjing with a master's degree in 1988 and she earned her bachelor's degree in 1989. During his childhood Wang often traveled by train between his hometown and relatives in Beijing. Those four-day-long train rides, each way, made him acutely attentive to both fundamental and seemingly imperceptible details of a great variety of landscapes he enjoyed drawing from his bunk bed. Chinese traditional landscape paintings, Wang's single strongest inspiration behind his architecture, remind him of his childhood. Lu was born in Shanghai and moved with her family to Xinjiang at age six. After graduating from Nanjing, the couple moved to Hangzhou, Zhejiang province. While Wang worked at Zhejiang Academy of Fine Arts doing research and building small experimental works, Lu worked at the East China Hydropower Design Institute with over 3,000 engineers and a small architecture department of two dozen architects where she was in charge of many large projects. In 1997, Wang founded his practice Amateur Architecture Studio with Lu, referring to his independent position and intention to work outside of the professional system with the emphasis on investigating Chinese culture and history, reviving tradition of craftsmanship, and dealing with salvaged materials in his resistance to the ongoing erasure of historical buildings in China. In 2000, after completing his PhD at Tongji University in Shanghai, Wang became a professor at the China Academy of Art in Hangzhou and together with Lu started designing its new Xiangshan Campus (Phases I & II, III 2002–13), a collection of 30 academic buildings. In 2003, Lu left her Institute to start teaching at the Academy and became a full partner at the studio. Wang became dean of the School of Architecture at the Academy in 2007. Their other most significant projects include the Lin'an Museum in Hangzhou (2020), the Fuyang Cultural Complex in Anhui province (2017), Regeneration of Wencun Village in Zhejiang province (2012-16), the Restoration of Zhongshan Road in Hangzhou (2012), the Ningbo History Museum (2003-08), Five Scattered Houses in Ningbo (2005), and the Library of Wenzheng College on the Suzhou University Campus (2000). In 2012, Wang became the first Chinese citizen to win the Pritzker Prize. Lu Wenyu joined our conversation with Wang Shu only in the very beginning and remained as a listener to the end.

ACHIEVING GOOD ARCHITECTURE
IS LIKE FLYING A KITE

In conversation with **WANG Shu** and **LU Wenyu** of Amateur Architecture Studio, Hangzhou
WeChat video call between New York and Hangzhou, October 23, 2020

028 Wang Shu & Lu Wenyu © Iwan Baan

Vladimir Belogolovsky: Is it true that architects working at your office don't come before lunch time, leaving the mornings to just two of you to think, discuss, and reflect?

Wang Shu: Yes. Usually we start our days with drinking tea. [Laughs.] We cut trees and plants in our garden. I draw and we discuss our recent designs. My wife, Wenyu is the only person who criticizes my work. But we are very relaxed here. Right now, there are 10 architects, including us. All our assistants are local architects. In the past, we had some foreigners.

None of them are students. We don't plan to grow; we are quite happy with our size right now. We are big enough to undertake any project and control its quality. We don't need to work on many projects at the same time.

VB: Wenyu, the two of you met at Nanjing Institute of Technology. How do you remember Shu as a student? I read that he stood out from everyone else as a rebel against the system, right?

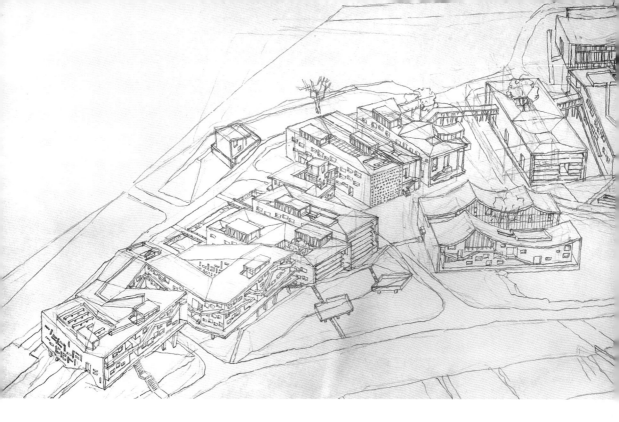

Lu Wenyu: We met quite late at the university, just before Shu was about to complete his master's degree. Before that, of course, I heard rumors about this student Wang Shu being very special, rebellious, and with erratic behavior. [Laughs.] But when we finally met, I realized that he was a very different person from what people said about him. My personal impression was very different. He was on a mission, for sure, but very genuine and true to his convictions from the beginning.

VB: Both of you grew up in Xinjiang. Why did you decide to move to Hangzhou to start your careers there?

WS: That was my decision. Hangzhou is a famous city in China for its beauty, ancient poetry, and painting. It is the most beautiful city in China for its scenery and landscape. This city on a lake was always in my heart. And after 2000, when I completed my PhD, everyone was surprised when I went back to Hangzhou,

where we lived since graduating from Nanjing. We didn't stay in Shanghai because Shanghai is not China, but Hangzhou is China.

VB: Shu, I understand that during your student time in Nanjing and in the early years of your career you were interested in deconstuctivist architecture. Could you talk about that?

WS: Yes, in my third year we had an assignment to design a hypothetical housing project. I modelled my proposal on the famous Fujian Tulou, a cluster of round residential buildings in Fujian province [009] I designed it in a deconstructivist style. The project attracted a lot of attention. It was even christened as the first post-modernist project in China. Our school had a very comprehensive collection of books and periodicals coming from all over the world. So, it was possible to follow the works by leading architects in America and Europe. I particularly recall following projects by Peter Eisenman, Bernard Tschumi, Wolf

029 Xiangshan Campus, China Academy of Art, Hangzhou, Phase II, 2004. Sketch drawn by Wang Shu from left to right without a stop over a period of four hours. Courtesy of Amateur Architecture Studio

Prix, Daniel Libeskind, and early paintings by Zaha Hadid. I was also interested in studying Chinese calligraphy done in various styles–from restrained to very expressive, which are somewhat similar to deconstructivist projects. I was also interested in the work of such architects as Aldo Rossi and Mario Botta and I even argued with my classmate who of them would become the master to be followed. Another architect who caught my attention was Tadao Ando.

VB: What specifically made you abandon that direction and dedicate your efforts to exploring local traditions?

WS: That fascination with Chinese culture started when I was young, even though there was no special training or influence from my family. I started doing calligraphy when I was in elementary school. I had no particular references then. So, I felt I had to invent my own style. I practiced a lot by writing Chinese poems from the Tang dynasty. But in college everybody

around me was fascinated mostly by Western ideas. In contrast to that, with a friend of mine, we liked to study and discuss Chinese paintings. I remember how strange that was to our fellow students. They even called us crazy. [Laughs.]

VB: In your work you deal with history in a very direct way–through the use of salvaged materials. How did you come to it, as your first major project, the Library of Wenzheng College [018] on the campus of Suzhou University, perhaps the first uncompromisingly modern building in China, was quite different, right?

WS: My earliest works were done before that, starting from my years as a master student. First, there was a hotel in Nanjing, which started in 1986 and completed in 1988. I would not consider any of those early projects, including the Library, as modern. They are rather post-modern, simply because of the time and multiple references used, although not historical ones. The hotel was probably the first post-modern building in Nanjing. What was special about it was the inclusion of a courtyard, a public space fully integrated into the street, which was very unusual in China at that time. Another project was the Children's Palace or Youth Center in Haining near Hangzhou, completed in 1990. That was a neo-modern building with influences by Rossi and elements of deconstructivism. It was a five-story white minimalist volume with a small red insertion at an angle. Then there was an interior project, an auditorium, in which I used old bricks as an echo and a dialogue with the existing old building, also made of bricks. Then there was a theater in Hangzhou, another deconstructivist work with timber elements, all constructed in a single day as a continuous performance of sort. But it was deemed as an illegal construction and taken down soon after. So, that was a period of about ten years of hibernation and incubation before Wenzheng College Library was built in 2000.

The Library was my first attempt to build a modern building influenced by an idea of a Chinese traditional garden, as a system of fragments. Yet, the result was very clean, very modern, or rather post-modern building. But the quintessential point of the project was to fracture a single object into smaller ones. That idea was taken from the southern gardens in Suzhou. Particularly, the Yipu, a small garden lost in the alleys. There is a small pavilion on a lake at the center of that garden, which is the whole essence. It echoes teachings of my professor in Nanjing, Tong Jun, from the first generation of Chinese architects. He talked about the importance of seeing the big in small and seeing the small in big. So, I borrowed ideas from the Chinese traditional garden system by introducing a small building to destroy big buildings. That was the idea–to integrate a large structure with something that's very personal, intimate, and emotional. That's the essence I want to capture in all my buildings. During the construction of the Library the person in charge of the construction asked me about one of those small pavilions, "What is this?" I said, "It is a reading room to study poetry and philosophy." His answer was: "Although I cannot stop you

from doing it. But personally, once it is built, I would want to detonate it." But it is still there. [Laughs.]

VB: I read about your concern that the Library's white volumes felt too Western and too abstract to you. What did you learn from that project that led to changing your direction, namely dealing with history through salvaged materials directly?

WS: I would say that the first reason, apart from the small auditorium project that I already mentioned, was when I started teaching at our Academy in 2000, there was an international sculpture symposium at the school, and I was asked to design the exhibition's layout and prepare my own piece for the exhibit by the West Lake, close to the center of Hangzhou. During that process I had a chance to observe the participating sculptors working on their pieces. Many of them used stone and stainless steel, which meant they had to build foundations to hold them up. These foundations would have to be dug out quite substantially with a lot of soil being removed to pour concrete. I felt the whole process was energy-consuming, quite wasteful, even damaging. My first reaction was to find use for that soil from the ground for my own piece to construct two rammed earth walls with a narrow path between them. That was the first instance when I explored the idea of recycling. And because the weather in Hangzhou is quite wet, I decided to use tiles to pave the path between the two walls. Although there was no roof, there were openings and a place to sit; the whole thing evoked the most basic representation of a house.

The piece became a tiny prototype for my new architecture. It was at that time when a famous old street in the city was being demolished and a lot of beautiful Qing dynasty tiles could be salvaged from there. In fact, those priceless tiles were treated like trash. They had no value. The scene was shocking to me. It was like a war zone, a barbaric demolition happening in the heart of such a culturally advanced city. That shock made me question the purpose of an architect, about morality of architecture. It would be unethical not to respond to that situation. That was the moment when my white period ended. After that I transitioned into my black or dark period. I am referring to the natural colors of such traditional materials as soil, bricks, pottery plates, and tiles. I also call these materials breathable. I decided to create my new architecture with natural, living materials that breathe.

VB: What happened to that prototype?

WS: It had no roof, so about a month later it started to be effected by the weather, and little by little, in a few months' time, after some parts were dismantled, whatever was left of it, completely disintegrated back into the nature. It was called *Wall Gate*. But many of the other sculptures are still there.

VB: Ningbo Museum [020] and your other buildings seem to diffuse a notion of a single authorship. Could you talk about diversity, anonymity, and multiplicity of voices in your architecture?

WS: I pursued this concept of anonymity in my PhD at Tongji University, during which I worked on the idea of anonymous architecture. And already in my Wenzheng College Library I incorporated this idea. For example, by introducing small volumes that accompany the main large structure. This is what you can see in traditional houses in Suzhou–they are delightful and beautiful, but not in a personal way. They are a product of a very organic language. That is what's moving about these structures. And that's what I was trying to express in a different way, particularly in the Ningbo Museum. I call the facades of this building–architecture completed by thousands of hands. I refer to the diversity of techniques in the construction of that building. And we mixed new and salvaged materials side by side. I wanted to build a small town with its own life, which could once again, wake up the latent memory of the city that was built over the demolished ancient villages.

VB: How did you try to achieve that and are you happy with the result?

WS: When we started laying bricks there, we went around the region to discover many bricklayers who use different techniques. Each can be identified by a particular pattern or rhythm, all very dynamic. So, I wanted to use many such techniques to bring the idea of variety and anonymity.

Ironically, when the builders started laying the bricks their work was quite rigid and formulaic. It was not organic. So, we had to do a lot of negotiations with them directly on site. Eventually, if I am entirely honest, I would say that there is only one wall, a small section, the area of five or six square meters, where the workers achieved the kind of quality that I was hoping for. There is a lot in the construction process that is beyond the architect's control. There is an abundance of diverse materials. There is a sense that you are dealing with a puzzle, a maze. I tried to build a diverse world as a resistance to the uniform world. I wanted to avoid the kind of singularity that comes from a design by one architect. Anonymous diversity might be designed by time; no human being could do that. But I tried. In a way, the final building in Ningbo is both ideal and far from what I originally imagined.

What I also must mention here is that the workers were very expressive about their skills and they were very proud of the work they've done. But, when they all went back to their villages and tried to carry on their work in similar ways to Ningbo, the results were very poor because they were self-conscious in their creations and they lost a sense of anonymity, which is so moving in traditional architecture. The success in Ningbo was in achieving the right balance between the architect's intervening too much and letting the workers be free, to a point. Achieving good architecture is like flying a kite. There is always a string attached to the building process. I would like to call the result of the Ningbo History Museum an anthropological fact in existence.

VB: In your 2011 lecture you said that architects are not building in the countryside. Since then a number of independent Chinese architects started working on projects in the villages. What do you think about their work there, in a way, triggered by your example?

WS: The countryside is a very important issue in China because it is crucial to preserve and develop traditional culture. The cities are being destroyed by the break-neck speed of development, accompanied by widespread demolition over the past two decades. That's why I encouraged our architects to go into the countryside. There are many people in rural China with building skills. It is not wise for architects not to use their knowledge and skills. Yet, when many of our leading architects went to the countryside they were

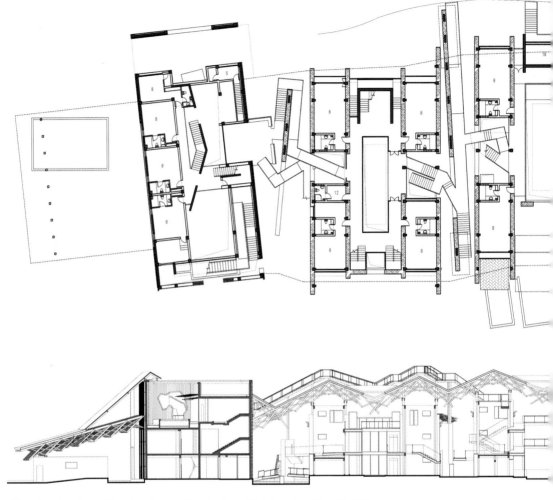

030 Wa Shan Guesthouse, Xiangshan Campus, China Academy of Art, Hangzhou, Phase III, 2013.
Ground Floor Plan and Longitudinal Section. Courtesy of Amateur Architecture Studio

still building for the urban class and tourists, not the villagers. Most of their projects are hotels, museums, libraries, resorts, children camps, or ostentatious apartment buildings. None of that serves people who live in these villages. What I particularly want architects to pay attention to is what constitutes the majority of these villages, which is the housing and the facilities that accompany them, spaces that they use in daily life–community centers, public toilets, shops, public squares, and infrastructure.

In my own attempt I went to Wencun Village in Zhejiang Province to design two dozen houses while inserting them into the historical fabric. That's when I realized that typically clients are very abstract, but in a village, you have to confront villagers directly. So, there is a very different level of responsibility on the part of the architect. I also like the potential to continue the dialogue between the villagers and the architect over a long period of time in their collaboration on working on many projects in the community. In my Wencun Village projects I am dealing with the totality of the village; there is a continuity between projects, whereas in cities architects are accustomed to dealing with one site at a time, quite independently of its context.

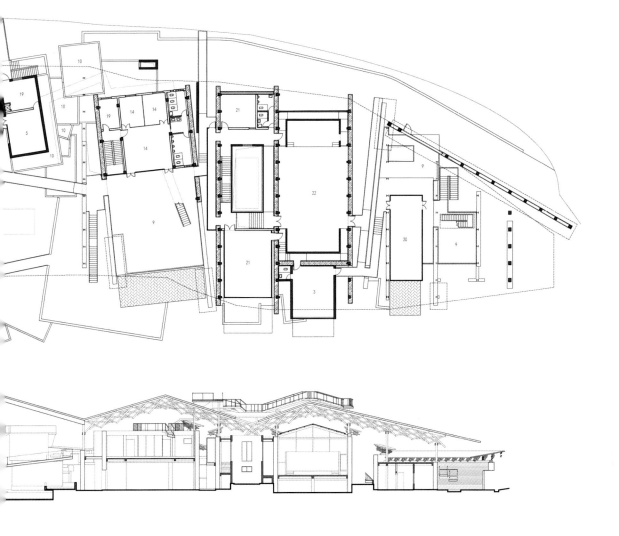

VB: What do you think about the current creative moment in China and about some of the leading independent architects and their achievements?

WS: There have been a lot of changes over the last 20 years. Having our own independent practice, I recall that around the year 2000, we were still rather lonely. If I had to make a list of good architects, back then I would probably name no more than five or six practices of note in the entire country. Right now, you can probably find 100 good-quality practices. So, this is a good direction because architects are focusing on doing a better quality architecture. There is also a trend among younger architects who are building both in cities and in the countryside. And they are concerned about historical parts of these cities and villages in a form of small interventions rather than large commercial complexes. This is a good development. Where I see a real threat is in the development of what I call monstrosities, buildings that cause irreversible damage to the environment and history. We are discussing wrong issues. Rather than discussing how to do large, out of scale buildings better, we should think whether we should do them at all. Imagine, one building can potentially destroy

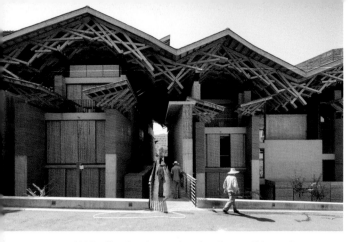

031 Wa Shan Guesthouse, Xiangshan Campus, China Academy of Art, Hangzhou, Phase III, 2006-13 © Iwan Baan

032 Wa Shan Guesthouse, Xiangshan Campus, China Academy of Art, Hangzhou, Phase III, 2006-13 © Iwan Baan

033 Wa Shan Guesthouse, Xiangshan Campus, China Academy of Art, Hangzhou, Phase III, 2006-13 © Iwan Baan

an entire street in a city's fabric. I also don't understand when some villages try very hard to look like cities. It is the other way around–cities should learn from the countryside. The countryside is China's last chance. We need to go to the countryside to recover our traditions, our original taste and culture.

VB: Could you talk about your Guesthouse on the Xiangshan Campus? People say that they are getting lost there. Was that intentional?

WS: To respond to your question, I need to refer you to my dissertation project again, where I explored the idea of a flaneur, an urban stroller. I remember watching a documentary on an ancient city in Morocco. The narrator said–there are 1,000 streets and alleys there and every visitor gets lost there. But the city's inhabitants never get lost." There are many signs and hints that they use to find their ways. That's what I like about historical architecture, which is designed for overall cohesiveness and long-term use rather than serving an immediate purpose, and there is a tendency nowadays for everything to stand out as a contrast to everything else. So, when I was designing the Guesthouse the idea was to create a building that has a sense of belonging to history and time, not merely representing its purpose in our own time.

VB: Speaking of time, you said, "Feeling about time is more important than feeling about space. Architecture is more about time than space." Could you elaborate on that?

WS: If you explore my buildings on the Xiangshan Campus it is hard to grasp the four faces of each of them [005-008]. The most memorable experience is when you walk in-between two buildings at a time. That's when spaces become fragmented into bits and pieces. They create patterns of repetitions that contribute to the sensation of getting lost and coming back to the same place at times. That's a kind of temporal experience that I was trying to achieve in my design. These ideas reflect my fondness of the works by French screenwriter and film director Alain Robbe-Grillet. He dealt with such notions as memory and imagination, and among his teachings there are fractured plots, repeated passages, and odd details. I think architecture can and should create its own

034 Regeneration of Wencun Village, Zhejiang Province, 2012-16 © Iwan Baan

time, but the sense of time does not need to be told as narration but come through the work and can be felt subconsciously. Every time I am building a building the intention is to create a world and a path that leads us back to nature. Getting lost in this world is a recurring theme in my work. But you are right, there are some staff members who sometimes complain that they can't find an exit. There is another academic block, in which people also sometimes feel lost, even though there are eight exits there! Also, the way I see the campus is like a border between the natural and the artificial. It is a very intimate conversation between architecture and nature. I always recall ancient grottos where giant buddhas are carved into the cliffs with visitors following one another and navigating along steep and narrow stepped paths, hanging dangerously close to the edge to see them. So, walking around the campus is, in a way, like walking along the edge, right on the border between these two worlds–architecture and nature.

Then there is the idea of recycling historical materials. That idea serves as a pedagogical tool for students to make them aware of how architecture can play a role in preserving both nature and history. Architecture is not merely about inventing things from scratch. Speaking of other unconventional features here, some staff members complain that some of the rooms are not bright enough. But in fact, it is quite common in Chinese traditional houses for the domestic interior spaces to be somewhat dark. It is the darker spaces that are better suited and stimulating for the mind, when you are more acute and observant of light, unlike the kind of spaces you typically find in modern-day hospitals. Another intention there was given to creating a variety of spaces for students and teachers to avoid any geometric rigidity, particularly for teaching. These are very special places under trees, on rooftops, or within corridors with nooks and corners. All these intimate situations are created very intentionally for the diversity of uses. What's also very important is that at times you can't distinguish where the architecture starts and where the nature ends. That is their very special relationship.

VB: Ai Weiwei said that your academy is the best art and architecture school in China because you built both pedagogy and the campus. Could you talk about your pedagogy?

035 Fuyang Cultural Complex, Fuyang, Anhui Province, 2017
© Iwan Baan

WS: When I just started teaching in 2000, there was the intention to develop a different concept for architectural education, which meant that it was very difficult to find teachers. I was given cart blanch. I could decide what I wanted to teach, how to teach it, everything! So, we combined the contemporary art system with the craftsman system to develop a totally new type of Chinese architecture. The reason Ai Weiwei was so generous with his complement is because he was the first person who I asked to teach here. In fact, he was the first person I thought of who would be suitable for such new school. Two of us started teaching the first class. The first assignment that we gave to the students who had no prior experience in architecture was to build an architectural project using non-traditional building materials, especially materials that are recycled. This is just one example of how we tried to get students out of the expected building environment. The idea was to let students' imagination be entirely free and to let them build their ideas using real materials with their own hands. Ai Weiwei could only teach one class and then I had to look for other teachers. In the beginning, I invited some of my former students, as well as some "interesting people," meaning not only professional teachers and architects. We also had some foreign teachers from Europe and elsewhere in Asia.

Wenyu, of course, was teaching with me from the very beginning. It was not until 2007, when the school became stable and we finally had a permanent staff of 10 teachers, half of whom where my former students. Also, it was intentional to encourage a continuous flow of new teachers, especially young architects who also studied overseas and returned to China. They keep coming here to join our effort to avoid any rigidity in our methods. Now, we have about 40 teachers and 700 students. Personally, I teach a core module, accompanied by other modules taught by other teachers who have a certain autonomy and flexibility. They prepare their own briefs rather than follow a particular standardized teaching program. Coming out of Chinese high schools our students go through years of systematized teaching, which I call brainwashing. [Laughs.] So, first, we start with a kind of reeducation. One of our typical assignments is to work on live drawings in a garden using traditional ink to capture primary architectural emotions to develop students' sense of intuition. We also teach students how to work with wood and brick. And we work with our master students on building projects at full scale in the field.

VB: I am interested in your idea of re-composition–using salvaged materials in new ways. What would you say is the essence of your architecture? What is it primarily about?

WS: The essence of my architecture is in trying to maintain a cultural continuity. You can't protect and preserve culture as is. That is not enough. You have to find a dialogue between tradition and continuously changing life. Each generation has its own understanding of traditions. It is important to be conscious that all of us are taking part in re-composing traditions as we know them–in how we carry on different stories or re-compose and interpret the language. We may not be aware of it, but we are continuously re-composing the reality we know. And how can we forget about such notions of human nature as passion, creativity, inventiveness, and originality that play a definitive role in the design process!? So, the main goal of preserving traditions is not about following or copying them, but to find constructive ways to achieve the main purpose–not to allow traditions and classical knowledge die. I am not interested in the past and traditional things; I am rather interested in the difference between the past and our own contemporary time.

VB: Which building built in China since the turn of the century, either by local or foreign

architects, would you nominate as the most significant achievement and why?

WS: Perhaps my answer may be surprising, but I would name my own Xiangshan Campus. [Laughs.] Why? Because it is a collection, an encyclopedic attempt that presents different ways and methodologies of Chinese architecture over different periods of time. It is an urban experiment. I don't believe in such sentiments that decisively state that architectural types cannot be invented. I believe my Xiangshan Campus is a successful example of a typological invention. It is a prototype for a new kind of city where boundaries of urban and rural merge. Chinese architecture is a product that was born out of a highly sophisticated civilization and it maintains a highly natural quality. What's important is how to sustain and keep that quality alive–in the use of materials, construction techniques, and workers' crafts, which goes beyond artistic and specific expressions of singular projects. I think this project is one particular path that can lead Chinese architects into the future. The other building that offers another, very different path, is Rem Koolhaas' CCTV in Beijing. It is a completely different approach but just as valuable.

It would be a mistake to think of any one direction as the "correct" one.

VB: We know that over the last 20 years Chinese architects had a lot to learn from Western architects. What do you think is the main lesson that architects from other cultures could learn from what the Chinese architects have discovered?

WS: China, in its continuous process of urbanization, has been serving an important testing ground for the whole world by providing both positive and negative examples, especially for developing countries. As far as architecture, Chinese architects have to negotiate between different civilizations. In China, we are still much closer to more traditional methods of construction. We are closer to nature than the building industry in the West. For example, wet construction–the use of brick and mortar or concrete in erecting structures–is very much viable in China. So, the Chinese architects can use these traditional techniques in very creative ways and that could be shared with more developed countries where these practices are no longer common.

036 **Fuyang Cultural Complex, Fuyang, Anhui Province, 2017** © Iwan Baan

Philip F. Yuan
ARCHI-UNION ARCHITECTS

Shanghai-based architect and Tongji University professor Philip F. YUAN (b. 1971, Harbin) received his education at Hunan University in Changsha, Hunan and Tongji University in Shanghai. His master's studies at Tongji (1993-96) occurred precisely at the time when digital, computer-aided technologies were being just introduced into architecture, namely at Columbia University in New York. Yuan started teaching at his alma mater in 1996 and founded his practice, Archi-Union Architects in 2003, the year he completed his PhD at Tongji. He has been a visiting professor at American universities, including Harvard's GSD, MIT, and the University of Virginia. The architect is known for his research on digital design, fabrication, and intelligent construction technologies in architecture, such as brick and timber robotics, and large-scale 3D-printing robotics. Yuan's real breakthrough is a group of small, socially impactful structures in Daoming, a bamboo-weaving village in Sichuan province. These buildings include the In Bamboo Cultural Exchange Center (2017), summer camp facilities, hostels, shops, and restaurants. They attract tourists, campers, and other visitors. More importantly, they generate new jobs. These buildings are built and assembled by the villagers themselves who are taught to operate robots at a specially set up local factory to produce various building components. Inviting leading architects to rural areas has become a trend in China, supported both by regional governments and businesses. The goal is to prevent locals from leaving for major cities in search of better paying jobs. Yuan imagines one day being able to build his digital factories all over the country, each serving its own region and to entice those villagers who already left to come back home to restore local economy and their families. Yuan's other works include the Light of Internet Expo Center in Jiaxing (2019), the Inkstone House OCT Linpan Cultural Center in Chengdu (2018), the Lanxi Curtilage Club in Chengdu (2011), and in Shanghai the FAB-UNION SPACE on the West Bund (2015), Tea House at J-Office (2011), and Silk Wall at J-Office (2010).

I AM INTERESTED IN SEEING THE FUTURE

In conversation with **Philip F. YUAN** of Archi-Union Architects, Shanghai
Archi-Union Architects' studio in Shanghai, March 7, 2018

Vladimir Belogolovsky: First, let's establish your roles because you have so many–an educator, researcher, theoretician, practitioner, writer. Could you talk about these directions and interests, and how they intersect?

Philip F. Yuan: Architecture for me is beyond just professional building design. Architecture is my way of life. I am in search of my own role within architecture. Architects may be preoccupied with design and building but I worry about a bigger idea: What will the future be like? Why do we build buildings? How do we build buildings? How can we produce better environments and build a better world? I am particularly interested in improving the environment for regular people, for the majority of the people, not just for the elite. That's why I don't want to be just a professional designer, even though we have a very active practice here with about 70 designers. I am interested in much more–writing, research, and teaching. Particularly teaching is important to me, which I started over twenty years ago at Tongji University here in Shanghai because it allows me to see my work critically and to test new possibilities. A typical practice of architecture is based on efficiency, budget, communication, and so on. But in the environment of the university architecture is all about experimentation and I am interested in seeing the future. Writing is very important because it forces you to think. In the last 10 years I have produced at least one book every year. Every book is a record of what was done in one year in terms of teaching, research, and practice. I am interested in both pushing the experimentation and reading history because I want to learn from history. So, I try to combine historical research with critical thinking because new theories are never entirely new; new theories are coming

037 Philip F. YUAN. Courtesy of Archi-Union Architects

from history. I view writing as part of research, it helps me to define my position in the profession because there is no practice without theory.

VB: Peter Eisenman told me that you can call yourself an architect only if you build, write, and teach. You do all three and more, since you also have a gallery and you are interested in popularizing architects' ideas. This is rare among architects. Why are you interested in so many aspects of architecture? Why not concentrate on fewer directions? What is behind this diversification?

PFY: Everyone is different. I am not Peter Eisenman or Rem Koolhaas. I grew up in an artistic family. My grandmother is a pianist. My sister is a violinist. My other sister is an accomplished dancer. My family is very diverse, but we all have strong roots in art. I am also an art collector, as many of my friends are artists. So, art is an important part of my life and many of my inspirations come from art, not from theory or science. I can't imagine being just a practitioner, working on design alone. I think every architect needs to have a theory and to have a theory you need to be open to many different directions such as research, writing, teaching, history, art, and so on.

VB: Would you say that architecture is art for you?

PFY: I would like to say that, although I am very much focused on technology. If we want to create structures that last for a long time, they need to be thought of as art. Everything I do here is all about using very sophisticated technology, but the goal is to produce something relevant, meaningful, and inspiring. Architecture as art is a major concern of mine. And to me, the goal is not only to produce a beautiful result but also a beautiful process. The process of construction can be elevated to the level of art performance.

VB: You are very eager to talk about the future. Your work is all about pushing architecture forward. You mentioned your goal to improve the environment and the way buildings get built. Does this mean that you are not satisfied with the architecture in the present? What makes you so anxious to want to change the way we build buildings today?

PFY: I work in a particular context after opening my practice 15 years ago. At the time, I looked around and saw the entire country booming with construction popping up everywhere. But I did not like the process for two reasons. First, everything was done very fast. Second, the whole construction process was based on human labor. Villagers were leaving for cities to earn more money and many ended up on construction sites. What I noticed in the last few years, is that many of these people are going back.

The urbanization in China is slowing down and the overall growth is becoming more stable. What I want to change is not just aesthetics of architecture. I want to change the construction process. I want people and machines to collaborate in this process.

VB: You offer a new form of practicing architecture based on the idea of collaborating with machines in design and construction. Could you talk about this model, what are the advantages, and is this the future for everyone?

PFY: We live in a new era. Not just in architecture, but in many spheres, such as medicine, transportation, or manufacturing. Humans can no longer operate on their own; they are being assisted by machines, so there is a collaborative relationship between humans and machines that defines our time. Computers and robots can enhance quality of construction and production and enable us to make new possibilities.

VB: You just mentioned quality. We are sitting now inside one of your spaces, the Tea House within an artist studio here at your office complex. It is a beautiful space with sculptural concrete stair. But what is it that makes this space truly contemporary? It reminds me of Ronchamp chapel by Le Corbusier built more than 60 years ago. We just talked about art. That building is a pure work of art. It was not the product of computers and robots as in the case of this building. How do you think new technology can enhance architecture? Are you using machines to achieve something more artistic than Ronchamp?

PFY: It is a valid question. Ronchamp was one of Le Corbusier's last works. It was his way to see the future in how light and space could be captured artistically. This space here is my way of seeing the future. From your perspective this building is similar or derivative, but from my perspective it is different. We want to push the technology to achieve results not simply made by the designer as an artist but to be based on various parameters. Originally, I wanted to do this curvilinear interior in white but when we took the wooden scaffolding out and saw beautiful wood grain in the concrete, I decided to leave it unpainted.

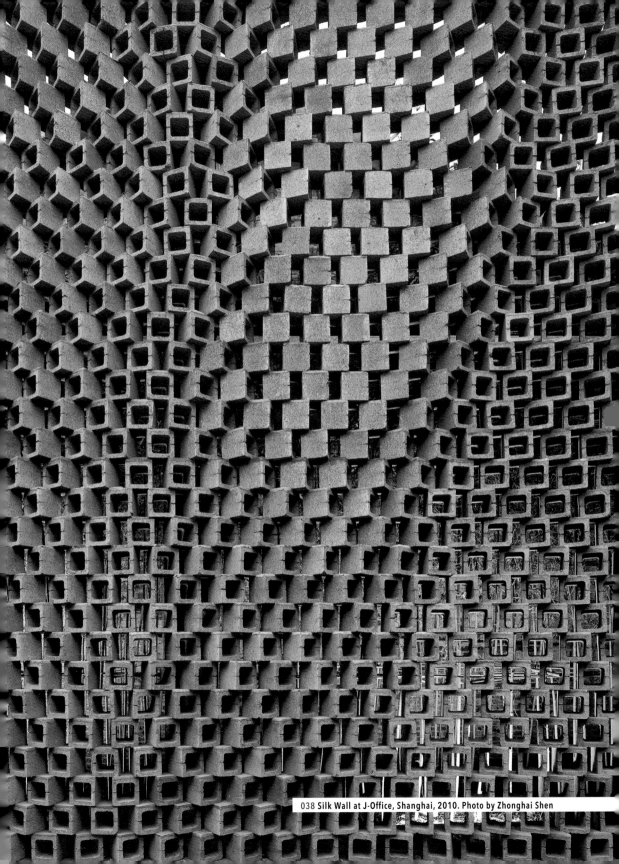

038 Silk Wall at J-Office, Shanghai, 2010. Photo by Zhonghai Shen

039 Tea House in J-Office, Shanghai, 2011. Photo by Zhonghai Shen

It is the roughness of the concrete that reminds you of Ronchamp but otherwise it is a very different building. How did we progress in 60 years? Well, Ronchamp is not based on structural logic alone; it is primarily driven by an artistic vision. But this building is based both on my vision as an artist and on structural logic.

VB: Where does the importance of logic come from? Didn't you say before that you are inspired by art? Logical in this case would be a box. We have a curved space here. What is so logical about something so poetic and complex?

PFY: The form was developed as a piece of sculpture, you are right. But the final form was defined by logic. Once we knew the direction, we calculated the absolutely most efficient way of constructing the curve and how many people and how much time it would take to build it. Le Corbusier could not calculate such complexity. We totally mastered the form-finding process.

VB: What you are saying is that today we can control the process of designing and building very complex forms and analyze and adjust them in every detail before the construction even starts. Your FAB-UNION SPACE here

in Shanghai is also built in concrete and its interior features very complex curved geometry. Speaking of this project you said, "The analysis leads to a form-finding process throughout the geometry of the site." Could you decode this phrase? What is a form-finding process? How do you typically discover the origin of the form that then guides you through a particular project?

PFY: The form-finding process is based on many parameters and the specifics of the site. We take into consideration every detail—how we want the light to come in, how the tree branch is going to cast its shadows, what will be the circulation, and so on. Another important aspect is that in our FAB-UNION SPACE the stair needed to be not only self-supporting but structural and carrying loads across the building's span. So, there are many decisions that define the final form. The original idea is artistic, but then it becomes very specific and the process of finding the final form is very logical, site specific, and parametrically driven. The computer responds to the design architect, but the process is all based on the collaboration between me and my computer. As a designer I don't know the final form, just a general direction. The computer makes it specific. The form is never settled before the form-finding process. The form is always a result of responding to many specific objectives.

VB: Let's talk about your intentions in architecture. What is it that you are trying to achieve because you clearly have an agenda and every commission helps you to achieve it, right?

PFY: For me it is important to show materiality in every project. I only designed one project early on that was all white and concealed. But typically, I use the materials in such a way that the building's structure is exposed. There is a dialogue between what the building is and how it is put together. In all my designs I first think about what the most appropriate material would be to use. I try to find the identity of each project in the right material. What I am looking for in architecture is not my personal identity but the identity of each project. I want all of my works to have different identities. And I search for these identities in the material and building process. Unlike other architects I spend most of my time in factories and labs to examine and explore the building and manufacturing process. These identities are rooted in each project's site, which leads to the right choice of material. It is the identity of the site and the identities of particular materials that together make up the identity of each project.

VB: Would you rather develop ideas that could be used by other architects or discover your own unique identity, and even techniques?

PFY: Of course, I would be happy if other architects used technologies and techniques developed by my studio. Look at the legacies of Mies and Le Corbusier. Their work opened up architecture and possibilities for many generations of architects. And now, I believe, a new machine revolution is coming; namely, the collaboration between architects and machines. It will change the profession entirely. The form-making process, which is what architecture is about, will be coming from the building industry, meaning from the collaboration between human and machine. We will always have signature architects but in the future their work will be altered or even defined by machines. Sure, such conditions as social

aspects will be very important reasons for shaping architecture. Still, I believe that it is new digital tools that will give us critical feedback and ultimately define architecture of the future.

VB: Let me ask you something. Before we sat down here, you showed me all the amazing tools and robots that can achieve all these fascinating forms and shapes in just about any material. The conclusion that I want to make is this: Okay, now I know that technologically anything is possible. As a designer, I can be totally free, which takes us back to how architects always worked–they dreamed about not what was possible, but what was impossible. Look at the Sydney Opera House. The technology eventually caught up with the design. Sure, such approach is not efficient but that's what ultimately pushes the technology forward–an original idea that challenges the reality. Why are you so concerned with responding to what machines can do? If you let your imagination be totally free the machines will eventually catch up. What do you think?

PFY: I work with machines to know their limits. That helps me to push my imagination. The imagination will always be ahead of what is possible but what I am doing is this–I am going in tandem with technology. I am going back and forth between my ideas and analysis of what tools can enable me to do. One pushes the other. A few years ago, I worked with a robot that could put together identical bricks in a variety of patterns. Now I am working with a more advanced robot that can deal with bricks that are all different. I am interested in this collaborative process. I use tools to direct my imagination. I want to imagine new possibilities in partnership with machines. We are imagining new architecture as partners.

VB: Is there one particular breakthrough project in your portfolio that you could call your manifesto?

PFY: I like to think that it is my latest project called the In Bamboo Cultural Exchange Center in Daoming, Sichuan Province. It is familiar and it is different. There is a good dialogue between the place,

040 FAB-UNION SPACE on the West Bund, Shanghai, 2015
Photo by Shengliang Su

tradition, culture, innovation, and use of technology. The onsite work was all done in just 52 days. That is because everything was prefabricated in the robotic factory that we set up nearby. All elements of the project were put on six trucks and delivered to the site and then assembled.

Many Chinese architects go to villages and build interesting buildings with local materials and labor. But I do more, I am teaching local people new techniques. And now that the local government agreed to build a number of other small projects in the same village we are going to use our new factory for these other new projects, which will include water infrastructure pavilions, education center, internet center, package-delivery station, hotel, children's summer camp, and public restrooms. All of these projects will be done in collaboration with the villagers. This will completely change the quality of life of so many people in that village. Also, the factory that we set up will be growing and it will be used for other projects in China. It will become our studio's second base. In Bamboo, as well as all other our projects that are going to be built in Daoming demonstrate how

industry, technology, craftsmanship, and aesthetics can merge to produce meaningful and new kind of architecture.

VB: Let's talk about the In Bamboo project in more detail. Who was your client and how did you receive this commission?

PFY: Well, here in China we have this tradition–regional governments give tax refund money back to villages. But the money is not given in cash. It can only be spent on the maintenance of these rural places. Typically, these villages paint their street walls and public buildings in white. All over the country these places look very similar because that's what so many villages choose to do–paint everything in white. So, what you see are these freshly painted white walls, gray tile roofs, and green trees. It was my idea to change this tradition. I talked to the mayor of Daoming and said that the money should be invested in new construction and public programs, not just painting every year. Then this town could generate its own income and improve its situation.

VB: Particularly the demographic situation because so many young people are leaving villages and small towns in search of jobs.

PFY: Yes, once young people leave for college they rarely come back. Daoming is losing its young people constantly, so there are mostly elderly and children who live there. Young people are leaving for Chengdu, the capital of Sichuan Province and other fast-growing cities such as Shenzhen and Guangzhou. This is, of course, not just a local problem but the same is happening all over the country. It is hard for the young generation to find jobs in the countryside. Regional governments are acutely aware of this problem and are looking for ways to reverse this trend. Building new community centers is one of the solutions.

VB: Yet, Daoming is a special case due to the fact that it is a regional center for bamboo weaving craftsmanship.

PFY: Yes, every family there has been involved in producing bamboo products for over two thousand years. They generate their income by making baskets,

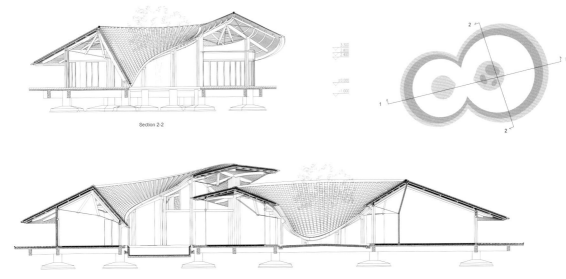

Section 2-2

041 In Bamboo, Daoming, Sichuan Province, 2017. Courtesy of Archi-Union Architects

furniture, and all kinds of souvenirs. The problem is that they don't know how to market their products. In Bamboo has become an important outlet for promoting this local industry. One of the main components that we designed in our center was the exhibition space to showcase the local crafts. It was this space that became our starting point for the new center.

VB: Let's talk about the center's planning. What kind of programs does it offer and how were they originally planned?

PFY: In Bamboo is not a big building. It is only 1,800 square meters or less than 20,000 square feet. Apart from an exhibition gallery there is a space for community gatherings and conferences, a restaurant, a tea house, and a souvenir shop to sell local crafts. The planning came out of many meetings between the villagers, regional government, and me. It wasn't that I was given the program; it took many discussions to arrive at developing it. There was a process; once the program was defined, I started working on how to organize different spaces to accommodate it.

VB: Who was the driving force behind this project?

PFY: As in any good project, it must be the client. In this case, the client was a developer working on behalf of the regional government. Usually, projects are driven by whoever pays for them. But it was my conversations with the villagers that determined the shape and content of this project. The program was open, which is how it should always be. Because as an architect, I can only react to what is needed by the local community. I can't just make up architecture and dream up its program. And it was important not only to discuss the building, but also how it would be managed once it is built. Right now, if you visit the center, you will find about ten local people working there. They organize the events, clean the rooms, and the most important part is the restaurant where they serve local spicy food. That's what generates income and makes the whole center sustainable. Other new facilities that were built after In Bamboo also have about ten people working there, which is a lot for such a small village. The initial investment came from outside, but the management is done by the local efforts. The model here is non-profit because all proceeds go into maintaining the center and other public projects in the village. It is a beautiful ecosystem.

VB: If there are now all these new jobs that attract back some of those who already left this village, we can say that architecture in Daoming is being used as a social tool to repair one village at a time, even one family at a time.

042 In Bamboo, Daoming, Sichuan Province, 2017. Photo by Fangfang Tian

PFY: I would confirm that.

VB: How do you think In Bamboo and other facilities in Daoming could serve as a model to other places?

PFY: When I talk about In Bamboo serving as an example, obviously, we are not talking about architecture and design because that is very specific to Daoming and to its region. But what can be followed is the business model, which could be relevant not only in China but even internationally. First, you need to have funds to start such project. In China, it is our system of tax refunds that villages are already getting from the regional governments. That's a starting point because you can't do anything without financial support. Second, it is important to develop a strategy for how such center would be managed, so the project could become sustainable. That requires an experienced team of professionals who can develop a program based on local requirements. Third, would be the design. Otherwise, people will not come. The new structure needs to be local and well-integrated into its environment, and yet, it needs to be different, so it would attract interest and curiosity. A new building must represent a kind of utopia. Whether architecture can become attractive to local people entirely depends on architect's talent. A new building has to have good spatial qualities.

VB: Could you talk about your other buildings in Daoming?

PFY: Once we finished In Bamboo, we were asked to design more projects. We just finished Bed and Breakfast with eight rooms. They are modeled after traditional buildings and are covered by double-curvature roofs. There is also a new tourist center that serves as a gateway to the village. There is a new summer camp for teenagers with classrooms, equipment rooms, and a restaurant. And we are now building a number of new buildings with community services, including an internet center, canteen space, and package-delivery station. Apart from these projects we also did public restrooms and we were even asked to design several water pavilions.

VB: If you were to summarize–what is the main lesson from doing these community projects in Daoming and what would you like other architects, whether in China or elsewhere, to learn from it?

PFY: The most important thing is the attitude that architects should have toward their projects. You can't start any project pretending that you are an expert and that you already know what to do. You have to be ready to learn from people who will be using your building. Architecture should be about investigation and communication. There should be discussion before designing. We had many meetings and every time there were new people and new ideas. A good designer is not only someone who can design something beautiful but also who can listen, communicate, and persuade others. Of course, you need to be lucky with a client. If your client is only motivated by profit it is impossible to arrive at a strong building. Developments should start with a good heart and civic mindset.

VB: Do you try to produce work unlike anyone has ever seen before?

PFY: Absolutely! I particularly focus on plastic printing. Why plastic, because it is a kind of material that is difficult to reuse and here in China, we have so much of it. We must come up with a solution for its reuse and plastic printing is one such solution.

VB: You teach architecture. Could you talk about your way of teaching and what kind of assignments do you give to your students?

PFY: This semester we are going to design a chair in the first half and a pavilion in the second half. The chair assignment is done individually, while the pavilion is a group project. We do research on important historical precedents. My students then try to design a new chair that they need to invent based on new tools available today. They don't just design it, we produce it either at the university or if it gets too complicated, right here at my office. And as part of this semester, I teach them how to use at least twenty different software programs. We also discuss inspirations such as forms found in nature and again, in the process of making things. Most professors at my school are not very fond of my methods because they have their settled ways of teaching and I am constantly changing what and how I am teaching, which is, of course, necessary.

VB: Let's talk about the digital paradigm in architecture. It was Columbia University in the early 1990s under the leadership of then Dean Bernard Tschumi and such young professors as Greg Lynn and Hani Rashid that digital architecture emerged in academia and in such practices as Gehry Partners and Zaha Hadid Architects. Where was China at that point and where is China now?

PFY: Well, China was far behind. But at this point China is where I am because my team represents the most advanced digital design and production techniques in the country. What you describe about the emergence of new digital technologies at Columbia is correct. But at that time, two important components were missing. There was no integrated link to production and there was no social impact. These technologies were meant to serve the elite, not the masses. I am working on integrating all three of these components–design, production, and building for the masses, as well as engaging local laborers and educating them in the process. Honestly, I don't see this kind of interest in the West even today. What I see is that these new technologies are used as artistic, self-centered expressions. They don't make a social impact. What I am doing is all about mass production and building for as many people as possible. Also, what I am doing today is a model. In the near future, I hope, this is how the whole of China will operate. Imagine, if every city in China will have a robotic factory like the one we set up in Daoming!

VB: What do you think about the Chinese identity? Do you think it is important for China, and for you personally, to read it in your architecture?

PFY: Not at all. If I lived in another country, I would address that country's regional conditions. Architecture making is influenced by where you are. Why does my architecture look Chinese? Because I am here. Architecture is all about understanding local technologies and building process. I am concerned with reflecting on what is around me, not necessarily with who I am.

VB: Could you talk more about this idea of collaboration between a human and machine? Who is the leader? Who is in control?

PFY: At this point it is us, people. We set up all the rules. But ask me this question in twenty years and I am not so sure that I will know the answer because of the advancement of the artificial intelligence. Perhaps in the future the relationship between humans and machines will be on par. Creativity is expressed in being able to set up the rules. Intelligence of the machines is constantly being improved. We need to learn how to use it. Look at the wind tunnel technology; it allows us to create very smart forms that perform best in various circumstances. Again, creativity is all about setting up the rules. For example, the romantic idea of catching up the sunlight–how do you do that? Once you set this goal the machine can do that much more precisely than we can. But we are the ones who set the whole process in motion.

VB: Your architecture is informed by performative principles. And you mentioned this phrases–structure performance simulation. Could you talk about it?

PFY: Structure performance is responsible for the most beautiful shapes in nature. Why trees are so stable and can withstand tremendous pressure? They are based on this principle. Modernist structures were sometimes inspired by nature. But they were not concerned with simulation, which is a strong direction now. Simulation helps us to find a form–formation, simulation, optimization. That's why process is so important in our work. We learn by analysis. Machines inform us. They expand our thinking and push our imagination. The results are very interesting if you know how to set up the process and how to control it. The question now is–How do we collaborate with the machine? It is totally different from Le Corbusier's time. He only relied on his own intelligence. But our intelligence can surpass his because we know how to accumulate intelligence. Our imagination today is so much more powerful.

VB: What words or short phrases would you use to describe your architecture?

PFY: Digital tectonics, cultural orientation, design identity. I think we should not erase what architectural history has accumulated before us. We need to balance traditions and new technologies.

VB: Do you think your work is beautiful?

PFY: I think so. I have seen some surveys in which ordinary, non-professional people identified my buildings among the most beautiful buildings recently built in China.

VB: Why do you think we need architecture to be experimental and progressive? What is so compelling about this idea of looking for something completely different from what we know and what we are accustomed to?

PFY: I believe in the idea that every generation needs to achieve something new. It is always a dream for the younger generation to have new things–new clothes, new gadgets, new everything. It is the most natural thing in the world. It is important for every generation to produce something new, something that can be identified with them and no one else–new technology, new style, new fashion, new beauty.

VB: I want to talk about your inspirations. When I talked to Hani Rashid and Lise Anne Couture we discussed their inspirations such as digital delirium, film, computer animations, clouds, aerodynamics, high performance cars, organic

tissues, flying, movement, speed, amorphic shapes, infinite space, etc. Are you driven by any of these inspirations? What makes you want to experiment and create something new? What feeds you?

PFY: Hani Rashid and Lise Anne Couture are futurists. I am half futurist and half traditionalist. I think any new creation should have a linkage to history and traditions. Nothing should be totally new. There should be a certain harmony and continuation between the future and the past. So, I am inspired by all of these things, but I am looking both forward and into the past because history has so many great ideas that we can still use.

VB: In one of your slides in your recent lecture at Columbia University you compared the forms of an apple and a pear and talked about what an ideal form for a hanging fruit would be. When we talk about an architectural form why do you think it is important to think of something that is precisely calculated, efficient, economical, and ideal versus something that is original, artistic, dreamed up, and idealistic?

PFY: It is all about the identity of each product. The shapes of an apple and pear are different because the seeds are different. The seed is the identity of the fruit. Everything has an identity. We can shape anything anyway we want to. But every object has its own identity, its own internal logic. Technology can help us to better define identity of each object. We need to embrace the new technology. In the past eight years we organized digital workshops here at my studio, which have become the most important events both for my studio and Tongji University. It is important to exchange new knowledge and educate each other. We cannot slow down this development. Architecture must keep up with the latest technology. And for China, what's important now is not just to master new technologies but to create them. What we are creating is not simply the subject of a research in a lab. We are building real projects and engaging many ordinary people in the process. Here in China, we have the opportunity to employ new technologies on a massive scale.

043 In Bamboo, Daoming, Sichuan Province, 2017. Photo by Bian Lin

VB: What kind of architecture do you strive to achieve?

PFY: To me every building should strive to be a manifesto, if not for the far future then at least for the near future. I want to know how we can build differently and how we can push architecture beyond what we know. I don't like commercial architecture that follows the market. I am always interested in this question—what is next? I am no longer inspired by contemporary buildings. I am inspired by history, art, and technology. And every year I travel to one new city purely for pleasure and in search of new inspirations. I just came back from Mexico City where I visited several magical projects by Luis Barragán, so my inspirations are very different.

VB: If you could meet one particular person from any time in history who would that be and what one question would you ask him or her?

PFY: That would have to be Zaha Hadid. I am a good friend with Patrik Schumacher, her partner. But there is a difference. She was an artist who predicted the future. He is theorizing on what she has predicted. I like her original instincts. I like her bravery. I am inspired by her a lot. And I know that if I asked her a question her answer would not be very specific. But one question I would want to ask is this—what drives you?

STRUCTURING WITH LANDSCAPE
UNIQUE ATMOSPHERE
INTERDEPENDENCE
UNCERTAINTIES
MINDSCAPE

LIU Yichun & CHEN Yifeng

ATELIER DESHAUS

LIU Yichun (b. 1969, Haiyang, Shandong province) and CHEN Yifeng (b. 1972, Kunshan, Jiangsu Province) founded their Shanghai-based Atelier Deshaus in 2001. The architects describe their architecture as buildings that turn into landscapes and landscapes that turn into buildings. Their architecture stands out in China's newly emerging constellation of independent architects with a strong body of public works–museums, schools, kindergartens, promenades, pavilions, temples–that don't seem to be concerned with Chinese roots. Their regional identity is ambiguous and intentionally suppressed in favor of audacious modernity. These buildings are prominently located in urban settings, they are large in scale, and they are all formally inventive, rigorous, and liberating. Liu earned his Bachelor of Architecture at Tongji University in 1991, then worked for three years at Guangzhou Architectural Design Institute and returned to Tongji for his Master of Architecture (1997). Before co-founding Deshaus he worked as chief architect at the Architectural Design Institute of Tongji University. Chen also pursued his degrees at Tongji, obtaining his bachelor's in 1995 and master's in 1998. Prior to co-founding Deshaus he worked alongside Liu at the Architectural Design Institute of Tongji University. The atelier's built works include Taizhou Contemporary Art Museum in Taizhou, Zhejiang Province (2019) and several projects in Shanghai: the Minsheng Wharf Silo Exhibition Hall Conversion (2017); the Modern Art Museum, Laobaidu coal bunker transformation (2016); the Huaxin Wisdom Hub, a conference and exhibition center (2015); and Site D at Innovative Port of Anting International Automobile City (2015). Yet, it is their Long Museum (2014), also in Shanghai, that has become a true milestone for Chinese architecture. Some leading critics and architects call it their favorite recent building in China. The following interview with partners Liu Yichun and Chen Yifeng was recorded at their studio in Shanghai with the help of a translator Doris Deng. We discussed the role of identity in the architects' work and how they try to connect their buildings to context, a fleeting notion in China.

THE IDEA IS NOT TO CREATE AN OBJECT
BUT TO CONSTRUCT A PATH

In conversation with **LIU Yichun** and **CHEN Yifeng** of Atelier Deshaus, Shanghai
Atelier Deshaus studio in Shanghai, January 12, 2018

Vladimir Belogolovsky: I read that you each design different projects in the studio. Could you talk about that?

Liu Yichun: This is true since 2010. Before that we always designed everything together. There were endless discussions and too many disagreements and arguments. That's why we decided to pursue two parallel paths. This approach led to greater efficiency and it helped us to formulate clearer ideas of our independent views of architecture. It also helps us to diversify our work and to avoid forming one recognizable style.

Chen Yifeng: It is important for us to express our solutions differently, even though we are fundamentally working in one direction and pursuing one family of ideas.

VB: Could you talk about the origin behind your studio's name?

LYC: "Atelier Deshaus" is a play of words. "Das haus" means "the house" in German, while "Des" is a reference to Dessau, home of the Bauhaus school. We both studied German when we were students at Tongji University. Also, the sound of "Das haus" resembles Chinese phrase "Da She," which means a big house. There is another phrase made up of some of the same characters, "Da She Da De." It means abandon much, gain much, which is similar to Mies's famous dictum less is more.

VB: How would you describe the intentions of your work? Do you have your own agenda apart from your clients' particular requirements?

044 LIU Yichun & CHEN Yifeng. Courtesy of Atelier Deshaus

LYC: Of course, we try to go beyond a particular program. We focus on structure and site, form and place, and how to connect them. We work on integrating humanmade with landscape. We focus on what we call objecthood and situatedness. In other words, we don't just see architecture as a pure sculptural expression but as a direct response to a complex juxtaposition of many layers of specific conditions such as the site, program, culture, and other meanings.

CYF: We concentrate on doing public architecture rather than commercial. We focus on two main

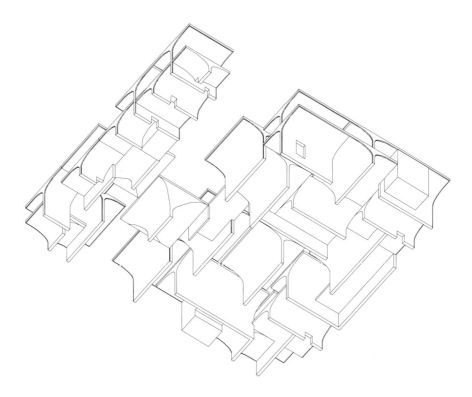

045 Long Museum, West Bund, Shanghai, 2014. Axonometric. Courtesy of Atelier Deshaus

categories–exhibition spaces such as museums and educational projects–mainly schools and kindergartens. We avoid working for commercial developers on such projects as offices or residential, as they are all about the market and maximizing profits. We are not interested in that.

VB: And what about houses? Wouldn't you agree that this is where architecture begins? It is a house that is a kind of microcosm, which is a perfect exercise for formulating a particular holistic vision.

CYF: Here in China, the land cannot be owned, so a private house is not possible, or very rare. You can say that private houses in China are all about interior design, not architecture. We both live in generic apartment blocks. The market situation is changing, as there is a high demand for new developments, so there may be opportunities for building freestanding

houses in the future. The other key focus for us is on people. Of course, we design spaces that are artificial, but they have to be comfortable. And the goal is to create a particular atmosphere for every project. We focus on uncertainties between abstractness and concreteness, interior and exterior, between solid and void. For example, in our Huaxin Wisdom Hub the lack of significant context led to creating an introspective world by proposing an outer wall that wraps both interior and exterior spaces. Inside and outside are completely intertwined and blurred, which is accentuated by lifting this outer wall off the ground, so pavement and grass go back and forth, in and out. We like these uncertainties.

VB: You seem to avoid composing your buildings into freestanding, clearly defined objects. Is that the idea? Your architecture seems to refuse to be defined by clearly perceivable edges.

LYC: The idea is not to create an object but to construct a path. Our projects are not about proposing new forms but about how they are explored and experienced. They are about the space and movement around, inside, on top, and through without any particular sequence. And often it is not clear where the entrance is; you need to discover it. A building is a path. You encounter and experience it before you realize that you are already inside of it. A building turns into a landscape and landscape turns into a building.

VB: Speaking of perpetually evolving urbanization in China you said, "We are confronted with the process of drastic urbanization; the surroundings are always unknown. Even if there is planning, it is always subject to unpredictable and constant change. Eventually, we have to resort to our own totality." You just compared your buildings to landscapes, but these landscapes seem to be quite autonomous; they float independently of the context around and they establish their own context, right?

LYC: We try not to tie our projects directly to the context since, as you said, it is typically in flux. But we always engage with the outside and try to create many opportunities for observing outside or engaging from inside and we are interested in these dialogues that often evolve beyond our control. We use our architecture to express and embrace this uncertainty, not to escape from it.

CYF: Many of our projects are built in suburban areas with no context whatsoever and we are often forced not to respond to the context but to create it. Sometimes we decide to isolate our buildings by creating a boundary to protect them from the constantly changing environment.

VB: In one of your texts you said, "We believe that pragmatic solutions related to contemporary architecture in China require a rational approach that is linked to a personal touch." Let's talk about this "personal touch" in more detail. What do you think differentiates your work from other architects'?

LYC: This is not a question for us to answer. We don't focus on creating our own identity. We simply work on projects, hoping that our identity will come through.

CYF: Of course, we have a particular way of doing architecture, so our hand becomes apparent. Our work has many uncertainties, but they are our uncertainties.

LYC: Any building, apart from responding to the specifics, is about the architect's own life experience, education, and interests. Architecture for me, should manage well three things: first, it is designed to be used; then it should be suitable for the site; lastly, it must be emotionally touching. The solution might be varied for each project, but fundamentally, all are related back to the theme of time, place, and people.

VB: You said something quite interesting, "Constructing a new place and experience is a task that every good architect should complete." Would that be accurate to say that in each of your works you intend to provide a unique experience? Could you talk about your design process? What are some of the initial questions that you tackle?

CYF: We focus on pragmatics and specifics. We work on creating experiences, particular views, and so on. Our focus is not on newness, but on being suitable and specific. For example, in the Spiral Gallery [Shanghai, 2011], the question we tried to answer is how to *see* the outside. So, we came up with this up-and-down route for the users to have a closed-open-closed experience along the path, as a better way to visually connect with its surroundings. The Huaxin Wisdom Hub is another story. The environment there is not exactly pleasant at the moment, so we created a wall to separate our building from it. Yet, the wall is not completely closed, but "floating" from the ground, to bring ambiguity and uncertainty.

LYC: Namely, there are two things that we care about. One is how an architectural work builds up its relationship with its place, whether it is cultural or contextual. And the other one is more relevant to modernity, issues that are global and shared by all people.

046 Long Museum, West Bund, Shanghai, 2014 © Shengliang Su

047 Long Museum, West Bund, Shanghai, 2014 © Shengliang Su

VB: It is ironic that you are saying that your work is not about newness. In just one generation Chinese architecture went from being generic and impersonal to self-consciously experimental and strikingly new. Being one of the most original architects in the country, you say that newness is not what you are interested in? You seem to downplay your role as creative authors. But let me assure you that when I go into your Long Museum or any one of your built works, they are about something I have never seen before and that is probably because you set that as your goal. You are pursuing architecture without any established rules. You are setting up those rules as you go, and you expect me to believe that you are simply solving the pragmatics? There must be something you are not telling me.

LYC: You are right, our architecture is about newness. But the new is the result, not the starting point.

Primarily, we focus on context and program. The new is a subtext. But sure, it is there. It is the focus on the specifics that leads to something new, not the other way around.

CYF: What leads to a unique solution is our recognition of something particular and unusual in the site or program. Unique conditions lead to unique solutions. We are after creating unique atmospheres in each project. These atmospheres must have memories of the past and look into the future at the same time.

VB: Your Long Museum is based on a pattern of repeated forms that you call vault-umbrellas or umbrella columns that mimic an existing ruin on the site. What was the main design idea and who was the leading designer for that project?

LYC: I was, but we intensely discussed this project together. The repeated patterns originated from a response to the context. There is a segment of coal-unloading hopper bridge that remains on the site. The museum's structure is made up of repeated units that represent an abstracted version of that hopper bridge. The idea was to form a clear dialogue between our new building and the remaining ruin by using a language of industrial production. That's why we came up with these umbrella-shaped units. Although the scale is different, the construction logic is the same. Our solution, for sure, was influenced by such masters as Mies and Kahn, but the main idea was to challenge a typical sequence of spaces in a traditional gallery, which is linear and hierarchical.

VB: Since Long Museum is an art institution its program is not very precise, as far as spatial requirements. Would you say that you designed this building as a ruin, somewhat independently of its function, imagining how the structure may look like in the afterlife of the museum?

LYC: Absolutely. The goal is to achieve a certain freedom and even a sense of eternity because I think a ruin is a kind of space that offers most freedom and is associated with eternity. So, the project was more

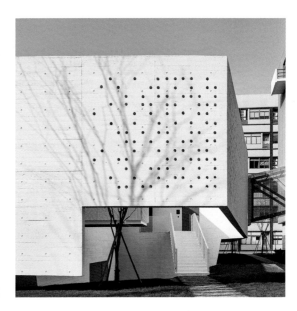

048 Huaxin Wisdom Hub, Shanghai, 2015 © Eiichi Kano

about the space itself, not simply a response to the museum's particular needs.

VB: Are you curious about what other architects are up to? Who do you pay attention to here in China or around the world?

CYF: I am very much inspired by Chinese traditional buildings and classical western architecture. As for the living architects, I enjoy the work of Alvaro Siza the most. I visited his projects and I am very much inspired by them. I feel like my interests are very much similar to what is reflected in Siza's works. Then, of course, Louis Kahn who is very inspirational to both of us.

LYC: In addition to Kahn we also both follow the works of late Japanese architect Kazuo Shinohara. If talking about the Chinese local influence, I would particularly cite a book titled *The Garden Treatise* (*Yuan Ye*, 园冶) by Ming dynasty garden designer Ji Cheng. In this book, he proposed a design theory called *Yin Jie Ti Yi* (因借体宜), which might be translated as interdependence, borrowing, suitability, and appropriateness. As is discussed before, we

049 Shanghai Modern Art Museum, Shanghai, 2016. © Fangfang Tian

need to take advantage of existing context to design the kind of architecture that would be suitable for a particular site.

VB: And what do you think about contemporary architecture here in China and about such internationally visible architects as Wang Shu or Ma Yansong?

LYC: I think their works are somewhat biased on the idea of Chinese architecture, or, architecture in general. Both offer quite literal representations of a place. In case of Wang Shu, his buildings are read somewhat like paintings. His architecture's primary concern seems to be in achieving a particular image. Contemporary architecture in general, is largely driven by an image. I don't think it should be the goal. And Ma Yansong's architecture is also pursuing an image, but his tools are different; he is using digital and parametric techniques to achieve that goal.

VB: You don't think their works offer spatially rich and engaging experience? You are right about the image as the main draw but in my experience of visiting their buildings there is never just a single dominating image. Wang Shu's Ningbo Museum may be a series of compelling facade images, but they draw you in and ultimately become a stage for unique architectural experience. Who do you think is particularly important among architects here in China?

LYC: I would name Yung Ho Chang, the founder of FCJZ with Lijia Lu. He is a former head of the Architecture Department at MIT and now professor at Tongji University here in Shanghai. Also, architects like Wang Shu and Ma Yansong are important, but they are not the architects that we follow.

CYF: We are searching for our own direction, and it is not important to us whether we are perceived as Chinese architects. We certainly don't want to fit any expectations of what in the West may be perceived as Chinese architecture. Of course, we are Chinese architects, but we don't reinterpret any "traditional symbols" consciously. The traditional design philosophy will be naturally revealed in our works. We are working on contemporary issues and we want to be a part of contemporary discourse.

VB: Do you think architecture is art?

LYC: Absolutely! Architecture should be thought of as art. Finally!

CYF: Of course, architecture as art is our goal. If it is not art, then it cannot be called architecture.

VB: Is there one particular building in Shanghai built in recent years that you enjoy most?

LYC: Our Long Museum! [Laughs.] Well, for us it is very important and enjoyable. In a way, it has become our starting point, as it incorporates many of

our ideas and interests that we experimented with in various projects but never so holistically.

VB: If you were to describe your architecture in single words what would they be?

LYC: Structuring with landscape, mindscape.

CYF: Poetic, contextual, usability.

VB: If you could meet any one person in history who would that be?

LYC: Alberti.

CYF: Kahn.

VB: What would you ask them?

LYC: We always ask the same question: What is architecture? We think it is important to ask this question quite often.

CYF: And we don't want to come up with the same answer every time. Every situation and every moment in time requires different solutions.

050 Minsheng Wharf Silo Exhibition Hall Conversion, Shanghai, 2017 © Atelier Deshaus

051 **Taizhou Contemporary Art Museum, Taizhou, Zhejiang Province, 2019. © Fangfang Tian**

Yung Ho CHANG

ATELIER FCJZ

Beijing architect Yung Ho CHANG (b. 1956, Beijing), together with his wife Lijia LU (b. 1960, Wuhan), started their practice in 1993 under the name Feichang Jianzhu, Atelier FCJZ, which literary means "not ordinary architecture," a symbolic name for what became China's first independent architectural studio, laying the foundation for contemporary practice in the country. Therefore, despite the architect's still evolving career he is referred to as the father of contemporary Chinese architecture and, according to many of my interviewees in the book, is regarded as the single most respected and influential architect in China. His Split House (2002) at the Commune by the Wall near the Great Wall outside of Beijing is among the earliest uncompromisingly modern and concept-driven buildings in China. Chang grew up in a prominent architect's family. His father was one of the chief architects of the Beijing Institute of Architectural Design (BIAD) and designer of many prominent buildings in the capital. Chang studied architecture at the Nanjing Institute of Technology (now Southeast University) before receiving his Bachelor of Architecture degree from Ball State University in Muncie, Indiana, and Master of Architecture from the University of California at Berkeley. In 1999, Chang founded and headed the architecture program at Peking University. He has taught both in China and America, including at Harvard's GSD and headed MIT School of Architecture from 2005 to 2010. In 2012, the year he joined the prestigious Pritzker Prize Jury, his fellow countryman Wang Shu became the first Chinese architect to win the Prize. Chang's work is unusual in China. It constitutes a kind of resistance not only to the ordinary and pragmatic, but also against everything that tends to be purely visual. He pursues architecture as an autonomous project. His buildings have their beautiful stories to tell. They are contemplative, introspective, and always beyond their first impressions. Among Chang's other important projects are the Forbidden City College renovation in Chongqing (2020), the Jiading Mini-Block in Jiading Industrial Park in Shanghai (2020), the Brick Pavilion/Information Kiosk in Shenzhen (2017), the Jishow Art Museum in Hunan (2019), the Vertical Glass House in Shanghai (2013), the Museum Bridge in Sichuan (2012), and the Xishu Bookstore in Beijing (1996).

I FAILED TO BE AN ARTIST BUT I BECAME AN ARTISTIC ARCHITECT

In conversation with **Yung Ho CHANG** of Atelier FCJZ, Beijing
Atelier FCJZ in Beijing, November 28, 2018

Vladimir Belogolovsky: Let me start with your quote, "I believe architecture is something more down to earth, and ultimately relates to how people live." Tell me you were kidding when you said that because it seems to me that your architecture is anything but down to earth. Down to earth is something that we tend not to notice, right?

Yung Ho Chang: Well, maybe something was lost in translation from Chinese. [Laughs.] What I meant is that architecture is tangible. It is about our physical world. Architecture for me is about enjoying life. It is very much about the way we live. And for us architecture is so much more than just buildings. You know, we design furniture, industrial products, clothing, jewelry, everything. For example, a couple of years ago, since architects like to solve all kinds of problems, I was asked to design a cake. There was a problem–traditional Mille-Feuille tends to get softened by the moisture of the cream between puff pastry layers. We solved it by separating the pastry and the cream, which was placed in a chocolate box in the center, so you can dip the pastry into the cream as you like. This is what I mean by tangible design. I don't enjoy reading philosophical books on architecture. It is too abstract for me. And I am not trying to expand on designing everything. I enjoy life and from time to time it gives me a lot of pleasure to design not just buildings**.** Still, it is buildings that I focus on primarily.

VB: You also said, "I don't think architects can just fly around and build structures anywhere, but rather they need to anchor themselves in one place. Architects should sit in their studios

052 Yung Ho CHANG © Fangfang Tian

and work with materials and their teams." Is that what you do yourself?

YHC: Well, I used to fly around, you are right; but not anymore. I continue to fly for construction sites and client meetings but not nearly as much. What I meant was that if you have the ambition to discover something in architecture and push the discipline you really need to spend time at your practice on daily basis. You need to learn how to put buildings

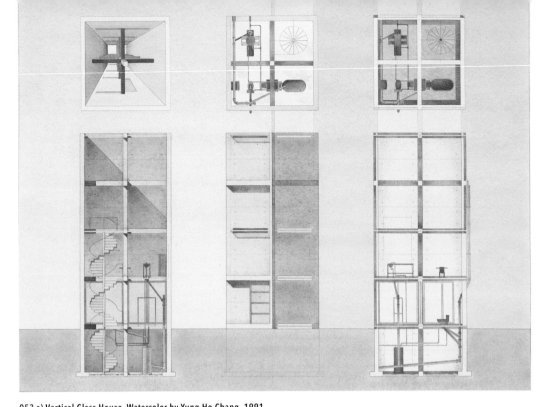

053 a) Vertical Glass House, Watercolor by Yung Ho Chang, 1991
From L to R: Plan of all floors looking down; Plan of all floors looking up; Planar Perspective. Courtesy of Atelier FCJZ
b) Vertical Glass House, Watercolor by Yung Ho Chang, 1991
From L to R: Day Section, Day Elevation (left) & Night Elevation (right), Night Section with Artificial Lighting. Courtesy of Atelier FCJZ

together. Good buildings are the ones that are put together well. Maybe I am getting more conservative. [Laughs.] Of course, you need to be curious and open, but at some point, you need to anchor yourself and focus on work. You must develop what I would call an autonomous architecture. Of course, as an architect, you need a client, you need to be engaged with society, you need to follow certain conventions about structure, climate, materials, and so on. But you should also try to develop your own sensibilities as an author.

VB: Speaking of what you called autonomous architecture, can you expand on that by perhaps referring to your Vertical Glass House that you built in Shanghai in 2013? This project has established a strong autonomy from its place. It is a fascinating play on seeing and being seen, as well as your refusal to reduce architecture to its function. Isn't it a good example that your architecture is anything but down to earth? It is quite an invention; one may even call it a novel that can be read spatially and experientially. You stayed there with your own family for a short while, right? Did you enjoy living in this house as much as designing it?

YHC: You are right, it is an invention in a certain way. Yes, I enjoyed living there very much. [Laughs.] Now that I think about it, among other references, I must have been influenced by John Hejduk's project *The House of the Inhabitant who Refused to Participate.* I do have a desire to stay in that theoretical house by Hejduk. And one of my intentions in the Vertical Glass House was the desire to experience space alone. It came from an architectural proposition, the glass house, which, of course, preoccupied many architects in the past, such as Mies van der Rohe and Philip Johnson. So, I took their glass house, whether

Mies's Farnsworth House or Johnson's Glass House and literally turned it 90 degrees. I flipped the materials–solid roof and floor were replaced by glass, while entirely transparent facades were replaced by almost windowless concrete walls.

VB: This was originally designed as a paper project back in 1991, as an award-winning entry for the annual Shinkenchiku Residential Design Competition organized by the *Japan Architecture* magazine. This project is such an idealistic and theoretical vision. Why do you maintain that your work is down to earth?

YHC: Because this house has a down to earth moment. [Laughs.] Let me tell you. I really wanted to experience being in this house. But I also wondered: Who else?

VB: Who else?

YHC: [Laughs.] May I suggest, today the notion of a glass house doesn't belong to Germany, the U.S., Mies, or Johnson. It belongs to everyone. There is a literary figure in Chinese history, Liu Ling. He was a Chinese poet and scholar in the 3rd century. He was one of the Seven Sages of the Bamboo Grove, the Taoists who enjoyed and celebrated personal freedom, spontaneity, and nature. He was said to be walking around his home naked. He explained to the surprised visitors, "The sky and earth are my architecture, my house is my clothing." When I worked on this project, I thought he would be my ideal client. The top of the house has a room that is meant to be completely empty. It is a pure space. You sit in the room. You look up and you see the sky. You look down and you see through the floors all the way to the earth.

VB: Now that you describe it, it feels like a very Chinese house, right? You turned an idealized Western house into an introspective Eastern house. The whole house is an autonomous courtyard with this very intimate connection to the sky and the earth. It also represents a kind of resistance to anything ordinary and pragmatic.

YHC: Maybe. But I want to think of it as a universal house. You know, I don't think the world of architecture should be divided into East and West. I want to think of it as divided into north and south, climatically, not culturally. I would say that all projects we have done are really intended to be used by anyone. The house was built in 2013 in Shanghai and was operated by the West Bund Biennale as a guest house for visiting artists. But it is largely unoccupied. So, in a way, it remains a theoretical project.

VB: Your father was an architect. What kind of architecture did he do?

YHC: I guess, I could put a label on him. My father, ZHANG Kaiji [Yung Ho Chang's Chinese name is ZHANG Yonghe] was a classicist, and a good one [017]. He was trained at the same architecture school in Nanjing where I studied. He returned to Beijing around 1950, which was, of course, already a new Communist China. Soviet Social Realism was a popular model then. He was one of the chief architects of the Beijing Institute of Architectural Design and the design architect in charge for what is today the National Museum of China on Tiananmen Square. It was completed in 1959 vis-à-vis the Great Hall of the People to complement it. Both were built the same year to mark the 10-year anniversary of the founding of the People's Republic of China. He also designed the stands in front of the Forbidden City for watching the military parades.

VB: These are very prominent projects. But this architecture was not very attractive to you, or was it?

YHC: Of course, he influenced me in terms of art and culture, but not directly with his architecture. My parents were unusual for China. My older brother and I, we were given a lot of freedom. We didn't study all the time like other kids, so there was a lot of time to play, but also to think. And when I studied in the U.S., I was totally transformed and became a modernist. Also, politically, I tried to be apolitical because I had enough of it here in China. [Laughs.] For a while, later, I accepted capitalism. However, after spending so much time with professors in American universities I became a liberal. [Laughs.]

054 **Vertical Glass House, Shanghai, 2013** © Fangfang Tian

And then when I came back to China and experienced very brutal changes caused by the unleashing of the market economy, I realized again that capitalism is not all that good. [Laughs.] Anyway, what I wanted was to get involved in the making of this new culture that was unfolding in front of my eyes right here, at home. My father didn't quite understand my intentions, as he was like many young people today. To him architecture was about going after success. But I am working on so many small projects…Well, I ask myself—by accepting one project or another, what is the project? What can I learn?

VB: You ask these questions before accepting every commission?

YHC: I do. Otherwise, I am not interested.

VB: You established China's first independent architectural office in 1993, laying the foundation of contemporary practice in China. Could you confirm this and talk about how you succeeded?

YHC: Yes, when together with my wife, Lijia Lu we started our practice, there were already some semi-private offices that began forming in the late '80s. But they were connected to the government,

so they were very similar to what was very common before—large state-owned design institutes. And when we first started our practice it was not even legal. So, when independent practice was allowed, we opened right away. We were one of the very first studio practices in China and, for sure, the first in Beijing. Later we started to meet other independent architects all over the country.

VB: When you started your practice, you said you were less flexible than others because you had your principles. Could you talk about these principles? What would you say your architecture is about?

YHC: Well, my problem is that I have too many. [Laughs.] To me architecture is not about ideology. It is an autonomous project. Architecture is about making a building with intelligence and wisdom, which is more important than personal formal expression. Architects have a core knowledge that they can offer to the society to make people's lives better. If I had an opportunity, I would make a whole city a better place. Does that sound like I have strong principles? Well, if a client makes a particular proposal and I disagree, I will stand on my ground because I have my firm believes.

VB: Some architects prefer not to interact with clients at all. They know what they want and how their buildings should function and look like.

YHC: We don't work like that here and our clients like to be involved. It is expensive to make a building; it should really function well. When we just started, the good part was that our clients didn't know much about architecture, so we could educate them. But the bad part was that they didn't have much trust in us. [Laughs.] Today our clients are very sophisticated. They travel, and they are very well informed. It really makes architects' lives harder. For me it is always hard to bond a particular relationship with a client, which is very important for working toward designing a project. Toyo Ito once told me that the most important thing for him in architecture was singing; that's what brought him and his clients together when they went out for karaoke. I don't have any such social skills. I don't drink. I don't play golf. And I can't even sing. [Laughs.]

VB: So, you are implying that you have no choice but win your clients' hearts by doing good architecture, right? You have many fantastic clients, so you must be doing something right.

YHC: Oh, God…I am really, really lucky. You know, my very first client for a small Xishu Bookstore in Beijing, that's no longer there, told me when the project was completed that he was not convinced by anything I told him in the meetings. But my eagerness and sincerity moved him so much that he could not say no to me. [Laughs.] I don't know what makes my clients to come on board, but they do seem to enjoy the process of working with me.

VB: And I read that in the process you often ask the following primary questions: "Where does a building end? Where does a city begin? How are their structures and organizations similar?" I am interested in your design process; where do you begin? What are the first questions that you pose?

YHC: Once we get a project, depending on what it is, I would spend time exploring various issues. If it is a university campus I would research about the educational system and the design would follow because I do believe that there is something bigger than architecture. For most projects, I would think about materials and structure first. For a while, I tried to explore new materials such as fiber-reinforced polymer. Today, I have some doubts about that. Not because I shouldn't explore new materials, but because so many projects are on a fast track. So, there is less time to experiment. I don't really have a favorite material, so I tend to experiment and use all kinds of hybrid combinations. But more than materials, I like to work on interesting details and invent ways of how different parts could be put together.

VB: You are never satisfied, always searching, questioning, exploring, and experimenting. Where do you think this urge to come up with something new, exciting, or specific comes from? For example, you said that you attribute your success to the fact that, as a young architect, you were in doubt. You did not agree with many things. Could you talk about that?

YHC: It is very simple–if I don't know the answer, I search for it.

VB: Imagine, if we only knew all the answers, then architecture would be all the same.

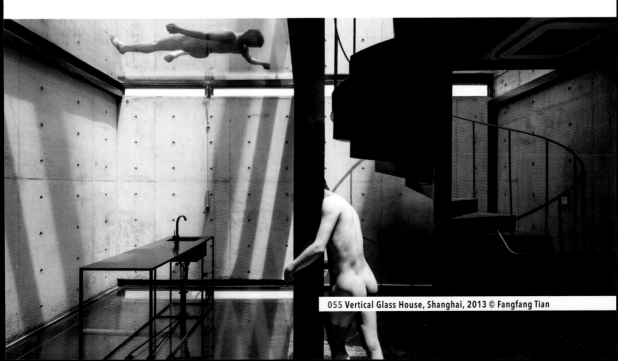

055 **Vertical Glass House, Shanghai, 2013 © Fangfang Tian**

056 Jishou Art Museum, Jishou, Hunan Province, 2019 © Fangfang Tian

YHC: We used to have a popular Russian magazine here in China that had this dictum, "Knowledge is our strength." But today, I believe the opposite is true–ignorance is our strength. [Laughs.]

VB: Could you talk about the current state of architecture in China? On the one hand, there is so much energy and so many young practitioners doing beautiful work, which can immediately be identified as Chinese with a good balance of looking back and bringing into their work local culture, history, and traditional materials. And on the other hand, they are looking forward and incorporate advanced technology. This was so clearly demonstrated at the Venice Biennale this year at the Chinese Pavilion, as it put on display so many of these, mainly small-scale projects in the countryside. And yet, I wonder if there is a lack of variety in this approach? So many projects seem somewhat formulaic, almost like the production of a single practice. What do you think?

YHC: I would agree with your observation. Yes, there is a kind of renaissance of creativity here in a big way. There are a lot of very good buildings all over. However, if I could refer to my own approach, I am a risk-taker. More so than a lot of my colleagues here. You are right, we started to do good work collectively. But, in a way, good work is not enough. These days,

architects know how to do a good building. But it is also important to work in areas that are less explored in our discipline. It is important to work outside of one's own comfort zone. Maybe you fail. Maybe you are not going to produce something pretty. But it is necessary to challenge yourself. I can see issues with offices when it is just about production. We need to be critical. There are forces that contribute to these similarities. One is the market and speed, with which buildings are being designed and built. The other one is the media. There is a lot of congratulatory press, both in China and around the world. That distracts architects from being critical.

VB: The positive press has to do with the fact that China discovered its own identity exactly at the moment when in the West critics almost gave up on the possibility that architecture in contemporary world could be something other than global and interchangeable. There was Colombia with their low-tech, social works in the poorest neighborhoods that could only be done there. Then there are some isolated works in Africa, built out of materials that the West forgot even exist. And for a number of years now we have Chinese architecture that is not only social and regional but also high-tech. And the fact that these projects are similar to one another only makes the case stronger. I agree with you–it is the market and the media, which

are, of course, global forces that now shape architecture.

YHC: Let me add to this that many Chinese architects, including myself, were educated in the U.S. and, in general, in the West. When they come back, they bring a particular language developed in those countries but also with socio-political awareness, which is positive in general. And yet, it pushed them into a particular way of talking about architecture. Because there is certain conformism in how architecture is discussed in the West, at least in the leading architectural schools, especially in the U.S. I am talking about the use of architectural jargon and theory. As a result, we are now producing many small-scale projects, while there are so many urban regeneration projects that are undertaken by mainstream architects. Our office is also getting some small-scale redevelopment projects in the hutongs. Well, we'll see where these projects will take Chinese architects and how long the construction boom and media attention will last.

VB: You once said, "I'm not very good at making exaggerated forms, that's not me, but I can do different architecture and still have a sense of discovery."

YHC: When I was a student at Berkeley, I had a Swedish professor, Lars Lerup. I always admired his work on habitation and narrative. One day, I was looking at his designs and realized that he was not a good form-giver. I was young and silly, so I said to him, "The reason you work with these conceptual ideas is because you don't know how to create forms." And he replied, "Of course!" He was very generous with me and this is also true with me. So, I am not a good form-giver. However, my ideas are rather formal ideas. I am very much influenced by artists, especially by such conceptualists as Marcel Duchamp and modernists as Kazimir Malevich. I have been interested in painting and now I am working on ideas of bringing abstract painting into architecture. Meaning, I want to explore such qualities as a brush stroke and paint texture. I am using these ideas to exaggerate or compress spaces. I like to think that I failed to be an artist, but I became an artistic architect.

VB: You have so many ideas, but it contradicts another one of your quotes, "After almost 20 years, I may just settle rather than find some more acute ideas about architecture."

YHC: Well, this is about bringing myself back into my practice and gathering my old ideas.

VB: Would you say architecture is art?

YHC: My personal, subjective answer is yes. But objectively speaking, of course, not. We live in buildings. So how can they be just art? Spaces must be livable. So, there are two contradictory answers… For me, it is. I try. Sometimes, there is a chance for architecture to rise to that level. But more than art, architecture is a discovery.

057 Forbidden City College, Chongqing, 2020. Photo by DID Studio

058 Jiading Mini-Block, Shanghai, 2020© Fangfang Tian

LI Xinggang
ATELIER LI XINGGANG

LI Xinggang (b. 1969, Tangshan, Hebei Province) heads Atelier Li Xinggang since 2003, which is one of five autonomous architectural studios within China Architecture Design & Research Group (CADG) in Beijing, a leading government-run design institute with 240 registered architects and over 3,000 staff that includes engineers, urban planners, designers, technicians, and researchers. Li studied architecture at Tianjin University from 1987 to 1991 and started working at CADG immediately upon graduation. In 1998, Li was selected to take part in French President's program that invited 50 young Chinese architects to pursue advanced studies in France for three months that he combined with practice at the Paris office of AREP. In 2003, Li led CADG's effort to develop the design for Herzog & de Meuron's Beijing National Stadium, the Bird's Nest [002]. From 2006 to 2011 he undertook PhD studies in architectural design and theory at his *alma mater*. A photo of Li's swimming pool [064] in the Gymnasium at the New Campus of Tianjin University (2015) won 2017 Architecture Photography Award by World Architecture Festival (WAF). Li is now the vice chief architect of the Institute; his namesake atelier consists of more than 30 architects working on museums, sports venues, housing complexes, metro stations, and community centers. For the last couple of years the studio has been leading the design of the Yanqing Zone at the Beijing 2022 Winter Olympics. Located 74 kilometers northwest of the capital, the zone will be home to National Sliding Centre and National Alpine Ski Centre to host competitions for alpine skiing, bobsledding, skeleton, and luge. Other prominent projects by Li include the Camping Service Center in Louna Village, Xingyi, Guizhou (2017), which evokes ancient Mayan temples in miniature; "The Third Space," a two-tower housing complex in Tangshan, Hebei Province (2015) with duplex apartments and jutted out pavilion-like covered balconies of various sizes and colors; and Jixi Museum in Jixi, Anhui Province (2013). I spoke to Li Xinggang about particularities of working within a design institute, the architect's philosophy referred to as "poetic scenery and integrated geometry," and his role in the design of the Bird's Nest and why he thinks it is the most important piece of contemporary architecture in China.

YOU OPEN YOUR DWELLING'S DOOR AND YOU SEE THE MOUNTAINS

In conversation with **LI Xinggang** of Atelier Li Xinggang, Beijing
WeChat video call between New York and Beijing, September 8, 2020

Vladimir Belogolovsky: Could we start with your experience at CADG? I understand that this is where you started your career at the very beginning and you decided to stay there and build your practice within this very large company, is that right?

Li Xinggang: Yes, when I just started working at CADG 30 years ago, it was the best design institute in China. I always wanted to work at CADG and came here as an intern even before I graduated. I liked the company's collaborative spirit. As soon as I graduated, I decided to go ahead to start my professional career at the Institute.

VB: What about BIAD, the Beijing Institute of Architectural Design? I am sure they would argue with your opinion about CADG being the best design institute in the country, right?

LX: You are right. [Laughs.] These institutes are quite competitive. Both were modeled after Soviet design institutes. CADG is under the leadership of the Ministry of Construction and is controlled by the national government, while BIAD is under the control of the Beijing Municipal government. So, while they focus on projects in Beijing, we work all over China.

VB: What could you say about CUI Kai [b. 1957, Beijing], the director of CADG? Some architects refer to him as a big brother-like figure for Chinese architects.

LX: He is the chief architect here. He is my leader, tutor, and mentor at the Institute. I worked directly with him when I just came here as an intern. Cui is also a graduate of Tianjin University. He inspired me

059 LI Xinggang. Courtesy of Atelier Li Xinggang

to start my professional career here at the Institute. He always encouraged me to make progress in my career and invited me to study in France. And it was him who recommended me to head the work on the design development of the Bird's Nest, on which I collaborated with Herzog & de Meuron from the very beginning. Cui is one of the most prolific and respected architects in the country. Now he leads his studio called Land-based Design and Research Center, and I lead my own Atelier.

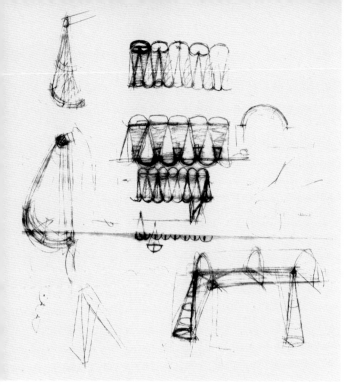

060 Gymnasium of the New Campus of Tianjin University, Tianjin, 2015. Sketch by Li Xinggang; Courtesy of Atelier Li Xinggang

VB: What are the advantages and what are the limitations of working within the institute system?

LX: When studios were first initiated, the idea was to create an independent-like spirit and autonomy, even though, bureaucratically we are a part of a bigger group. Of course, one of the key advantages of being a part of our group is to have access to all necessary support and resources. There is a strong cooperation among various disciplines, and we are able to retain control over quality, which is a difficult task for independent practices that have to form their teams for every project by themselves. This allows our studios to bid competitively for a variety of jobs–from very small to very large public projects such as the Olympics. And we have full autonomy as far as design freedom. There is a lot more stress for independent architects working with other consultants. But CADG is like a family. And within this family our Atelier is entirely autonomous.

VB: What are your thoughts on a certain competition between architects working within the institutes and those who are independent? Wouldn't you agree that they have a certain resistance to the so-called mainstream? What do you think about the mainstream architecture in China?

LX: I am actually a good friend with some of the leading independent architects such as Zhang Ke, Dong Gong, Li Hu and Huang Wenjing of Open Architecture, Liu Yichun and Chen Yifeng of Atelier Deshaus, and many others. We see each other as contemporaries rather than competitors. The difference is that we are working in different environments. We have mutual interests and common goals. If you say or feel a certain resistance on their part against the mainstream, I don't feel that I represent the mainstream either. I would say that perhaps 20 years ago independent architects had inferior positions toward the institutes. But over the last decade they received a lot of acknowledgment, recognition, and media exposure all over the world and in academic circles. So, perhaps the table has turned and now it is the independent architects who are in a more advantageous position. So, if anyone of the independent architects still maintains the rhetoric of going against the mainstream, they are overexaggerating the issue. In fact, some of them have become the mainstream.

VB: But let's be realistic for a moment. If you go to Shanghai, you will see some major projects such as several art museums by Atelier Deshaus. Also, Open Architecture did another popular museum Tank Shanghai on the West Bund. You may see some cultural projects in Shenzhen by URBANUS. But these are the exceptions. You may walk all day long in most major cities in China and you will not see projects by these leading independent architects. You either have to make special trips to remote villages to discover them or you need a guide to help you find these hidden gems in Beijing: galleries, kindergartens, boutique hotels, restaurants, artist residencies, and so on. And if you go to China as a tourist, you will miss these projects entirely. So, how can

you call their work mainstream? They are well published; they are talked about. But they have no real street presence. These architects are somewhat invisible. They are, in a way, paper architects. Agreed?

LX: When I talked about the "mainstream," I referred to these architects' authority and status internationally. Of course, if you talk about mass construction in the country, most projects are done by the institutes. And in most cases, they lack good quality, which is regrettable. Still, I can predict a gradual conversion taking place of our forces–projects designed and implemented by design institutes and projects led by independent architects. I can only hope that the quality of projects designed by both groups will become less and less distinguishable over time. The idealist visions of the independent architects will be matched by more imaginary projects by the institutes. At the same time, more and more independent architects' works will gain a more noticeable presence on the streets of major cities. In the future these groups will not be seen as opposing.

VB: Could you say a few words about Tianjin, a fast-growing metropolis, yet in the shadow of first-tier cities. Many famous Western architects are now working there: Diller Scofidio + Renfro, Bernard Tschumi, MVRDV, KPF, GMP, and others. It is a very ambitious place with many great opportunities for architects, right?

LX: Today, Tianjin is one of five most populous cities in China after Shanghai, Beijing, Chongqing, and Shenzhen. Having a rich history dating back to the middle ages, Tianjin is a major seaport on the Bohai Bay of the Yellow Sea and a gateway to Beijing. The city became open to international trade in late 19th century. It had foreign concession territories, which distinguished it as a particularly open city, similar to Shanghai. In the 1990s, the government made a commitment to develop the city's bay area around the port, known as Binhai New Area. Now work is being done on connecting it to the old historical center. So, it is a dual-core city. This new district is being developed on a similar scale and as ambitiously as Pudong in Shanghai. Yet, the city is situated

061 **Gymnasium of the New Campus of Tianjin University, Tianjin, 2015. Photo by Sun Haiting**

062 Gymnasium of the New Campus of Tianjin University, Tianjin, 2015. Photo by Sun Haiting

very closely to Beijing. So, there is a siphon effect taking place, as a lot of attention is focused on the capital and, therefore, limits the amount of resources the city could have. Tianjin is being developed on a grand scale with very large complexes that seem to be very autonomous and detached from each other to stimulate a vibrant urban life. So far, the Gymnasium of the New Campus of Tianjin University is my second project there. It is located on a sort of belt that connects the old city and the new one that's being built on the bay side. The idea of building the new university campus was to bring more people to that part of the city, which remains undeveloped. The university area will become the new center around which that part of the city is being planned.

VB: Let's talk about your design process and inspirations in relation to your Gymnasium project.

LX: The most important question and the genesis of the Gymnasium is, of course, a kind of *tabula rasa*. It was planned like a new settlement. The question was: How do you settle students, professors, and staff in this place? There was literally nothing there before. To give the place a sense of belonging became the most important issue. When I first visited the site, it was just flat land with a river and highways. There was almost nothing to relate to. But in just three years it was going to turn into a development of over one million square meters to house 30,000 students. It is a daunting thought.

I remember going to an exhibition in Beijing on post-war Italian architecture–five case studies by three architects' projects in Milan and Genoa. They were insertions into the existing historical urban fabric. There was a lot to respond to. It was all about expansion, reconstruction, and regeneration. But

063 Gymnasium of the New Campus of Tianjin University, Tianjin, 2015. Photo by Zhang Qianxi

here the situation was different. In fact, in China, this situation is a lot more relevant and typical. This is what the Chinese architects have to deal with all the time: how do you start something from scratch? This is surely the main aspect that many independent architects are resisting. But that's the situation we are in. Very often architects have to invent reasons for their designs because they work in the absence of any tangible context. That's what leads to very quick and random designs. Another problem is the speed of construction. It makes quality suffer, which is very regrettable. I am fighting and resisting this reality with my own projects.

VB: I understand that you related your design idea to physical tension that occurs in the human body to poeticize its movements when engaged in different sports. Could you elaborate on that idea?

LX: Yes, the initial concept for the design was to come up with structural components to create a kind of settlement, even a series of settlements. How do you initiate a settlement to give a certain significance to such an empty site? The idea was to create a variety of concrete shell structures of different scales to accommodate different kinds of activities and movements of the human body. So, it is a response to creating a settlement out of nothing, and a response to the body movements characteristic of different sports. It creates a kind of poetic atmosphere in the space.

VB: You used wooden formwork to build concrete structures, which is rarely used now in the West and is long replaced by steel construction, which is more economical. Could you go over your reasons for using concrete?

LX: First, unlike similar sports arenas, this complex was built primarily for recreational use and training, not competitions. So, there was no need for creating long span spaces. Therefore, the complex is rather a series of mid-size spaces, which can be achieved more economically by using concrete rather than fabricated large steel members produced in factories. And unlike in the West we have a lot of human-power in China, so it is much more affordable to use labor intensive technologies such as building wooden formwork. In general, it is more economical to construct a building out of smaller elements that can be produced on site rather than fabricating large elements that would have to be brought to the site to assemble. Still, the Gymnasium is a combination of structures. For example, there is a running track suspended in the space that required a large open space. For that we used steel frame construction. And when I use concrete structure, I tend to expose all surfaces to demonstrate how spaces were constructed to achieve a direct communication–it is always informative to show how the whole structure was put together. The complex has a sense of plasticity. That's what I wanted to communicate to the users and different spaces are done with different elements to achieve a variety of forms.

VB: What I like about this project is that it is not imposing a singular image, form, or perception. In a way, it is almost like a small town of interconnected neighborhoods with different characters, spaces, and elements. The result is a community of buildings, each distinguished by its own unique roof, expressed with the same material but different geometries. It is an exhibition of varieties of elements, not something repeated again and again. A variety of forms and ways of assembling them. Didn't your client question this strategy as uneconomical? I wonder what arguments you used to defend it?

LX: First, the different structures and geometries reflect different spatial needs of different sports. There are different spans, depths, and heights. Second, from the beginning, the idea was to create a variety of forms because there was nothing there before. The complex was planned as several neighborhoods, as you observed, a family of characters.

Every family consists of related members, but they are not the same. To achieve a certain diversity and richness was intentional. This one complex initiated a large development on campus and right away it had to look quite complex. There are different uses, different positionings on the site, different ways for the sunlight to enter, and, therefore, there are different forms. Natural light is a very important component of the design. Another important point is that the building was designed in such a way that it could

064 Gymnasium of the New Campus of Tianjin University, Tianjin, 2015. Photo by Zhang Qianxi

be naturally ventilated. And for that you also need to create a variety of airflows. So, each side of the building looks very different.

VB: How did you arrive at the half-cone units? If barrel vault roof is more or less expected, half-cone unit geometry is quite rare, especially utilized both for roof and facades. Did you rely on any particular inspirations?

LX: My intention was to find a kind of unifying geometry that could be identified as a sort of DNA for the whole project. There is both repetition and variety in this project. Therefore, I relied on a shell system. There is a variety of forms but what all of them have in common is that they are based on the use of ruled surface. In other words, all these barrel vaults and hyperbolic paraboloids belong to one family of forms. Their curves can be achieved by building wooden forms in a very simple way—with a lattice of straight elements. I like this kind of straight forward, ordered geometry that can produce very rich forms and spaces.

VB: There is also something that you call "poetic scenery and integrated geometry." Could you talk about that?

LX: Yes, that is the concept that describes this project's design strategy. Integrated geometry means that structure, form, space, materials, and construction techniques are all integrated. They work together as an integrated system, and this system is interacts with the movement of the human body to create an exciting space and atmosphere.

VB: There is another thing. If you look at this complex it is not apparent at all that it is situated in China. The forms and materials are not referencing the culture of its place. You were not trying to tie this building to its cultural context, right?

LX: That's true and it is because the focus was on underlying universal qualities. The idea was to create a variety of spaces on different scales that would be attuned to many sports activities occurring within. As you said, we tried to express different body movements instead of assigning symbolic Chinese characteristics to these buildings.

VB: While designing this project did you rely on any particular historical precedents, as far as the use of concrete and brick? I am always interested in architects' use of specific inspirations. For example, Gaudi's undulating facades and roof for his Sagrada Familia Schools in Barcelona next to his famous basilica served as a model for such architects as Felix Candela, Santiago Calatrava, and some others.

LX: Of course, Gaudi is a great source of inspiration, particularly for his organic language, structural logic, and for innovative handling of the brick. Yet, when the Gymnasium was finished some people likened it to the Kimbell Art Museum by Louis Kahn because of similarly designed cycloid barrel vaults. But the main reason for using them was their economic structure and to work with the idea of how to admit and filter sunlight into the space in a variety of ways. While designing this roofscape I did not think of any specific precedents. The comparisons came already when it was built. So, they must have been present in my mind subconsciously. But I am not denying the influence of Gaudi and Khan, as well as some others on my work. I admire their architecture very much. Yet, when I am designing, I try to push beyond what I know to discover something new.

VB: Now, let's talk about your Jixi Museum. Unlike the Gymnasium that project reveals the fact that it is based on Chinese cultural references. Could you talk about the main design concept?

LX: First, the difference in my design approaches comes from the site. The Jixi Museum is situated in the center of the town, which is over thousand years old, and is surrounded by beautiful mountains and rivers. Jixi is a typical historical Chinese town in the southeast. So, the atmosphere is completely different. The main concept for this project could be described by a poem by Hu Shih, a philosopher, essayist, a leading intellectuals, and a former Chinese ambassador to the United States from late 1930s to early 1940s. His ancestry comes from Jixi County and he was educated there, as well as in Shanghai and in America. He left an extensive legacy and there is a collection of his writings at this museum. One of his poems talks about the relation of humans to nature and mountains, about emotional connection between dwelling and landscape around it. You open your dwelling's door and you see the mountains. The museum design was inspired by this visual and emotional sentiment. The site, which was used for Jixi County government throughout history was cleared in the 1940s to build half a dozen government buildings. More than 40 trees were planted at that time. One of them survived from ancient times. It is over five-hundred years old.

All those buildings were removed in 2010, when the government relocated its offices to the new part of Jixi. All trees survived that demolition. We were not obligated to keep the younger trees, but I decided to keep all of them, no matter whether old or new. So, our design was formed around them, which led to the layout reminiscent of a village with courtyards, artificial ponds, and internal streets running along the fragmented buildings that are all covered by a single continuous roof. The new roof was designed to evoke mountains, visible in the distance. The entire roofscape is made up of a series of pitched roofs—all sloped at one fixed angle of 30 degrees, reaching to different heights and spanning different volumes. This slope profile is characteristic of local houses. Visitors have access to the roof terrace with panoramic views over the ancient town and mountains in the background. This project is also based on the idea of "integrated geometry and poetic scenery." Poetic scenery is expressed in the roofscape itself and how it is viewed by visitors from the roof terraces. And integrated geometry is expressed in the triangulated forms that constitute the structural logic of this entire project. So, even though these two projects—Gymnasium and Jixi Museum—look very different there is a relationship because each represents a family of related forms.

VB: One of the gardens within the museum is particularly interesting for its geometrically cut, thin concrete blocks that form a mountain-like profile against a whitewashed garden wall. That feature reminds me of a similar composition at a garden inside the I.M. Pei-designed Suzhou Museum [2006], which is also positioned against a whitewashed wall and reflected in a pond in front of it. Could you touch on that?

LX: Of course, this is an ancient traditional design device. These compositions of stones represent miniature mountains. In the Jixi Museum the idea was to create miniature mountains to play with the scenery of the real mountains in the distance. In a way, there are three scales, in which mountains are represented here: the miniature mountains expressed in stone compositions in the garden, the roofscape represents mountains in the middle, and far away in the distance there are the real mountains. So, there are close mountains, in the middle, and far away. It

065 *Jixi Museum, Jixi, Anhui Province, 2013. Photo by Xia Zhi*

066 Jixi Museum, Jixi, Anhui Province, 2013. Photo by Qiu Jianbing

Weiwei who was an artistic consultant during the early stage of the project. The project was unique and complex. It involved the use of the most advanced technologies at the time. It was a historical milestone and not just for China but globally. For us, it was an extensive research and a great learning experience. What I learned from that collaboration with Jacques and Pierre is the idea of integrating the structure, form, and space together. That's a very important design logic that I admire and try to follow in all my work, which is consistent with my own philosophy of integrated geometry and poetic scenery.

VB: What would you say your architecture is about and what kind of architecture would you like to achieve?

LX: I am pursuing the kind of architecture that would interact with nature in the most meaningful way. And when I talk about nature, I mean not only the actual nature but also artificial nature. The goal is to make people enjoy interacting with nature in architectural space. Our architecture is for people and their enjoyment. We want to be both idealistic and realistic.

VB: What do you think about the current creative moment in China? Whose work do you pay particular attention to?

LX: I think it would be fair to say that the general quality of architecture improved a lot since the early 2000s. We have passed that moment when architects began feeling confident about their work. That moment took place back in 2008, when the Olympic projects were finished. At that point we achieved the completion of a number of symbolic and iconic projects. Now we are preoccupied with projects that are much more sustainable. We are thinking about ecology, sustainability, and environment. Architects' skills have become much more developed and sophisticated and architecture is becoming a lot more complex with the use of AI, robotics, parametric design, and so on.

VB: Which building built in China in the last 20 years would you call as the most significant achievement?

is like being inside of a painting. And, of course, the miniature mountains at this museum are abstracted and made of concrete, not natural rock and soil as in Suzhou or other ancient gardens. The pond and area all around it are also done in geometric concrete panels. There is no attempt to achieve natural likeliness. It is an unmistakably humanmade garden.

VB: How was your collaboration with Herzog & de Meuron on the Olympic Stadium? It started the year when you just formed your studio in 2003, right?

LX: That project was the reason for forming my studio. In fact, the stadium was my first independent project. Before 2003, CADG did not have any design studios, just different departments. Initially, three design studios were formed. Now there are seven studios–five architectural and two of structural engineers. These architectural studios consist of anywhere between 10 and 50 architects. As far as my experience of working with Jacques Herzog and Pierre de Meuron, it was very special and memorable. I worked with them from the very beginning and was stationed at their office in Basel during the competition phase. At that time, we also worked with Ai

LX: It is difficult to pick just one building, since there are so many great projects realized all over the country. But the one that stands out would have to be the Bird's Nest. I think this building played a very important role at a very special moment for China. It was the building that helped to project a very positive attitude to the whole world. And Western architects used that special moment to elevate their creativity to a new level. The building is unique. Its structure, form, and architecture are all intertwined into one integrated system. It is a kind of building that could not be built without the most advanced technologies such as BIM (Building Information Modeling). And if you let me name one more project designed by a Chinese architect that would be West Village in Chengdu by Liu Jiakun [093-095]. I nominated this project for this year's prestigious City of Humanity Awards as the best public space in China. He invented a new urban typology that generates a new kind of public space. It is loved by people who live there and around it because it is open and welcoming. It is a true center of life, a great achievement for architecture. This is a great example for all architects to follow by aiming at making a city a more desirable place to live.

VB: Interestingly, when I talked to Liu Jiakun, he cited the same two buildings—his West Village and the Bird's Nest. I agree about these choices as being at the top of the list of the most important buildings in China. And I can also say that based on my own visits to the most iconic buildings in Beijing it is the Bird's Nest, which stands out as the most striking and memorable. Yet, we can't ignore a strong criticism of this structure by such prominent critics as Kenneth Frampton who insists that the stadium is excessively overdesigned by using too much steel, concrete, and resources in general. How would you respond to that criticism?

LX: No, I don't think it is overdesigned. I took part in the entire design process from the very beginning. I can say that the final result of the stadium is based on rigorous research. From the beginning the brief asked the stadium to have a retractable roof. The initial idea was to make the stadium porous. But the retractable roof structure is very heavy and required massive supports. To hide the supports additional random-looking steel members were introduced. Then when the project's design was close to being finished the government decided to eliminate the retractable roof due to cost concerns and, more importantly, safety concerns. That was a response to the 2004 collapse of a section of a roof at Terminal 2E at the Charles de Gaulle Airport in Paris. As part of that decision 9,000 seats were removed to bring down the stadium's capacity to 91,000 seats. By then the building was already under construction. The structure was adjusted and simplified somewhat, but the system could not be changed. It was too late to completely redesign the project. And if we had to redesign the whole project it would no longer be the Bird's Nest, which was the symbolic image that won an international competition and full support of the people.

As built, the building brought a lot of pride to China and its citizens. It was hugely important for boosting self-confidence in China at the moment when the Olympics opening ceremony became the attention of the whole world. And after the Olympics the stadium was used in other major events. It continues to be used regularly and will be used again for the upcoming 2022 Winter Olympics. Of course, now the times are different. We no longer need to demonstrate our confidence. That moment has passed. Now we are focused on sustainability, integration with nature, and serving people. But the Bird's Nest will remain useful. Its criticism is not justified because it is a long-term project unlike many other Olympic venues around the world. The stadium is criticized for being overdesigned and much bigger than it needed to be. But the fact is that it has been serving people and its generous structure can be used and adapted to a variety of needs in the future. When we question whether a project is sustainable, we need to consider how it is used in the long run. To build something economic for a single event is not the answer.

FAMILIAR STRANGENESS
SIMPLE COMPLEXITY
UTOPIAN IDEALISM
DIRECTNESS
NEUTRALITY

ZHANG Lei
AZL ARCHITECTS

Nanjing-based architect ZHANG Lei (b. 1964, Jiangsu Province) does not believe in history, only time. He is convinced that history is something that is taking place in our own time, being shaped by particular circumstances, current programmatic demands, the latest building techniques, and contemporary sensibilities. History is not what actually happened but is our understanding and interpretation of it. There is no point in looking for specific solutions from the past. Whatever is being built today will inevitably fit into history. Only truly contemporary projects have a chance to become a part of history. Yet, the architect does not believe in starting each project from scratch. He gets his inspirations from vernacular architecture, not from specific architects who left their stylistic mark. Therefore, his focus is on finding rational, technologically advanced, environmentally sympathetic, and spatially poetic solutions. Zhang pursued his architectural degree at Southeast University in Nanjing. Young Ho Chang and Wang Shu also studied there. After his graduation in 1988, Zhang started his teaching career and went to

ETH-Zurich in 1991 for his post-graduate studies and teaching. He returned to Nanjing in 1993 to resume his teaching position at his *alma mater*. In 2000, Zhang joined a group of young professors, also ETH-graduates, to start a new department at Nanjing University–School of Architecture & Urban Planning as an alternative education to the traditional model at Southeast University. The next year he was asked to head Nanjing Design Institute, which enabled him to establish his design studio–Atelier Zhang Lei, the position he combined with being the vice dean of the school. However, in 2009, he resigned from both positions to focus on practicing architecture by starting his own independent studio, AZL Architects. The architect's most renowned projects include the Ruralation Retreat & Spa in Tangshan (2019), the Ruralation Shenaoli Library in Zhejiang (2015), and several works in his hometown: Shitang Village Internet Conference Center (2016), Wanjing Garden Chapel (2014), CEPIA 4# House (2011), Slit House (2007), Brick House (2007), and the Model Animal Research Center (2003).

HOW DO YOU ESTABLISH A CONNECTION BETWEEN PAST AND FUTURE, BETWEEN HUMANS AND THE ENVIRONMENT?

In conversation with **ZHANG Lei** of AZL Architects, Nanjing
WeChat video call between New York and Nanjing, June 19, 2020

Vladimir Belogolovsky: After graduating from Southeast University in Nanjing you went to ETH-Zurich. Why did you decide to go to Europe rather than America where most leading independent Chinese architects pursued their degrees?

Zhang Lei: Southeast University has an exchange program with ETH-Zurich. After graduating in 1988, I worked at the school as a teacher and in 1991, my school sent me to Zurich for one year as an exchange scholar. But I remained there for three years because I stayed as a teaching assistant with Professor Herbert Kramel. In 1993, once my teaching assignment was fulfilled, I went back to Nanjing to continue teaching at Southeast University. In 2000, I moved from Southeast University to Nanjing University to start a new school of architecture together with a group of young professors. All of us spent time at ETH and we thought that we had a chance to do something differently from Southeast University, which is one of the oldest schools in China. We said, why don't we try a new way?! In 2001, I was named the director of Nanjing Design Institute at Nanjing University.

VB: First, you became a teacher and then practicing architect, right?

ZL: Yes, I transitioned from initially teaching and doing research to practicing architecture. In China, every university has a design institute; these institutions always work together. And university professors typically work at Local Design Institutes. They are very closely integrated. Within the university, I headed my own design studio with my own projects. In 2009, I resigned as the director and vice dean at

067 ZHANG Lei. Courtesy of AZL Architects

the Architecture School to start my own independent practice. So, as an independent architect I've been practicing for a little more than ten years but in reality, I started my practice almost 20 years ago.

VB: Referring to your Research Center in Nanjing, your first completed project, you said, "My ideas were clear since the beginning; I wanted to express the qualities of the modern, contemporary space. I did everything I could to avoid traditional or cultural concepts. So, the

068 CEPIA 4# House, Nanjing, 2011 © Yao Li

like life itself, like rain and sunlight. And context is also just another substitute for time that connects the past, the present, and the future. Civilization is more important than context and culture. Civilization reflects the way we progress as individuals and collectively over time. The progress of civilization is recorded materially by architecture. So, architecture continuously has been pushing the boundaries of civilization. Time is neutral and objective, and it is a job of the architect to discover certain spatial possibilities. It is up to the architect to establish links between the past and our own time, human and nature.

VB: Wouldn't you agree that what you say is a very contemporary view of history, particularly in China where traditions used to be followed very attentively. It was a matter of inheriting historical models–letter by letter. That's why I want to know more about the source of your inquiries. What are the roots of your convictions?

ZL: My understanding of time and contemporary condition doesn't come from studies but from practice. There are no particular influences that I would cite, either from my time in Nanjing or Zurich.

VB: Would you say that your understanding of time and history is similar to other young professors who took part in establishing the new Architecture School at Nanjing University with you back in 2000?

ZL: I don't think so. We all have very different theories and ideas about contemporary architecture. What's common is our search for alternative models to a singular traditional system that we experienced ourselves when we were students at the Southeast University.

design was just the result of a combination of function and space. Nothing related to traditional materials or ancient typology. In order to support these ideas, I used minimalist architectural language." Is this still your position? What formed this need to be liberated from being bound to local culture and place?

ZL: First, I believe that the world doesn't live in history. History is something that gets formed much later. There is only time. So, architecture, and culture in general, should not be limited by certain expectations. Architecture should be fluid and organic, just

VB: You mentioned that your Research Center was one of the earliest projects by Chinese architects entirely focused on space in a clear and rational way. What was it that initially brought your attention to these issues–any particular projects or texts of any architects that you came across in Europe? Wouldn't you agree that before you went to Europe and others,

mostly to America, architecture was done very differently in China? It was only after your generation started coming back from abroad that radically new visions of entirely new architecture stared to emerge in China.

ZL: I would argue that my Research Center was a result of my own teaching experience both in Southeast and Nanjing universities. There is a design course that I developed with focus on pragmatic and practical solutions. In fact, the pedagogy in Nanjing and Zurich were quite similar. Both were based on a rational, problem-solving approach. It is an anthropological method of gathering and interpreting information in order to solve issues through architectural means such as space and material. Another aspect of that project was the client's demands. The client then just returned from the U.S. with the program that reflected particular needs for laboratories to work with rats. There were such demands as the need for gardens and abundance of sunlight. The client brought many observations into the project from other existing laboratories in the U.S. and China. In addition to this programmatic analysis we had to deal with particular site conditions. That's where the idea of staggered gardens and courtyards came from. So, the result is based on the relation of the interior spaces to the site and how light is distributed in the interiors. Architecture responding to sunlight was always one of the most basic aspects of our design curriculum. So, this first project became a kind of transfer of knowledge from teaching a class to the real-life project.

VB: I like your observation about how buildings are built in Switzerland. You said, "You make a building like you make a watch." Is that something that you want to bring to China? Is that a kind of personal mission for you?

ZL: I really respect the level of professionalism in Switzerland. So, I would compare people working in building industry there to watchmakers. There is almost religious dedication to precision, which is lacking in commercial mass-produced building industry in China. As far as my mission, I believe architects are tasked with a responsibility to reshape and expand the boundaries of our civilization. So, in

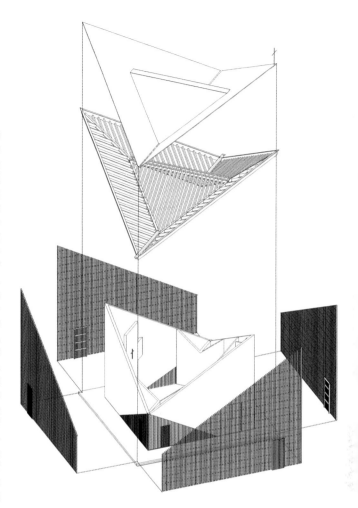

069 Wanjing Garden Chapel, Nanjing, 2014. Exploded Axonometric
Courtesy of AZL Architects

my very first built project, the Research Center one would find both pragmatism and utopian idealism. In architecture, you can observe the world and make a better version of it.

VB: "Architects have a responsibility to reshape and expand the boundaries of our civilization." Could you elaborate on this very poetic idea?

ZL: I see the material world as the conduit of culture. We, architects shape the material world.

VB: Shape, expand, and transform… And apart from materiality and achieving such obvious objectives as high quality of construction and light ambiance, what are the main concerns that you pursue? How would you summarize what your architecture is about?

ZL: After many years of practice, I am convinced that the most important concern we have right now in architecture is its position toward establishing a good relationship with the environment. The second most important objective is to find the right balance between form and content. There must be a strong consequential link between exterior and interior. They should be related to how we live and experience life, both individually and collectively. Architecture is about establishing a good and lasting relationship between everyone involved, including the public. So, every attempt to design a building is like a journey to establishing a particular relationship.

VB: You called your architecture "simple complexity" and "familiar strangeness." Could you elaborate on that?

ZL: By simple complexity I mean a coexistence of form and content, which results in spatial depth. Even simple forms must be built with deep and profound content. And a familiar strangeness is about connecting the strangeness of our future with familiarity of the past.

VB: You said, "To make an interesting image is not a challenge; our students can do that. The question is: why do you make it?" Could you talk about some of your inspirations?

ZL: Inspirations come from a filtration of information and our own system of values. Even 20 years ago, when I was teaching, I would encourage my students to learn from vernacular architecture, by studying similar architecture as exemplified by Bernard Rudovsky's book *Architecture Without Architects*. For the last seven or eight years I've been working in rural areas where such examples of traditional ways of settlements are more evident. So, my inspirations primarily come from local encounters. And if you look carefully into the work of the greatest master architects you will always find this link to architecture without architects transformed by personal visions and imagination. So, for me that's where inspirations come from, not from individual solutions of other architects.

VB: When I look at your built work, these buildings are all built in different materials and exploring different geometries and themes. For example, your Garden Chapel is about lightness, Slit House is about solidity and materiality, the Internet Conference Center is about relating the building's gestural form to its context, the Brick House is about the use of a single material, and so on. Each project seems to explore its own logic. So, I struggle to identify evolution of a single author in these very autonomous works. Is this intentional?

ZL: The projects that you mentioned may be very different but there is a consistency that I see in them. First, I use the kind of materials and techniques that speak of our own time. And second, there is always a strong relation between the building and the environment. For example, the Internet Center and the Chapel are very quickly constructed projects. Both were built in just 45 days each. So, in both examples we used composite materials in timber and steel that enabled us to build these structures very efficiently. The Slit House was built on site with very strict heritage regulations. It was the first modern-looking building in the area and therefore, the whole project was a search between the past and present of that place. The Brick House is a house for a poet, situated south of Nanjing and very close to a brick kiln where they are still producing bricks. And they have good bricklayers right there. So, the first and obvious decision was to utilize local brick. Each situation informs me as an architect and that's what effects my decisions.

VB: In other words, similarly to what you said that for you there is no history, only time– right now and right here, your own work is responsive to each situation. In a way, you don't allow yourself to develop a particular personal vision, you let it be driven by specific

070 Slit House, Nanjing, 2007 © Iwan Baan

circumstances–the site, program, client's vision, a certain material availability, and so on. In a way, you start each project with an open mind, without picking up the pieces from previous projects. Is that right?

ZL: I would say so.

VB: Could you talk about your Slit House? There is no such thing as a private house in China, right? There are certain exceptions, but it is very rare since land cannot be bought, only rented. Who was your client and how is the house used today?

ZL: The client for that project was a local government. The person who was in charge is an architectural fanatic who wanted a very special response to a very particular site. So, in the beginning, the project was about making a single-family residence for local officials. But during the construction and even following its completion there was so much attention to the house that it became unsuitable for anyone

to stay there. So, it was converted into a kind of social club for recreational use by the local officials. Traditionally, life in a Chinese house revolves around a courtyard with its link to the sky. It is a very direct and powerful connection between humans and nature. But the site was too small for a traditional solution and the slit in the heart of the house became an enclosed courtyard–symbolically and literally. All the public spaces of the house converge around the central staircase, which is lit with natural light through a series of windows and skylights that form a zigzagging slit.

VB: In a way, leading independent architects who now practice in China constitute a subculture. On the one hand, your work is done in opposition to the work carried out by Local Design Institutes, which control most of large-scale urban projects. And on the other, your architecture is a strong contrast to what foreign architects bring to China–signature spectacle

pieces, often unrelated to local conditions. I wonder how you see this situation?

ZL: Well, I think it is natural for small independent architects to start working on smaller scale projects that are not centrally located. For large prestigious projects, such as cultural institutions, the government demands very high standards, which prohibits most independent architects from qualifying to take part in such prestigious competitions. But in recent years the situation has been improving with more opportunities for us, especially since so many great projects designed by independent architects were built and attracted a lot of attention in national and even international media. More and more design institutes are willing to collaborate with independent architects. For example, AZL Architects is working on important cultural projects every year. And this year we were asked to take part in a prestigious international competition for a Natural History Museum in Shenzhen in partnership with the Nanjing Design Institute.

VB: You enjoyed your position at the Institute and Nanjing University, heading your own design studio there with access to many prestigious projects. Yet, you decided to give it all up and start your own independent practice. Why is that?

ZL: In 2009, I decided to quit both of my positions as a director at the Institute and vice dean at the University. I wanted to have more responsibilities and challenges as a practitioner. There was a requirement to maintain an equal balance between research, teaching, and practice. In contrast, I wanted to devote more time to practice under my own name and to channel all my energy into design. That's what I enjoy most–being challenged and take risk on my own.

VB: How do you see your own work in relation to other leading independent Chinese architects?

ZL: I would say that here in China, the work of architects reflects their personal qualities. At least according to my own theory [Laughs.] If I could describe my

position in the Chinese context, I would name such characteristics as simplicity, neutrality, and directness. And when I say neutrality, I don't mean that my work is neutral. It is not. What's neutral is my attitude toward culture, tradition, regional characteristics, and history that we discussed earlier. This position gives me a lot of freedom to address every work directly and independently of other projects and not just precedents by other architects, but even my own.

VB: I want to ask you about China's most controversial architect, Wang Shu who was your classmate at Southeast University. It seems that his work in some ways has become a model for many independent architects in the country. Yet, it is a strong contrast to yours. What do you think about his architecture?

ZL: We were classmates for almost eight years. Since the student days he was a rebel. He moved from a student dormitory where all other students lived to a hut at the foot of the Purple Mountain called Zijin Shan, a famous hill in the eastern part of the city. Since his student days every one of his projects has intelligence, wisdom, and strong criticality of various issues. His designs always have unique qualities of a literati. His architecture has assumed a form of resistance, particularly to the overwhelming global consumer-driven capitalism. That kind of criticality is rather rare, let alone his ability to persevere and be persistent at it for such a long time, realizing so many important projects.

VB: So, you think of him as a rebel. I am thinking: Who in the West would be identified as a rebel? Clearly that would be Rem Koolhaas. What is interesting is that both are rebels, but at the same time, both have a huge following. Both attracted attention for being unlike anyone else. Both changed trends and both achieved the highest level of recognition in the profession. Wang Shu is the reason for many architects to pay a lot of attention to the role of history and widespread demolition in China and beyond.

ZL: Absolutely.

072 Shitang Village Internet Conference Center, Nanjing, 2016. Photo by Hou Bowen

VB: What would you identify as the main issues or problems now for Chinese architects?

ZL: Speaking of the main issues we can't separate Chinese architects from everyone else. Architects have to face issues that are global. I don't believe in very special concerns that are only important to the Chinese architects. And the greatest challenge for all architects is time, as I emphasized repeatedly–to focus on issues of our own time and specific place and situation without borrowing ideas from the past or other places and projects. And what can be more important than to try to address and achieve the most sustainable relationship between humans and the environment?

VB: What one building built in China since the beginning of this century, either by local or foreign architect, would you call the most important and positive architecture?

ZL: To me clearly, it is Wang Shu's History Museum in Ningbo [020]. I think when you ask for a single project to be identified as the most important for our country it would have to come from a Chinese architect. This museum is clearly a testimony to what I think is the most important issues in architecture: How do you establish a connection between the past and the future, between humans and the environment? Wang Shu's building does that eloquently.

VB: I absolutely agree with you. I had a chance to see it in person and apart from being rooted in Chinese culture and instantly identifiable with China, it has a very powerful presence. It also came into being at a very precise moment

in recent history. It was critical for such a powerful building to be built precisely in 2008 with a strong message–contemporary Chinese architecture has arrived. It was the year of the Beijing Olympics, when a number of spectacular buildings by foreign architects were just finished in China. It was precisely that moment when, while global architecture was being celebrated in the country, its own original and distinctive architecture has emerged. His building signaled the sign of new times. And it was done on an equal scale, although not in the first tier city, which marked another shift of attention of the Chinese architects - moving from major cities to secondary cities and to the countryside. His project is a major protest against what you called global consumer-driven capitalism in China by putting his rebellious position on his building's facade.

ZL: It pointed to an alternative way for many local architects. Although, I already expressed my own position toward history and time, I still recognize the enormous importance of that building for many architects here in China.

073 Ruralation Retreat & Spa, Tangshan, Hebei Province, 2019 © Wen Studio

Binke Lenhardt & DONG Hao

CROSSBOUNDARIES

Interdisciplinary architecture and urban design firm, Crossboundaries was founded in 2005 in Beijing by Binke Lenhardt (b. 1971, Mannheim, Germany) and DONG Hao (b. 1973, Shanxi province). The two met in New York in 1999, while pursuing Master of Architecture degrees at Pratt Institute. Prior to their Pratt education, Dong had earned his bachelor's from the Beijing University of Civil Engineering and Architecture, while Lenhardt had received a Diploma in Architecture from the University of Applied Sciences in Dortmund, Germany. Before coming to the U.S., Lenhardt worked in Holland and Germany where she is a registered architect. After graduating from Pratt in 2000, the two architects worked at various firms in New York and moved to Beijing in 2002, at the time when the city was already preparing for the 2008 Summer Olympics. Once Lenhardt completed her intense course in Chinese at a local university the couple started working at the Beijing Institute of Architectural Design (BIAD). Being the only foreigner at this giant organization, Lenhardt soon became proficient in Mandarin. The architects worked their way up at BIAD and registered their own independent practice, while still working at the Institute. In 2006, they won second prize in the international competition for the design of Ningbo History Museum, which was won by Wang Shu. Crossboundaries currently employs 20 architects, a third of whom are foreigners. More than half of the studio's projects are educational—schools, kindergartens, childcare facilities, as well as youth, social, and cultural centers. Lenhardt and Dong also teach at the Central Academy of Fine Arts (CAFA) and Tsinghua University. The practice maintains a self-initiated design and creative thinking school for children, set up in 2017. It serves as a laboratory to test innovative ideas on how architecture can impact the learning process. In addition to the Beijing location, Crossboundaries established an office in Frankfurt, where Antje Voigt is a partner. The studio's most prominent built works, illustrated here, include Jinlong School in Shenzhen (2020), Beisha Kindergarten in Jiangsu (2018), and the Soyoo Joyful Growth Center in Zhengzhou (2015).

HOW CAN A BUILDING
PLAY A PEDAGOGICAL ROLE?

In conversation with **Binke Lenhardt** and **DONG Hao** of Crossboundaries, Beijing
Crossboundaries studio in Beijing, November 18, 2019

074 DONG Hao & Binke Lenhard. Photo by Matjaž Tančič

Vladimir Belogolovsky: You came to China in 2002, after acquiring your Master of Architecture degrees at Pratt Institute in New York. Could you talk about that experience and why you decided to work at the state-owned Beijing Institute of Architectural Design (BIAD), as opposed to either at foreign or local independent practices?

Binke Lenhardt: I chose to work at BIAD because I wanted to understand the system of planning and execution in China. Back then, I was the only foreigner at this huge institute of close to 4,000 people. Hao

and I worked there from 2003 on. In China, design institutes are responsible for almost 100% of all construction drawings done in the country. And independent practices typically must collaborate with so-called Local Design Institutes (LDIs), so not only foreign offices have to do this. Perhaps in the countryside some smaller projects stay under radar of the institutes and more independence is possible. In fact, there are many more opportunities for architects to work on small scale projects that may be neglected by large institutes. Having worked at BIAD for several years gave us invaluable insight into how the architectural profession operates in China.

Dong Hao: For me the experience was very different, as I spent most of the time collaborating with foreign architects, including such leading international firms as SOM, Foster + Partners, and OMA. I also collaborated with Zaha Hadid and Robert Stern, among others, mostly on competitions. While at BIAD, I spent many months at some of these offices abroad, so I learned more about how these international practices design projects and how they operate. I worked closely with them on coordinating the design and construction documents. I remember when Norman Foster flew in on his private jet to Beijing, coming to the office at midnight, just before the final presentation for the China National Museum competition. I worked with him until three o'clock in the morning, assisting him during our presentation the following day. So, while Binke was learning how the local system works, I focused on how to adapt projects designed by foreign architects to the Chinese reality. Going back and forth between China and the West gave us a lot of ideas about how to run our own projects at Crossboundaries.

VB: This information is surprising to me because none of the leading independent architects in China who I talked to here ever mentioned the fact that all of you must collaborate with LDIs. This means that all independent architects in China are recognized by local authorities as designers only, right?

BL: Yes, legally most independent offices are design consultancies, not full-service architectural offices, as is the case in the West. This is unless they hold their own license. An independent office, either foreign or local, no matter how big or influential, cannot legally complete a building in China without the approval of an LDI. Only LDIs can stamp construction drawings. There are different kinds of licenses, depending on the type and size of buildings. Only the institutes have the right to approve the construction documentation of all categories. If a client wants us to design, let's say, a theater, we would design the project and be obligated to work on the construction documents phase with the institute that is assigned to the project. The challenge then would be to keep the original design intention and avoid serious changes during the production of the construction documents. On our part, we go over every drawing by the institutes and we visit the construction sites diligently. Working with LDIs, as tightly as possible, is a must. Otherwise, a well-designed project may turn into a failure when built.

DH: One of the reasons that we decided to start working at the institute here in Beijing is that we wanted to understand how the whole system works. Now we know it from the inside and can maneuver through it. Very few leading independent architects in China have this knowledge, as most of them started their practices right after school or following their internships abroad.

VB: There are other reasons that make your practice quite unique here among leading Chinese architects. Namely, not only Binke was born and grew up outside of China, but Hao, you were trained at the Beijing Institute of Civil Engineering and Architecture, which is not one of the two elite schools–Tsinghua in Beijing and Tongji in Shanghai–where most leading architects in China were educated. Does this situation make you want to resist certain tendencies pursued by other independent architects?

BL: Well, I am a foreign national in China and the work of Crossboundaries does not fit into the aesthetics, which are currently attributed to much of the contemporary "Chinese architecture." For me it is not about "Chinese-ness," but about practicing our beliefs in a certain context. And for us this context is China. We think the authenticity of our projects lies in the specific set-up of the project itself, not in its poetic language or material preferences alone.

DH: Well, I never thought of our work this way. I thought we were just doing our work earnestly. And the visual aspects are not our only focus. But you are right, our work stands out here. The reason we called ourselves Crossboundaries is that there are many layers, interests, and meanings that we want to cross. We are constantly crossing boundaries, both cultural and in terms of our discipline. Maybe because we don't belong to this elite group you describe,

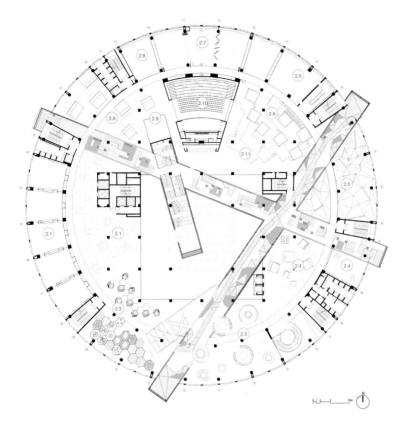

075 Soyoo Joyful Growth Center, Zhengzhou, Henan Province, 2015. Second Floor Plan. Courtesy of Crossboundaries

we were able to keep our attention focused on our own work, rather than being distracted by following others.

VB: What would you then say your architecture is about? What are your intentions?

BL: Most importantly, we don't see ourselves as merely creators of buildings. We are not just designing objects; we initiate discussions and interactions. Our buildings are done holistically–from inside to outside, and with attention to every detail. We are also involved in urban design, landscape, furniture design, graphics, exhibitions, and even the education process that's taking place inside our buildings. Architects can do so much more to influence our environment positively. But such broad and interdisciplinary hands-on involvement is unusual here. The profession is mainly understood as something very isolated. As an architect you are expected to work on your building's architecture. Such disciplines as landscape or interior design are viewed as outside the architects' expertise. We have proven that many different aspects of designing buildings can come from one team, that we are versatile.

DH: What we, as architects, provide to the society should be broader, deeper, and more meaningful, not just creating buildings. Here in the office we also organize various professional and social events. We want to have an impact on the society overall. We run a design school for children and people who work at our office teach these kids to think creatively. There is always an agenda behind our work. You can see it by going over the kind of commissions we undertake. We go after the kind of work that gives us a lot of power and freedom, not only as architects but also in terms of proposing our own visions for new kinds of programs. We involve clients in our design process. We are interested in architecture that

076 Soyoo Joyful Growth Center, Zhengzhou, Henan Province, 2015. Photo by Yang Chaoying

promotes communication and we push for opportunities to design hybrid programs. We believe that a 21st-century building is a hybrid building with fluid programs that cross boundaries in the most seamless ways.

BL: Architecture should be people-centered. That is the most important intention. Style is not important. We don't want to limit ourselves to any particular materials or means of expression. For example, our educational projects are designed as a result of many meetings and discussions with parents, teachers, as well as people in our own office. We want to empower people. Our work triggers attention and spontaneity. We want to encourage a new kind of experience. Many of our projects don't enjoy generous budgets or schedules to design them, so we focus on maximizing whatever resources we have. We sometimes struggle to balance between speed, resources, and quality, but we give our absolute best. If we see a certain potential, we never refuse a project just because there is not enough money to build it. We'll find a way.

VB: Could you talk about your design process?

DH: We always start with reviewing the briefs in depth. We ask many questions and get very precise. We challenge, and sometimes get back to our clients with suggestions to revise briefs. For example, take our Soyoo Joyful Growth Center project in Zhengzhou.

Initially, it was meant to be an interior renovation of just one floor within an existing round building of 30,000 square meters. The client had a vague vision for a playful learning environment. But we convinced him to do the extra step of a feasibility study of the original program, as well as the neighborhood and demographic characteristics of that part of the city. Eventually, he decided to go for the refurbishment of the entire building, its facade, and even public areas around it. So, as a result, it became the realization of a common vision and we were able to transform the building into a kind of hybrid, containing a high programmatic complexity with focus on education. The transformation of the building revitalized that whole neighborhood, which used to be quite disengaged.

BL: We look for weak spots in each brief, for "mistakes," so to speak, and push our clients to rethink and revise their original visions. We also function as a think-tank because why not take advantage of another opinion? We always welcome a discussion and collaboration. In the office we have frequent pin-ups and discussions, in which everyone participates. Our goal is to find the best possible solution, so it is a very collaborative process. I think the advantage is obvious. As a team, we can put forward perhaps twenty, thirty ideas and discuss the ones that have most potential to be developed. And I am interested in hearing other points of view and challenging myself. I am far from insisting on my solution always being the best. We try to apply this

077 Beisha Kindergarten, Jiangsu Province, 2018. Photo by Wu Qingshan

process to all our projects, no matter how small the scope. This attitude gives us certainty that the design direction is right and that all aspects have been thought through.

VB: Welcoming discussions, proposing hybrid programs, challenging and rewriting clients' original briefs. This is what many young architects from around the world say. Who would you credit most for influencing you to think this way?

DH: When I first came to New York–I've never been abroad before that–what first introduced me to this collective brainstorming process, was the experience at the design studios at Pratt. Before that my education was very technical and based on a lot of drafting. My Pratt professor Jack Travis was very instrumental in introducing me to challenging things and asking questions. He is like a mentor to me and we still maintain a good friendship. So, considering my own experience, it is relevant to mention that the Chinese system doesn't allow much space for challenging a particular tradition, system of values, and expectations. It is more about execution, not initiating a creative process.

BL: For me the method of "questioning the given" comes from my upbringing, my childhood, and particularly the influence of my father from early on. He never allowed me to form just one single opinion.

To this day he is like that. And, of course, I went to school and university in West Germany where there was a lot of reflection on your opinions and actions. As a student, I always had to consider ten different ways of doing something. We are also influenced by the works and writings of Rem Koolhaas, particularly on our way of questioning and expanding our clients' briefs.

VB: Let's talk more about the school that you started at your office. How did you come up with this idea and more importantly, why?

DH: The school idea is an integral part of Crossboundaries' work. When we were working on one of our first educational projects, we became interested in spaces of learning. We were commissioned to design a project called Family Box. Our client wanted us to come up with a new kind of school. The idea was to introduce the learning process through play quite physically. We used a color-coded solution, where each color indicates a particular zone such as a library, classrooms, play areas, café, and so on. Then we had more projects with this client and developed so-called smart volumes that feature a variety of elements to engage children in learning through play. There are slides, climbing zones, movable walls, soft-upholstered seating, and more. That approach became the model for our other projects and, eventually, expanded our potential as educators.

078 Beisha Kindergarten, Jiangsu Province, 2018. Photo by Wu Qingshan

BL: Our educational projects enabled us to do a lot of research and gain knowledge on the topic and we became interested in starting our own school where we developed our own curriculum and we engage our employees to teach here. The school is set up as a real business model. It is for middle school kids. It is a sustainable program, a private tuition-based school with a two-week afterschool design course, both in Chinese and English. It is totally unique.

VB: Why do you do all these things? Both of you teach at architecture schools. You lead a busy architectural practice, and now you run this school. What do you try to achieve?

DH: We decided to switch our focus from design only. We are architects and we want to achieve our own kind of architecture, but not only through architectural projects. That's why we teach. And that's the reason for creating our own school. We want to have an impact on how people think about the environment. We run events here that introduce people to more sustainable and responsible ways of living, and basically how to live with less. These events became so popular that it gave us a kind of community hub

status and people identify these qualities with our practice. We are interested in figuring out how to use our own space and that experience helps us to understand what kind of spaces work best. This is how we adjust and finetune our architecture.

BL: Another reason why we became involved in teaching is the fact that by the time many people get into universities it is already too late for certain things to emerge, especially creativity. We decided to do something about it. Now we teach at universities much less and we focus more on teaching at our own school. The existing education system does not allow to nurture creativity. This is what we observe when we teach. Students are selected based on how well they perform overall, but most of them don't know why they go into architecture in the first place. Our goal here is to focus on creative and analytical thinking. For us the process is more important than the outcome, so kids can experience the joy of learning.

VB: I understand that your own school serves you as a kind of laboratory. Creative education is in big demand in China and there is willingness to experiment on the part of

clients. So, when they ask you to design a school program you can test ideas right here in your own prototype. By now you have done a number of educational projects such as schools, kindergartens, and youth centers. Would you say that you are primarily interested in this building type?

BL: Education overall, both as a process and building type, is very important to us because even the way our studio works is like a school and it is not just about knowledge exchange alone—we also benefit greatly from our educational projects. In terms of our prime interest I would say that our goal is to work on hybrid programs with educational components that could be mixed with leisure, sports, art, retail, office, and so on.

DH: I believe it is a school that is perhaps the most influential building type, meaning that it can have maximum impact on people's behavior. It is true, to us this line of projects is like a laboratory. We test

different ideas in our own school and apply them in our projects. We don't aim at training architects or designers here. We teach our kids critical thinking and appreciation for design. We offer hands-on training with visits to significant buildings, examining various urban issues, and teach them presentation skills. We are developing a model for progressive interactive education. And we are interested in how this could push and influence architecture itself. We want to understand how architecture could influence the process of education. How can a building play a pedagogical role? Our goal is to develop such a compelling program that it would become a part of public education, perhaps all over China. We are interested in the development of such an educational program, as a whole, not just a look of a particular building. To us architecture is inclusive. Architecture is a result of an interactive process—it can be so much more than a building.

079 Jinlong School, Shenzhen, 2020. Photo by Wu Qingshan

XU Tiantian

DNA_DESIGN AND ARCHITECTURE

XU Tiantian (b. 1975, Fujian Province) earned her Bachelor of Architecture from Tsinghua University in Beijing in 1997 and Master of Architecture from Harvard's GSD in 2000. She then worked in the U.S. and at OMA in Rotterdam before opening her DnA_ Design and Architecture studio in Beijing in 2004. She stands out as one of the few independent female architects in China and the only one in this book. Xu is committed to building relevant public projects in rural areas, particularly in small villages in the Songyin river valley of Songyang County in Zhejiang Province. In this picturesque region, about five-hour drive south of Shanghai, the architect has completed nearly 30 projects to date, a rare feat for any architect. Visiting some of these buildings first-hand, I can attest that this architectural pilgrimage was one of the most memorable and rewarding experiences. Xu defines her socially engaging structures as "architectural acupuncture." But not only are they beneficial in the most direct social sense or even "healing," according to their most active advocates, they are most

definitely and undeniably beautiful. Yet, Xu insists every time that it is not their beauty, but a capacity to make a social impact that's important. Her buildings bring public programs and reveal culture and heritage of each village. The idea is to restore these villages' identities–infrastructure, industry, social structure, cultural facilities, and to bring jobs. Another important message here is that to be contemporary you no longer have to start from scratch. There is an attempt to build a more organic continuity between various historical layers. Among Xu's most renowned works here are the Water Conservancy Centre (2018), the Dushan Leisure Center (2018), Pine Pavilion (2018), Shimen Bridge (2018), the Tofu Factory (2018), the Hakka Indenture Museum (2017), the Bamboo Pavilion (2016), and, my favorite, the Brown Sugar Factory (2016) for its explicit and encompassing expression of modernity, universality, and yet, locality in the most compelling way.

WE TREAT PROJECTS LIKE PATIENTS.
EVERY PATIENT IS DIFFERENT, SO IS EVERY PROJECT.

In conversation with **XU Tiantian** of DnA_Design and Architecture, Beijing
DnA_Design and Architecture studio in Beijing, November 30, 2018

Vladimir Belogolovsky: I have visited a number of your projects built in the last few years in Songyang County. I particularly enjoyed my time at the Brown Sugar Factory in Xing Village.

Xu Tiantian: Because of the workers' choreography in their orange robes against thick, white steam. Everybody likes that.

VB: I enjoyed it for two reasons–the beauty and intelligence of your architecture. Because of the inventive use of details and the building's strong position. It is unquestionably modern and universal. At the same time, the building responds to its site and it is identifiable with its region and culture. There is a lot going on there for such a modestly scaled project. Also, each one of your projects has a strong vision of its own. They are very autonomous, and they seem to share little in common. These projects are very specific to their places, even materiality is expressed very differently every time. I didn't find any repetition in thinking or even detailing.

XT: I think this has to do with the overall story. There are over 400 villages in Songyang County. Architecture there is used as the acupuncture strategy targeting local rural symptoms. These buildings bring public programs and they reveal culture and heritage of each village. So, it's really case-by-case situation–to analyze the village, to diagnose the symptoms, and to find the right architectural intervention by setting up relevant programs at appropriate locations. This will impact the design of the buildings to be more about the place and people rather than a signature architectural style. And it's

080 XU Tiantian. Courtesy of DnA_Design and Architecture

more about the logic behind each project that is always consistent. The idea of architectural acupuncture is to look for a systematic, sustainable strategy. The goal there is not just to cater to tourists, which, of course, is a major impulse for local economic development, but to restore these villages' identities. We are talking about infrastructure, industry, social structure, cultural facilities, and so on.

VB: Could you tell me what first brought you to architecture?

XT: I was preselected to enter Tsinghua University here in Beijing. I just picked architecture, which was

081 Bamboo Pavilion, Damushan Tea Plantation, Songyang County, Zhejiang Province, 2015. Photo by Wang Ziling

at the top of the list of all the departments. Well, I suppose, I went by my intuition. As you can imagine, the list was pretty long, but architecture was the most interesting possibility to me at first glance.

VB: Did you know anything about it?

XT: No, I didn't! [Laughs.] And there were no architects in my family. I made this decision entirely on my own, without consulting my parents. But, you know, later I realized that my decision may have something to do with the house, in which I grew up, in Fujian Province on the southeast coast of China. It's a very old wooden house with a sequence of endless, open and closed courtyards, refined details, and very beautiful spaces. It once accommodated over 100 people.

VB: After Tsinghua you went on to the GSD at Harvard, then worked in Boston for several years and later for OMA in Rotterdam.

XT: I worked in Boston for three years and then at OMA Rotterdam for less than a year. I went there mainly because of their CCTV project in Beijing. But then I went on a short break to visit Shenzhen and was totally overwhelmed. It was post SARS and there was so much energy–people going out, stores and restaurants open around the clock. It was then that I decided to come back to China, especially since we

had to work very long hours at OMA. I hated that. [Laughs.]

VB: Well, you thought you were working long hours until you started your own practice, right?

XT: But we don't work long hours here! Our hours are very reasonable. I started my practice in 2004, after working with Ai Weiwei on Jinhua Architecture Park in Zhejiang Province. I collaborated with artist Wang Xingwei to design a group of public toilets in the park. And Songzhuang Art Center was my studio's first building.

VB: What would you say you learned most from your collaborations with artists?

XT: Architecture can provide practical solutions to a real problem. But most of the times projects are commissioned by clients. And artists, particularly conceptual artists, are working in a very different way–they identify important issues and address them with their work. This is what could be adapted into architectural thinking and working. The idea is not just to provide answers but raise questions. Yet, there is a difference between being an architect and artist. I don't want to make a statement. Instead, I want to find a practical solution to a real-life problem. My response should be practical and functional, that's

082 Brown Sugar Factory, Xing Village, Songyang County, Zhejiang Province, 2016. Photo by Wang Ziling

what architecture is. Architecture doesn't need to be overly expressive or theoretical. In other words, it is not enough for architecture to be about itself. Architecture can be something very real and right in front of you, not a shining, proud object. Not that I don't appreciate beauty in architecture. But it is not its most important value. It can be more.

VB: I can tell that it is important to you to have a good balance between life and work.

XT: You know, when I was expecting my third child, my son in 2009, I put my practice on hold for several years. Only after he went to kindergarten, I reopened it. I love architecture but life is not only about architecture. I call myself a part-time architect. Our studio is very small—fewer than 10 people, and I think it's the right size to keep a good balance.

VB: Let's go back to your projects in Songyang County. I remember, it was back in 2012, when everyone was still talking about ever-growing cities and increasing pace of urbanization, especially in China, when Rem Koolhaas pointed the other way by saying, "Half of mankind lives in the city, but the other half doesn't." When did you start paying attention to the countryside here in China?

083 Brown Sugar Factory, Xing Village, Songyang County, Zhejiang Province, 2016. Photo by Wang Ziling

XT: It was a coincidence that my work shifted to the countryside. I was first contacted by Songyang County officials a few years ago for a hotel project and then we were periodically asked by the county to serve as advisors on their village development issues. So, we worked for one year to take on these projects, pro bono. For example, the Pingtian Village Center was a cluster of abandoned small villager houses that most people preferred to be demolished. But we considered them as a crucial building fabric of this traditional village and proposed to offer our design for free, so that county government would sponsor its construction cost. It became a successful project for the village and started a pattern of working together with local communities and the county government on initiating programs to target different issues.

VB: And what started as a pro bono initiative, eventually led to a string of commissions, right?

XT: Yes, because soon, the demands grew, and we could no longer afford not to be compensated. So, after we did the first three projects that way, we accepted all subsequent projects in the villages as paid commissions. Eventually, we came up with the architectural acupuncture concept, which was accepted by the county and led to a systematic collaboration. The Songyang story is one singular project for us. And each of these small interventions is done with modest budget and local materials and building techniques to engage and motivate the local communities. These individual projects will also create interactions between the neighboring villages. I like to say that acupuncture is performed to release the trapped energy in various places to remedy the whole organism of a particular village.

VB: And each of these villages has its own character and distinctive culture.

084 Brown Sugar Factory, Xing Village, Songyang County, Zhejiang Province, 2016. Photo by Wang Ziling

085 Shimen Bridge, Shimen Village, Songyang County, Zhejiang Province, 2017. Photo by Wang Ziling

XT: Yes, unlike cities. So many of our cities have become alike, or homogeneous and they are losing their identities. But each village has its own history and focus. The goal is to use the architectural acupuncture strategy to re-activate one village at a time by restoring their identities, which will also reflect on their architectural identities.

VB: I understand that this project attracted a lot of attention in the media because already the results are very tangible. People are coming back to these villages, right?

XT: There have been many new changes in this region. Young people are moving back to their home villages and starting new businesses–from e-commerce on local products to new tourist programs. When we first started in Pingtian Village three years ago there were only 20 people left and mostly elders. Now the total number of inhabitants has increased to over 100. In Shicang Village, the Hakka Indenture Museum has attracted an investor from Shanghai to open businesses at what used to be vacant houses next door. Now local villagers are motivated to initiate various enterprises that have resulted in a significant increase of economic revenues. People are

086 Pine Pavilion, Huangyu Village, Songyang County Zhejiang Province, 2017. Photo by Wang Ziling

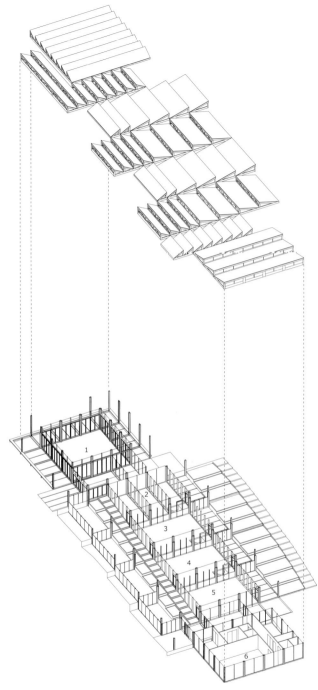

087 Tofu Factory, Caizhai Village, Songyang County
Zhejiang Province, 2018. Drawing by DnA_Design and Architecture

now proud of their heritage and are optimistic about their future.

VB: How would you summarize what your architecture is about?

XT: For me architecture is not just about crafting an object. I don't like when architects try to impose their own signature styles on a particular place. I think history itself is important—the place, traditions, construction methods. I want to work with these tangibles and react to real needs, which are different every time. Architecture is a tool to respect and preserve local history and to address specific issues. Architecture should be able to connect the past and the future. Most of our buildings in Songyang County are barely noticeable on the outside. You may discover them when you are already inside. Our forms come from the places where we work. There is nothing striking, foreign, or even personal. We try to be very careful. There are buildings that need to be seen and there are buildings that need to be discovered. There should be different degrees of expressions. As I said, we treat projects like patients. Every patient is different, so is every project.

VB: And how would you describe your work or a kind of architecture that you want to achieve?

XT: I never thought about that…It would be too easy, no? No, I would leave it open.

VB: Open is a good word.

XT: No, I mean I would leave any conclusions completely open. No conclusions. I am still exploring and learning. I really like to continue the Songyang story. We can explore the capacity of architecture and expand on it. You know, the real reason I stopped doing architecture for several years is that I no longer liked it. I wouldn't have stopped it if I really liked it. The real purpose was unclear then. And now I like it so much because architecture can have a real purpose. I came back after years of reflection, understanding that architecture can be something very tangible, a social engine.

VB: Do you worry about Chinese identity in your work?

XT: Not at all. What is Chinese identity anyway? China is too big to even have a particular identity. Every village I am working in claims to have its own identity. I think it would be too shallow to generalize it.

VB: Would you say there is a particular evolution in your work from project to project? Are you concerned with developing your own personal voice? Do you see a connection between your projects in different villages?

XT: When we work in villages, it is more important to integrate the program with the village history and the current needs, then to adapt the building techniques or material fitting with a given context and on budget. And we always respect architecture without architects. Every project is different. For example, the Brown Sugar Factory is about the celebration of life and production, a modern light steel structure, a common rural light industrial building form. It is used as a social space for the village and for performances. Whereas, the Indenture Museum in Hakka is a quiet place constructed out of the excavated nearby ancient stone to contemplate local history. It's about the weight and the ancient history of Hakka. Architecture is also about storytelling. Each project has its own plot to merge with its village context. I don't think you could swap them around. The consistency of the logic, the intellectual thinking behind each project, the message—all these aspects—are more important than the individual expression. In fact, we have been very cautious and skeptical about developing any particular style. But I think it's inevitable to leave certain traces in our projects. Certain commonalities come through; I am sure of it.

088 **Tofu Factory, Caizhai Village, Songyang County, Zhejiang Province, 2018.** Photo by Wang Ziling

LIU Jiakun

JIAKUN ARCHITECTS

LIU Jiakun (b. 1956, Chengdu) originally wanted to be an artist. He heard that architecture had something to do with drawing, so he applied to the Chongqing Institute of Architecture and Engineering, not fully understanding what his role as an architect would be. After his graduation in 1982, Liu worked at the Chengdu Architectural Design Academy for two years, which he did not enjoy. So, he set out on a journey that lasted for over a decade, spending time in Tibet and Xinjiang Province in Western China where he practiced meditation, painting, and writing, producing several fiction stories, while officially working at the Literature Academy as a writer. In 1993, Liu's former classmate Tang Hua invited him to attend his architectural exhibition. Encountering his friend's research-based projects, suddenly rekindled Liu's interest in the profession. He decided to give his dormant passion another chance. in 1999, Liu founded his practice, Jiakun Architects, in his hometown. His powerful buildings attracted universal acclaim that brought prestigious awards, including the 2003 Chinese Architecture and Art Prize. Liu's celebrated Rebirth Brick project, initiated after the 2008 Sichuan earthquake, was based on producing bricks and cement blocks from the rubble of the demolished buildings to facilitate the "rebirth" of culture and place. The project earned him a reputation of the "architect of memory." Another one of his influential projects is the West Village residential urban block in Chengdu (2015), a new building type–a maxi-courtyard that occupies an entire city block to maximize the inner area with sports activities and park, welcoming a diverse public life mixed with commerce. The architect's work was exhibited both at art and architecture biennales in Venice and in 2018, his inaugural Serpentine Pavilion Beijing was presented. Liu's architecture is rooted in social and vernacular traditions, oriental aesthetics, close observation of the everyday life, refinement of folk skills and wisdom, and is characterized as being fully integrated with nature. The architect's other built projects include the Renovation of Tianbao Cave District of Erlang Town in Luzhou in Sichuan Province (2020), the Suzhou Imperial Kiln Ruins Park & Museum of Imperial Kiln Brick (2016), the Chengdu Museum of Contemporary Art (2010), the Hu Huishan Memorial in Chengdu (2009), and the Luyeyuan Stone Sculpture Art Museum near Chengdu (2002).

I CAN ACCEPT IMPERFECTIONS

In conversation with **LIU Jiakun** of Jiakun Architects, Chengdu
WeChat video call between New York and Chengdu, April 13, 2020

Vladimir Belogolovsky: It is very unusual for Chinese architects to give their own name to their practices. But casually naming your studio by your given name is unique even for a Westerner's ear. What do you think?

Liu Jiakun: It is very simple–I wanted to be honest with myself and accountable for my work. I wanted an easy and straightforward name, then my given name is the simplest. But you are right, it is very unusual because when I first suggested this name, Jiakun Architects, there was a lot of resistance from the local authorities who had to approve my company's registration. They said, "Who do you think you are?!" They thought it was egoistic and eccentric. [Laughs.]

VB: You once observed, "If I run out of ideas, I just plant more trees." Was that a joke or do you believe nature can save architecture by hiding architects' lack of imagination or mistakes, as Frank Lloyd Wright famously pointed out?

LJ: Yes, this is true, particularly in the case of the Luyeyuan Stone Sculpture Art Museum, which was my first built project. I was asked not just to design the building but also to do the landscaping all around it. So, it was no joke for me because at that time I still lacked experience and expertise in so many areas! Additionally, the intention was not to overdesign certain parts of the building. So, as you can imagine, if I could cover them with trees it was to my advantage. Anyway, who would criticize a tree? You know, we all came from monkeys! [Laughs.]

VB: You are referring to the project where you lined up a row of concrete columns and one of them is replaced by a tree, right?

089 LIU Jiakun. Courtesy of Jiakun Architects

LJ: Actually, it was the other way around. The tree was there first, so I designed columns to align with that one tree, and I just cut an opening in the slab around the tree to let it continue to grow.

VB: After finishing university and working as an architect at the local institute you decided that it was not for you, so you went away and spent over a decade meditating, painting, writing, traveling, and basically observing nature and people. What was your main lesson from that experience?

LJ: What I discovered was that design and writing is not that different, after all. Actually, both are sort of forms of conspiracies, you know? [Laughs.] Well, in both cases, you lead your audience to a particular

090 Luyeyuan Stone Sculpture Art Museum, Chengdu, 2002
© Jiakun Architects

VB: I know that you came across an exhibition that made you want to go back to doing architecture after years of taking a break from it. Could you talk about that encounter?

LJ: In the late 1980s, I decided to give up on architecture altogether to become a full-time writer. But in 1993, my classmate from the university invited me to his solo architectural exhibition. It was a show of both built and unbuilt projects. That's when I came across my last hope, a possibility to express individuality through architecture. At that time, I fully gave up on architecture, but after attending the exhibition I decided to pick up my interest in the profession. But before devoting myself to architecture fully, I had to finish my book that was at the core of my imagination for a long time. Once the book was finished and out of my way, I started my architectural studio. That was in 1999.

VB: What was the book about?

LJ: For me the book was about Utopia and Anti-utopia. On the face of it, it contemplated how to build a new idealistic town, a utopian city. I was inspired by real new cities, similar to new socialist and industrial towns in the USSR. The book was not about laying out architectural strategies, but an exploration into politics, socialism, and revolution. I would call the book a political manifesto. You know, every Chinese architect has a small Mao within him; we see architecture as a tool to change the world, to make it better, but usually, things are counterproductive! [Laughs.]

VB: Your architecture is about making, building, and revealing the everyday, and what is authentic about living in China. What else is your work about? What is your main goal as an architect?

LJ: There are many issues that I am very concerned about, particularly with the juxtaposition of the utopian and the everyday, modernity and traditions, collective memories and personal memory, as well as sustainability. In every one of my projects I try to focus on all these issues. Although each project will face comprehensive problems, the focus of each project will be different. Again, going back to one of my first projects, the Luyeyuan Stone

outcome, a climax, so to speak. Interestingly, many of the notions we are dealing with as architects also exist in the literary world in terms of the necessity for structure, rhythm, surprise, even for balance and right proportions. We are operating with very similar tools. Of course, writing is more orderly, more linear—line by line, page by page, following a traditional plot structure—the beginning, climax, and ending. In contrast, architecture is much more erratic and spontaneous. As a writer, you know what you can achieve as an individual. You build up an anticipation, you create something that leads to something unexpected and provocative. But in architecture, it is about teamwork. You can surprise even yourself. There is more mystery to it.

091 Rebirth Brick Sample, Since 2008 © Jiakun Architects

Sculpture Art Museum, my key focus was on lyricism, on the poetry of space itself. But if you look at my West Village project here in Chengdu, you will see that the focus is much more on the social engagement of people, and not only on those who live there, but even those living all around it. In fact, many of my projects pay particular attention to how they fit into their surroundings. If Luyeyuan Stone Sculpture Art Museum is about "poetry," then West Village is about "sociology."

VB: Could you talk about your design process? In one of your lectures you said that in most cases you work with unskilled laborers and before initiating your design you meet with them to discuss what they are capable of. I heard that you do that even before starting your design. You said in one of your lectures, "Once I understand what the workers can do, then I can design my building." Is that right?

LJ: This is true, but not at the very beginning. At the beginning, I will still have a basic concept of the overall design. Of course, I want to know what builders are capable of, so I don't design something they can't build. But in the very beginning I spend time to discover various issues. First, I need to investigate the site and fully understand the context. During this stage I would decide on what the problems are and how to tackle them, and in what way.

VB: Ever since the 2008 Sichuan earthquake you initiated the use of brick or cement block reconstructed from the rubble of the demolished buildings to facilitate "rebirth" of culture and place. Due to the use of this technique you are referred to as the "architect of memory." Could you talk about this technique and do you rely on it in your other projects since then?

LJ: The origin of that rebirth brick idea was, of course, the fact that the earthquake left so much destruction and rubble. The immediate problem was rebuilding. So, it was important to come up with a creative and fast way to rebuild. And this technique proved to be very sustainable. I am very proud for being able to create my own, so-called building block for producing my own kind of architecture. And I kept using it for a while in a number of my subsequent projects, even years after the earthquake. To this day I sometimes use this technique, but the source, the ruble from the earthquake has become very limited over the years and there is not much left of it.

VB: So, your idea of the rebirth brick did not merge into your iconic and unique way of building? Isn't there enough rubble from the widespread demolition in China to keep this idea going?

LJ: First, I don't consider this technique as my unique architectural gesture because I don't want to be tied to a single architectural element and be recognized for just one kind of attitude. The idea is to use this technique strategically where it is appropriate. The other reason is very mundane, which is the cost of such process. Initially, right after the earthquake, there was a lot of readily available rubble and, therefore, the cost was very low. Whereas, now, if I want to continue using the same technique, I have to spend a lot of money and efforts to find the rubble from a particular demolition. So now it has become more challenging and from the standpoint of sustainability, it no longer makes as much sense as before.

VB: You just mentioned your focus on blending personal memory with collective memories. Could you elaborate on this idea?

LJ: Traditions, in general, is a grand overarching theme here in China, which we can't escape. It is the foundation on which many things stand. However, traditions may not be as vivid as personal memories. As far as this juxtaposition, collective memories are never as emotional and penetrating as the memory of a particular individual. That's why my project for the Hu Huishan Memorial was entirely based on creating a very personal perspective, not just to all victims, but specifically to one of those who perished, a 15-year-old high school student. The shape of the Memorial was inspired by a typical relief tent from the earthquake-stricken zone. The exterior walls of the Memorial are plastered in the most natural way to the local area, while the interior is painted pink, the

girl's favorite color, and decorated with her personal toys and objects. Of course, the Memorial is not only for Hu Huishan, but also for almost 100,000 other victims of that earthquake. After the earthquake, the relief tents were everywhere in my hometown. So, the Memorial reflects both collective memories and my own, personal memory.

VB: Going back to your "rebirth" brick idea, what do you think about the notion of authorship in architecture? Are you at all concerned with how to leave a particular trace, your own mark, as an author? For example, would you say that your reliance on using the "rebirth" brick, even if strategic and not universal, is what makes your architecture distinctive, unique, and identifiable with you personally?

LJ: I do care about authorship and personal character, and unique identity, but I don't think it needs to be conscious or contrived. It should come subconsciously and spontaneously, not deliberately. Of course, there are architects who are known for

092 Chengdu Museum of Contemporary Arts, Chengdu, 2010 © Longping Li

inventing their own formally recognizable language. But I don't belong to that camp. What I want to follow is not a fixed symbol or style, but a consolidated methodology and common spiritual temperament. Having a style is like a double-edged sword, it is beneficial for being recognized, but it puts a lot of limitations on what is possible.

VB: What words would you use to describe your work most accurately or the kind of architecture you strive to achieve?

LJ: I am not good at making conclusions with single words. Quite the opposite, as I like things to be inconclusive. Let me refer to Martin Heidegger's poem "Poetically Man Dwells." I like to think that poetry lies in the core of my work.

VB: What is a good building for you?

LJ: I often question this myself–What is a good building? What can we expect from good architecture? Well, it is like defining oneself, which is a very difficult task. I like different buildings for different reasons. But what I particularly like about

any building is when I stand in front of it and experience an emotional sensation. At the same time, I like certain unsettledness. Speaking of my own buildings, I like when I feel that I might have done something that's not quite right. In other words, I like buildings that welcome alternative readings. I don't like architecture that pretends to be perfect.

VB: A building that's unsettled and imperfect is a good building, right?

LJ: I would phrase it this way–imperfect buildings could be viewed as good architecture. I can accept imperfections because it is a strive for perfection that leads to rigidity. Perfection is all about closed system, whereas, imperfections open the system and enrich architecture with possibilities.

VB: You practice architecture away from other leading Chinese architects in Beijing and Shanghai. So, you must be the right person to ask: What do you think about the current creative climate for practicing architecture in China?

LJ: There are many more opportunities for the Chinese architects now than before. At the same time, I feel that so many architects are preoccupied with fetishizing their architecture, focusing on improving their skills and perfecting their techniques instead of continuously exploring and experimenting. There is less willing to be critical and to engage in making architecture more socially relevant. You can see more and more really exquisite buildings. This may seem that local architecture is becoming more mature, but to me it is less interesting. Overall, the atmosphere is perhaps no more different than it was a decade ago.

VB: In other words, what you are saying is that architecture has reached a certain level of relevance and creativity about a decade ago and since then it has not evolved much besides adjusting itself here and there, and it has turned into a formulaic style with all its rigidity and expectations, right?

LJ: You can say that.

VB: This is my perception–so many independent architects in China are focused on the issue of regional identity. This offers a great alternative to so-called global architecture, but don't you think this predominant focus on history, traditions, materiality, and regionalism limits architects' possibilities? There seems to be no such liberating and necessary premise that architecture could really be anything.

LJ: I agree that there needs to be a balance. Nowadays, we pay a great deal of attention to our history. However, we need to derive our ideas and inspirations from both–our local culture and from whatever is learned and developed around the world. In fact, I disagree with the view that globalization needs to be resisted. That would lead to a closure of ideas and attitudes. Ideas should be shared and multiplied. We should take what is quintessential about different cultures to enrich our own. Architecture should benefit from creative ideas, no matter where they come from.

VB: Together with such architects as Yung Ho Chang, Wang Shu, Li Xiaodong, and Zhu Pei you belong to the first generation of contemporary independent architects in China. I wonder how you see your own work–as moving in one direction and sharing a particular common ground or do you perceive your architecture differently?

LJ: Compared to some of the architects you mentioned I see myself as a latecomer. I went away for more than a decade and rekindled my interest in architecture when these architects were already practicing for quite some time. I think what we all have in common is a certain hunger for learning and opening up to many ideas that were out of reach before. And most of these architects were exposed to living and studying abroad for many years before coming back, so their work was infused by what they have learned overseas. And there was a kind of urgency to innovate and build after a long period of official government-approved style. Then in the '90s, we all became free. I relate more to Wang Shu because his focus is

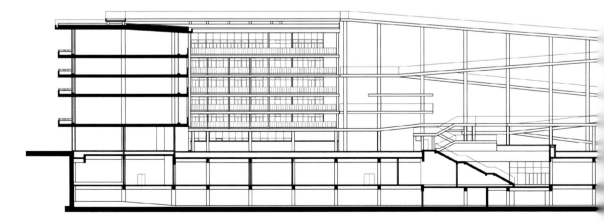

on analyzing and reproaching our own culture and utilizing traditions in new and innovative ways. One fundamental difference between my work and Wang Shu's is that I would never directly recycle ancient materials as entities. I respect tradition. I hope my work carries the spirit of Chinese traditions, but I don't want to bring ready-made traditional techniques and materials into my architecture. I prefer to use contemporary techniques and materials. There is no ambiguity about what is contemporary and what is not.

VB: In one of your interviews you pointed out that "Many contemporary buildings don't have shadows." What did you mean by that?

LJ: Let me correct that. I must have talked about the necessity for buildings to have atmosphere, as referred to in Junichiro Tanizaki's novel *In Praise of Shadows*. A shadow is a physical phenomenon, but I referred to qualities that may not be quite visible. Yet, they are very important. For buildings to project a particular atmosphere or aura is very difficult to achieve. It is necessary for buildings to contain stories, even secrets.

VB: You said that many architects rush to photograph their buildings right after they are completed and before they are "spoiled" by users. You said, "They don't realize that they have become the enemies of life itself." How do you bring your buildings in contact with real life?

094 West Village, Chengdu, 2015. Bird's Eye view © Chen Chen

LJ: It is very true, as so many architects are preoccupied with their pure compositions and stark visions of how their buildings should look like. But I believe that architecture should tolerate usage. Architecture should accommodate people; it is not about achieving a certain perfect composition in the architect's mind. When architects look at their buildings after they are completed, they prefer if there is no one around them. But if you look at such buildings as Luis Kahn's Parliament in Dhaka, for example, you will see many poor people going on with their daily lives–doing laundry, resting, feeding cows, and so on. It makes this building more vivid. It is important for buildings to tolerate activities that they are a part of.

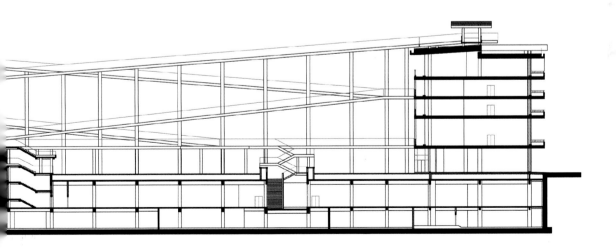

095 West Village, Chengdu, 2015. Crossed Tracks © Arch-Exist

VB: When I look at your projects, I can't avoid noticing that you hardly use any colors. Yet, you mentioned throughout our conversation that you want your buildings to be contemporary. But contemporary means to be able to use all kinds of materials and techniques that were not available in the past. Is this discipline and disposition to use a certain palette of materials and colors intentional on your part?

LJ: I tend to use natural materials, preferring their own inherent colors. I would not paint anything. And it is not my intention to produce something either contemporary or traditional.

VB: Is there a progression in your work? How would you describe your professional path– going from earlier projects to the most recent ones?

LJ: What I emphasize most in my work is oriental metaphysical character and how it can be interpreted today. This is my continuous preoccupation. But, of course, when I just started, I had to do a lot

of experimentation and I achieved certain results through trial and error methods. I feel that when I started, I was the least prepared and knowledgeable of the leading architects of my generation here in China. But once I became familiar with many techniques and the reality of architectural practice, I started paying more attention to each project's specifics and relation to its circumstance. More and more I set my focus on the process of making each project, which is very specific and relevant to each situation. The question of style is less and less interesting to me. Also, early on I was very concerned with criticism and feedback from critics and clients. That was due to my own lack of confidence then. I was trying to cover my absence of confidence by applying different theories and philosophies. Now I know what I am doing; it is based on my experience and confidence, as well as constant observation of everyday life and peoples' relationship to buildings.

VB: What would you say should be the role of a contemporary architect?

LJ: I am, of course, paying a lot of attention to the emergence of all kinds of new technologies, and for sure, some of them will replace many current traditions and ways of doing architecture. Architecture should be more inclusive and adoptive to what is coming. But what's important is not to give too much attention to mere aesthetics, forms, and styles, but to keep developing a critical attitude and to make architecture relevant to people it is designed for. I am convinced that architecture should carry a particular message. Technology helped us to make architecture very complex, sculptural, and advanced, but we should not apply them superficially. We should not forget about our roots and keep learning from the past examples of those buildings that possess spiritual qualities within them.

VB: What one building built in China since the beginning of this century, either by local or foreign architect, would you pick as the most important and positive example of architecture, and why?

LJ: Your question is not easy to respond to because there are so many good buildings that were built all over China in recent years. Thus, before coming up with my answer, let me try not to be very humble this time and introduce my own project first, West Village here in Chengdu. It is a very open project where the whole territory is accessible to the public to enjoy. It is a maxi-courtyard that occupies an entire city block to maximize the inner area with sports activities and park, welcoming a diverse public life. Its key feature is that the entire courtyard was built within the streets, and the elevated walkways along the perimeter, floating above the rooftops. This constant change of altitude is unique, and it activates a dynamic flow of energy within this whole neighborhood. I would call this attitude–form follows essence. I see this project as a typological innovation. It is a new way of living together, a new social structure, even an attempt to build a new kind of urban utopia. The other important project I would choose is the Bird's Nest Olympic Stadium in Beijing by Herzog & de Meuron [002]. I like its scale, innovation of structure, and the fact that it is embraced so much by the public. There are similar surreal moments between this project and the West Village.

096 Liquor Tasting Pavilion, Renovation of Tianbao Cave, District of Erlang Town, Sichuan Province, 2020 © Arch-Exist

LI Xiaodong
LI XIAODONG ATELIER

Beijing-based architect LI Xiaodong (b. 1963, Beijing) is considered to be a true guru and undisputed authority to many young Chinese architects, equally dedicated to practice and teaching. Li is a reflexive regionalist for whom architecture is a matter of debate and whose stance is firmly rooted in Chinese history, culture, and philosophy. He is the author of *Chinese Conception of Space* (2007) and is the chair professor of the architecture program at the Architecture School at Tsinghua University, for which he designed the New Building (2014). The architect seems to be unaffected by the rapid speed of development in China. He chooses carefully before undertaking only those projects that present opportunities to innovate and rethink architecture. The architect uses these projects to respond best to each place, program, and what constitutes his ongoing pursuit to express his own identity. Everyone of Li's very few and typically very small buildings is thoughtful, comforting, serine, and strikingly beautiful. They include

the Dragon Boat Museum in Foshan (2018); the Li Yuan Library near Beijing (2011); the Bridge School in Xiaoshi Village, Fujian Province (2009); and two projects in Lijiang, Yunnan Province–the Water House (2009) and the Yuhu Elementary School (2004). Li is currently working on the largest project in his career, a school in Shenzhen, which is under construction. After graduating from Tsinghua University with a Master of Architecture in 1984, Li spent 15 years outside of China–first completing his PhD at Delft University of Technology in the Netherlands (1989-93) and then teaching there and later at the National University of Singapore. He established Li Xiaodong Atelier in 1997, one of the first independent architectural practices in China, and to this day, one of very few namesake ateliers in the country. In 2010, Li became the first Chinese architect who won the Aga Khan Award for Architecture. We discussed Li Xiaodong's attitudes toward creativity, individuality, and the role of history in Chinese architecture.

IF SOMETHING HAS BEEN DONE BEFORE, WHY BOTHER REPEATING IT?

In conversation with **LI Xiaodong** of Li Xiaodong Atelier, Beijing
Li Xiaodong Atelier in Beijing, April 17, 2017 & October 30, 2019

Vladimir Belogolovsky: What was it that first brought you into architecture?

Li Xiaodong: I was 16, when my father realized that I would be a good architect because I was very good at building chicken houses out of brick. I grew up in a small village where we lived on the ground floor of an apartment building. I would often rebuild these structures, which was intuitive to me and very interesting. I was doing that since I was 12. My father was working at the Agricultural University in Beijing. It was his friend who suggested it to him. Curiously, that friend wanted to study architecture, but couldn't do it, as it was during the Cultural Revolution times, when architectural studies were suspended for ten years in the entire country. During that time, all universities in China were sent to the countryside. That's how my family ended up living in that village. The entire campus was relocated from Beijing to the countryside. In fact, it moved several times from one province to another, and so did we.

097 LI Xiaodong © Li Xiaodong Atelier

VB: How would you explain to a lay person what your architecture is about?

LX: I would say it is about organizing space in the most beautiful way. Organizing a functional, beautiful space for people to use it in the most enjoyable ways. Space should be beautiful, ordered, and functional. And spaces should be done economically. Money should not be spent on things that are unnecessary.

VB: In other words, you concentrate on what's necessary, on what needs to be done. But when I look at images of your beautiful buildings, such as your Bridge School in Fujian Province, I feel that the reason I like it is exactly because you, as an architect, have done something that goes beyond what's necessary. You have done something extra that has turned a mere building into architecture.

LX: That's because what's necessary is something that's difficult to define. What was necessary for that school in that village? The village needed something iconic at that time to bring up their spirit. That village had to be rejuvenated. It was necessary to inject aesthetic quality into the local community. The new school had to serve as a beacon. The reason I placed the school right over the new bridge was because it could act as the new center for the community. There are two old castles on either side of the creek. Historically, there used to be two communities that had been fighting one another. That's all in the past, so the idea was to connect these two places. The bridge, quite literally, is a symbolic metaphor for that unity. It was also important to make the connecting link with the school for young children because they represent the youngest and most energetic group of the community. The center is the right source for the energy to be spread all over the village.

VB: How do you see your role as an architect?

LX: I see myself as a reflexive regionalist. I address specific conditions such as budget, program, and climate. It is complicated and nothing is preconceived. What I am not interested in is to project a particular style. I am interested in identifying solutions to address very particular conditions. I resist using clichés in architecture. I don't like when architects approach every problem with a fixed solution. Architecture is not about a style; architecture is a matter of debate. Solutions in architecture should be based on analysis, not on preconceived forms.

VB: You describe your architecture as reflexive regionalism. Could you elaborate on that and how would you summarize the intensions of your work?

LX: Reflexive regionalism to me means to be sustainable. Architectural solutions should be based on reality. They should be natural and adapted to real life conditions. And when I say natural I don't at all deny the importance of individuality. Beijing is different from Shanghai and very different from Yunnan, and we, architects, all have our very different ways of understanding architecture. You can be natural and individual. There is no contradiction in that.

VB: You said that when you start working on a project you first analyze the site and the flow of energy through it. Could you touch on your design process; how do you begin?

LX: It is a secret. [Laughs.] Well, I have been practicing tai chi for many years, which is about

simultaneously looking inward and outward; it is a system of breathing and energy flow. It enables you to focus your mind so intensely that all your senses become more alert. So, I understand energy better than those who don't study it. The first thing I do when I start a project, I analyze the site and the flow of energy through it. Most people identify forms with shapes, colors, and materials. But I identify forms with energy. It is very abstract, but it is very real. Also, I try to be very minimal in my designs. And again, I only use what's necessary. The key difference between Chinese and Western cultures is that in the West people use all kinds of devices to be efficient. But the Chinese have to practice with the simplest tools we have to do very complicated things. Chopsticks is a good example–you can pick up anything with chopsticks if you practice well. You don't need to use a knife and fork. In my practice I try to reflect this attitude.

VB: What is architecture for you?

LX: Architecture is a creative solution that identifies a contemporary lifestyle. And it has nothing to do with a style.

VB: And what if I asked you this question in the beginning of your career, 20 years ago? Would you say that architecture has nothing to do with a style?

LX: You are right, 20 years ago, we were all looking for discovering a new style. But now I don't think that kind of approach would be sustainable. We know how limited our resources are. Styles cost money.

VB: Ever since the 2008 world financial crisis, architects have been talking about the importance of the economy of means. Yet, buildings are becoming only more complex and more expensive, despite of what architects say.

LX: My buildings are very cheap. The economy of means is one of my main concerns. Sustainability is composed of many issues and cost is one of its main components. For example, I often use an orthogonal grid that helps me to bring greater efficiency to my projects–both in terms of circulation and achieving the simplest structural support. I always avoid deep

098 Bridge School, Xiashi Village, Pinghe County, Fujian Province, 2009 © Li Xiaodong Atelier

cantilevers or special design forms. There is nothing special in my architecture in terms of forms.

VB: Why are you trying to downplay your work? If you say, there is nothing special in your forms, why would clients want to commission you? There must be something that makes your work special, right?

LX: I do want to achieve very beautiful and memorable environments. But I am not trying to create intentional iconic forms. I want to create architecture that is logical, sustainable, and that speaks of its time. But I don't believe in architecture as the expression of an individual style. I don't think it is sustainable. Architecture and painting are not the same things. A painting has a compositional logic. But architecture is functional. And architecture has neighbors, whereas a painting can be a world in itself.

VB: Let's talk about your Liu Yayun Library. In a way, it is also a world in itself, despite its very modest size. The recycled twigs on the building's exterior make the building very beautiful.

LX: Yet, the twigs were not used for decoration. They have a function. They filter the light into the interior. When I worked on this project, I found twigs everywhere in that village. It was the most important texture that touched me there. The villagers collect the twigs and use them for heating and cooking. Naturally, I wanted to preserve this feature, but not as decoration.

VB: When I think of your work the words that come to mind are the following: quiet, still, intangible, reflective, permeable, framed, open-ended, part of nature, and so on. What do you think? What single words would you use to describe your architecture?

LX: Natural, consequential, logical.

VB: You said, "This is what matters: we need to find ways of developing our architecture without aping Western models or relying on superficial imitation of traditional Chinese forms and decoration." When you say "we"–you are talking about the Chinese architects. Do you believe the Chinese architects need to have a particular unity or perspective on what should

099 Water House Club, near Yulong snow mountain, Lijiang, Yunnan Province, 2009 © Li Xiaodong Atelier

constitute contemporary Chinese architecture? Do you think there should be common ground among Chinese architects?

LX: I think every architect in China needs to think about how we can contribute to contemporary architecture. We share an incredible culture that we can turn to for inspiration to bring to our contemporary practice. Traditional Chinese architecture is not about form but about space. I wrote a book about this. It is called *Chinese Conception of Space*. It is about the intangible feelings of space. All of my ideas come from Chinese traditional architecture. I lived and worked for many years in the Netherlands and the United States, but I don't think anyone can find in my work any particular influences by the Dutch or American architecture. My work is rooted in Chinese culture, although I always try to express my architecture with contemporary means. My architecture is contemporary.

VB: And what you take from traditional Chinese architecture to your contemporary work is the focus on space, right?

LX: Right. You can see that the form did not change in traditional Chinese architecture for hundreds of years. Just like Laozi said, "Clay is used to make vases, but it is the emptiness they contain that makes them useful." In other words, the important thing is what's contained, not the container. Again, forms were never important here. It is more about identifying original conditions than inventing original forms. Throughout its history, Chinese society was largely agricultural, for which you need a collective mindset. For example, Confucius talked about the importance of hierarchy to insure political stability. Our society was not about expressing individuality but about how we could work and progress together. Otherwise, there is chaos. Creativity needs individuality, but individuality was never an important issue in Chinese society historically. Collectiveness was more important than individuality.

VB: And now individual ideas are quite popular here, right? Why is that?

LX: Because we don't have enough of good ideas. We need more and there is a will to contribute. We need to have more individuals and more original ideas. I think it is good to try to search in this direction.

VB: But you are not interested in creating unique, iconic forms.

LX: Not a bit. I think it is very selfish to create iconic forms.

VB: So, you are saying that it is possible to be very original without creating something iconic.

LX: Sure. For example, when I think about New York I think Central Park is the most iconic image that represents the city.

VB: You teach architecture here in China and internationally, and even won major awards for teaching. How important is teaching to you? What do you learn from teaching?

LX: I have to say that before I started teaching, I was very confused about my practice. I derived at my forms very randomly. That made me feel very

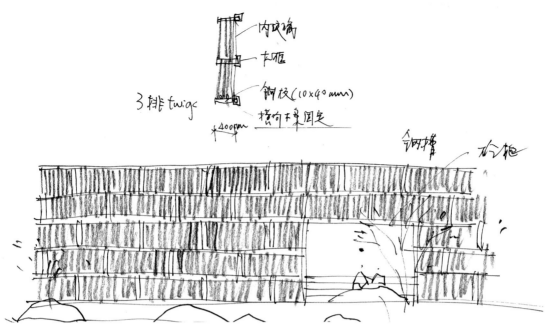

内玻璃
卡框
钢板 (10×40 mm)
横向本条固定
3排 twigs
400mm
钢板   卡框

100 Liyuan Library, Beijing, 2011. Sketch. Courtesy of Li Xiaodong

upset with myself. After spending seven years in the Netherlands, I stopped practicing and went to Singapore to teach and research for about eight years. Teaching is a way of understanding architecture holistically. What is your architecture? I think it is very difficult to practice before one begins to teach. When you teach you have to understand things completely; you don't teach architecture in pieces. It is impossible. So, teaching for me is about reflecting on my work and myself; it is about testing my ideas. Also, teaching is about transmitting ideas into younger architects.

VB: If you had to pick one most important recent built work in China either by local or foreign architect, what would it be?

LX: I don't think I could pick one dominating work that is right in the center and is profoundly more important than everything else. But to tell you the truth, I still like my own work the most. I think I am on the right track.

VB: So, you are not very happy with the work of your colleagues here?

LX: Yes and no. I don't think there are many architects in China who are doing research and practice at the same time. Still, there are a number of very good local architects. I would particularly single out Liu Jiakun, Dong Gong, Zhang Lei, Hua Li, Atelier Deshaus, and URBANUS.

VB: And could you name a single most important building built by any of these architects?

LX: This is hard. For sure it would not be a foreign architect because then it would be an iconic building. Such buildings are typically selected through government-initiated international competitions and that's what they want to keep building in China–Western-style iconic buildings. As far as one building by one of the architects I just mentioned, I like Long Museum by Atelier Deshaus in Shanghai. What I like is the transformative nature of this project, how it transforms from an industrial remnant found on site into something entirely different, new, abstract, yet, related to that industrial heritage and character. I also like the fact that this building has no clear Chinese identity. It is a true modern structure. There is nothing nostalgic about it.

101 Liyuan Library, Beijing, 2011 © Li Xiaodong Atelier

VB: Would you say that you achieved a great level of control in your work and are you satisfied with the projects that you had a chance to build?

LX: Not always. My very first building, the Yuhu Elementary School that was built in Yunnan in 2004, was a disappointing experience to me. It was a compromise due to a low budget. Still, it was a good test for me here in China after 15-year period of living abroad. But since then I gained control and I am very happy with the way a number of my projects were built, particularly the Liu Yayun Library, the Water House, and the Bridge School.

VB: On your website it says that you are focused on small and often self-initiated projects. Could you elaborate on how you initiate projects and why you focus on small scale?

LX: I do have some larger scale projects as well. Actually, the scale doesn't matter to me for as long as there is an opportunity to innovate and cast new ideas. I am looking for things I haven't done before. I am not interested in repeating something. And the reason for self-initiated projects is simple–I want to be able to control the design and construction; that

way everything is under my control. When you work for a client, you always depend on many approvals and inevitably, you have to compromise. But in self-initiated projects everything is up to me. Only then I feel empowered as an architect.

VB: And who is the client in those self-initiated projects?

LX: These projects are initiated directly–between me and the local people. In the case of the Bridge School, a friend of mine told me about this poor village, Xiaoshi in Fujian Province, and their needs. The money for construction came from a private foundation. This project is not unique in China because local governments are now aware of such examples and they invite architects and sponsors to stimulate the local economy. I was one of the very first, if not the first architect in the country who started doing such projects in the villages. The first project was the Yuhu Elementary School. Yuhu is a small Naxi village in Lijiang, Yunnan Province, an area under the protection of World Cultural Heritage Program. The school was established in 2001. I visited it in 2002, with my students when I was teaching in Singapore. It started as a research project. It was done pro bono on my part. The money for construction came from private donors in China and Singapore. The school was completed in 2004. Back then there were no independent architects working in the countryside in China.

VB: Many of the architects who now focus on projects in rural areas just started opening their offices in early 2000s: Zhang Ke started his studio in 2001; Philip F. Yuan in 2003; Xu Tiantian in 2004; Zhu Pei in 2005. Yung Ho Chang opened his practice in 1993, but his early projects in the countryside were all private villas. Wang Shu did his Library of Wenzheng College [018] in 2000, but that was a part of a university campus in Suzhou. His now well-known regeneration project in Wencun Village [022, 034] in Zhejiang Province started in 2012.

LX: That's right. At the time, I was still going between Singapore and China, and did not have clients here, so I had to be proactive about getting work.

VB: You said that you try to develop propositions for an appropriate Chinese architecture. Could you elaborate on that?

LX: What I mean by that is the issue of identity. And not Chinese identity overall, but particularly regional one. China has so many different regions, I don't believe there is such a thing as Chinese architectural identity. There shouldn't be one, anyway. China is too diverse as a country culturally and climatically for a single architectural identity.

VB: Yet, many Chinese architects avoid being personal, as opposed to many architects in the West. There is no strive here for establishing recognizable signature styles. And you just told me that you don't believe in architecture as an expression of an individual style. You said it is not sustainable. How do you then bring subjectivity to your work?

LX: Very easy–through the way you order space, how you work with materials, and resolve details. There are so many ways to be personal in architecture. I focus on spatial order. Sure, I am interested in my own interpretations, but not by inventing

102 Liyuan Library, Beijing, 2011 © Li Xiaodong Atelier

137

new, unseen forms. To me that's more relevant. But subjectivity is important. So, if something has been done before, why bother repeating it? I want to find my own way. I am looking for my own order, my own strategy, and my own attitude. This is what makes my architecture subjective. There is nothing special about basic materials such as brick or bamboo. But once you establish a particular order and find intriguing juxtapositions that's when architecture has a chance to become something special, even unique.

VB: Would you agree that there is a sense of collective thinking in Chinese architecture? So many architects have very similar preoccupations. Atelier Deshaus is rare exceptions. They are quite successful at being able to suppress their cultural identities and focus on issues that have no cultural boundaries. Yung Ho Chang told me that he prefers to divide buildings into north and south, as opposed to east in west, meaning–climatically, not culturally. What do you think about this lack of diversity and wiliness to reinvent architecture here?

LX: I think our architects are very conscious of the identity of the architecture they are producing here. There are similar concerns about using local materials, relying on traditional techniques. Perhaps architects are not quite free yet to explore very different ideas. We are preoccupied with similar issues. Many of us are moving in the same direction. We are not as diverse, as we could be. That's true. But more and more the Chinese architects are becoming sensitive to our own culture. We have gone through such drastic urbanization over the last two decades. So much has been lost, so we are preoccupied with our cultural identity and architecture is the best means to form it. This is what's more important now than pursuing individual identities. We need to be more confident about our culture collectively before we can pursue our ideas individually. One of the most critical issues now is sustainability. We have to be mindful of using resources rationally. And at this point, memory of our own history is important.

103 a), b) Liyuan Library, Beijing, 2011 © Li Xiaodong Atelier

VB: What is a good building for you?

104 Dragon Boat Museum, Foshan, Guangdong Province, 2018 © Li Xiaodong Atelier

LX: To design a good building you have to understand the site and to distill energy coming from that particular place in the most elegant way. Through your intervention, you make that particular spot uplifting spiritually. I do believe that architecture is spiritual, and architects should search for that particular spirit. Li Yuan Library is a tiny remote place, but every weekend 500 people go there. It has become a weekend retreat for city folks and many others come from faraway places just for the experience to be there. Why? It has nothing to do with the building's function or its form. But people find it uplifting spiritually. They recharge there.

VB: Is there one particular building, anywhere in the world, that you would advise every student of architecture to visit to encounter an ultimate uplifting experience?

LX: Fallingwater by Frank Lloyd Wright. I particularly love its sequence and layering of spaces, the relationship between the building and its site. I can't think of any other building that is so closely related to its place. It is just like he said–it is growing naturally out of its site. I would also recommend visiting Chicago as a collection of remarkable architecture as a true world heritage.

139

MA Yansong
MAD ARCHITECTS

Beijing-based architect MA Yansong (b. 1975, Beijing), the founder of MAD Architects, is known for his unconventional, undulating forms that helped him establish China's most successful global architectural practice with offices in Beijing, Los Angeles, Rome, and Jiaxing in Zhejiang Province with the total staff of 130. Ma was a graduate of the Beijing University of Civil Engineering and Architecture. He earned his master's degree in Architecture from Yale University in 2002. Before establishing his own studio in 2004, Ma apprenticed in New York at Peter Eisenman's studio and at the London office of his Yale professor Zaha Hadid. The architect's original work first attracted wide attention in 2006, when he won an international design competition for the Absolute Towers in Mississauga, a suburb of Toronto, Canada. The residential project composed of 56-story and 50-story high-rises was completed in 2012, making MAD the first China-based architecture firm to build overseas. The buildings are based on a repetition of an oval plan, slightly rotated from one floor to the next, to achieve an attractive sculptural silhouette that the locals aptly nicknamed "Marilyn Monroe" towers. The Canadian realization led to a number of prestigious international commissions in Europe, Japan, and the United States. In 2009, Fast Company named Ma Yansong one of the "10 Most Creative People in Architecture." In 2014, MAD was selected as principal designer for the Lucas Museum of Narrative Art in Los Angeles, now under construction. Ma's architecture is inspired by *Shan Shui*, traditional Chinese landscape paintings and is intended to establish emotional connections to nature. His Harbin Opera House, built in 2015, is conceived as a mountain-like building with a walkable path bringing visitors to an open observation deck at the top, accessible to the public at all times. Other important projects in China include the Yuecheng Courtyard Kindergarten in Beijing (2017-20); the Chaoyang Park Plaza office and residential complex in Beijing (2012-17); the Huangshan Mountain Village in Anhui Province, a large complex of ten linked buildings with retreat apartments that evoke a mountain range (2009-17); the Ordos Museum, a heroic sculptural form in Ordos City in Inner Mongolia (2005-11); and the Hutong Bubble 32 in Beijing, an alien-creature-like metallic bubble form, containing a toilet and stair access to a roof terrace of a renovated courtyard house (2008-09). Among many art projects, Ma collaborated with Olafur Eliasson on experiential exhibition *Feelings Are Facts* at the Ullens Center for Contemporary Art (UCCA) in Beijing in 2010.

SOME PEOPLE MAY SEE MY WORK AS FUTURISTIC, BUT I SEE IT AS TRADITIONAL

In conversation with **MA Yansong** of MAD Architects, Beijing
MAD Architects office in Beijing, March 27, 2017

Vladimir Belogolovsky: If someone wants to understand what your work is about, what project would you show and what would you say about it?

Ma Yansong: To tell you the truth, I don't mind if people don't understand my work or who I am. [Laughs.] ...It is hard to choose because I am a different person, while working on every project. Every one of my projects is about different emotions.

VB: One critic wrote that Harbin Opera House is the most beautiful building in all of China.

MY: Yes. But for me, I even think it is too beautiful... Because when I design, I don't really think about every line, proportions, or colors. For example, our Chaoyang Park Plaza, which just finished construction here in Beijing, contrasts greatly to its surroundings. If you think of the many buildings nearby or, in general, typical office towers, most of them are very similar box-like structures. They represent power and capitalism. Even Rem Koolhaas's CCTV complex wants to outdo them all, not by building taller, but by imagining the most original iconic form. But, as a result, it is a critique of the other towers, which makes his building even more dominant.

VB: You don't like that.

MY: My approach is different. The Chaoyang Park Plaza is very close to the park and lake, so I close my eyes, I close my ears, and I don't want to communicate with the humanmade world; I only want to relate to the nature in front of me. And, if you insert our building into a traditional Chinese landscape painting, it will fit just right. But if you look around and compare it to other buildings, you may see it as something very bold and conflicting. Some people even say it is ugly. I don't think so. Because

105 MA Yansong © MAD Architects

culturally, it fits very well. Yet, contextually, it is somewhat foreign because the urban context is not Chinese.

VB: The urban context here is imported from the West.

MY: Yes, but that's the context that we have now and there is judgment about my work not fitting in.

VB: You said earlier that you don't care if your work may be judged either as beautiful or ugly. What is it you care about? What is the main intention of your architecture?

MY: I don't like what has happened to our cities, as this is the result of us having followed modernism for such a long time. Everything has started to look the same and lacks inner spirituality. Nowadays, function is prioritized over nature and emotions. My architecture is about making a statement. But we are not making a building as an object. We are trying to create a landscape inside the urban environment. I derive my inspiration from traditional Chinese architecture where nature is an integral part of daily life in the city. I am looking for ways to adapt Chinese traditions of blending nature and architecture to contemporary architecture on an urban scale.

VB: You said your architecture is about making a statement. Now you have become a large office with projects being built all over the world. Seriously, how many statements do you need?

MY: [Laughs.] Well, despite that, I try to make every project differently and consider their cultural context, but the statement is always the same–I try to turn my architecture into a landscape and interweave its functions into the natural environment. Of course, this nature is artificial, it is humanmade. There is no pretense about that, but the intention is to create an emotional experience, to reconnect humans with nature. It is not about creating a building as object to display its functions or technology. When I talk about nature, I mean emotions, spirituality. Nature is not a tree or flower; nature is an emotional atmosphere–a place where one can seek their innermost being. One of my heroes, for example, is Louis Kahn. In a way, he is an anti-modern architect because in the core of his work there is a conversation with nature. I also love drawings and buildings by Oscar Niemeyer.

VB: Kahn and Niemeyer to you are anti-modern because…

MY: Because to me, modernism is associated with being new and different, and against what was there before or what's around. Even though they are architects of the Modern period, they had a profound ability to create architecture that better represents human aspirations, creating an allure that transcends time.

VB: You said, "We should discover new ways to make humans and nature closer."

MY: Yes.

VB: You also said, "I think it is important to practice architecture with an attitude."

MY: Yes, I did.

VB: What does it mean to you to practice architecture with an attitude?

MY: Drawing inspirations from culture. Being critical… Critical about the context…And really thinking about what kind of cultural impact we want to leave in our urban centers. Do you know what I mean?

VB: Not really…

MY: Well, when we started working on our Chaoyang Park Plaza tower I said–I don't like any of the towers around; I wanted something different. Not like CCTV, but something more beautiful. I wanted to build something that would bring nature into the city context and would make people re-think the approach we take toward future urban developments, both in China and around the world. That's an attitude.

VB: It reminds me the approach you just criticized…You look around and then you close your eyes, your ears…

MY: But I open my eyes to nature. That's my attitude. Many of my projects are built more in opposition to their contexts. Sometimes, they are more integrated. In my Hutong Bubble 32 project, built in central Beijing, the bubble-like, futuristic form that contains a toilet and stairs to the rooftop seems to be alien to its historical surroundings, but at the same time, it reflects everything around it with its shiny surface and, in a way, disappears entirely. Yet, this strange form attracts curiosity and opens possibilities for newly imagined spaces that promise to revitalize the historical fabric of the city. On the other hand, Harbin Opera House is isolated; it stands alone. My intention there was to create a mountain. There was no "crime" there before…

VB: You mean the site was pure.

MY: Yes, there was no "crime" committed by architects yet. [Laughs.] So, I tried to be gentle and we provided a path for anyone to climb to the top to make the building not just look like a mountain, but, in a way, make it part of nature.

VB: You first studied architecture at the Beijing University of Civil Engineering and Architecture and then at Yale where your thesis project was called "Floating Island." What was that like?

106 Harbin Opera House, Harbin, 2015 © Iwan Baan

MY: It was shortly after 9/11, in 2002. So, I proposed to rebuild Ground Zero in Manhattan. For my thesis project, I had the option of choosing either Frank Gehry or Zaha Hadid as my instructor. I chose Hadid because I think her work is more natural and ultimately, more beautiful. But in the beginning, it was a very rational approach, starting with the analysis of history of high-rises in New York. So, the question for me became: What is the next generation of high-rises going to be like? I had no clue. There was so much pressure and then there came a relief–I saw my project in a dream. It was something floating high above the city. The next day I sketched it and it was so strange that people told me I could not show it to Zaha. But I did, and she liked it. She said it was like a work of art and suggested that I look more to the work of such artists as Anish Kapoor and Olafur Eliasson. She also suggested that for my final presentation I should put some

dimensions so that people could identify it as "architecture." [Laughs.]

VB: Designing that project must have been a very emotional experience.

MY: It is always very emotional and intuitive for me. I never start with a diagram.

VB: Before opening your own practice here in Beijing in 2004, you studied with and worked under two leading Western architects–Peter Eisenman and Zaha Hadid. What did you learn from them?

MY: With Peter, I worked on his City of Culture project in Santiago de Compostela and the Jewish Memorial in Berlin. He is very analytical about history and form making. But he also has an emotional side despite being very systematic. I also interacted with him at Yale where

143

we discussed one of my projects. I tried to design it the way he would have done it. It was a tower growing out of a very restrictive site with a typical orthogonal footprint. But, as it went up into the sky, which is free of any constrains, its form became more organic and fluid, like a cloud. With Zaha, I worked on my Floating Island project, which I thought was already quite daring, but she still pushed me. She always encouraged exploring the artistic and emotional side of every project and that's my biggest lesson learned from her. We once worked on a competition in the UK. She said, "We won't win anyway, so why don't you do what you really like?!" [Laughs.] My impression working with her was that she did not want to repeat herself. Every project had to be different. For that project, I used brick, which she really liked. But other partners were skeptical because they haven't used brick before. [Laughs.]

VB: You didn't win the competition.

MY: Of course, not! [Laughs.] It was before she had any work in the UK and before winning the Pritzker. One quality that I really admire in her is the urge for experimentation. I think true experimentation is very rare for my generation. The previous generation of architects was more daring.

VB: Why do you think so?

MY: Well, when architects who are now in their late '60s, '70s, and '80s were my age they were much more adventurous than my generation today. They did not build as much, but their thoughts and projects were sharper. My generation's undertakings seem somewhat timid

and weak. The current projects are not as emotional as they should be.

VB: What do you think about your work's progression? For example, when I asked this question Patrik Schumacher he said, "It is a process. Every time you finish a project, you start thinking about other ideas. We look back at buildings built ten or five years ago and you see how they could be done differently now. So, I think we are getting better." Do you feel that about your work?

MY: Not at all. I would feel bad if I did that. I want everything to look new and different every time. The architectural landscape 5-10 years ago was different from what it is today. We should be constantly evolving. I don't want to look back and think about how things could have been done differently. I want each of my projects to look different every time.

VB: Why is that? Why not develop a style and perfect it?

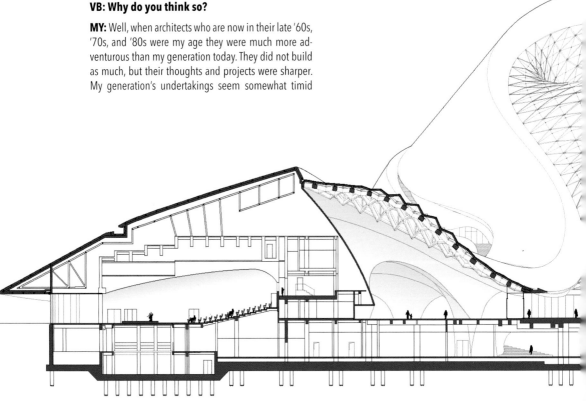

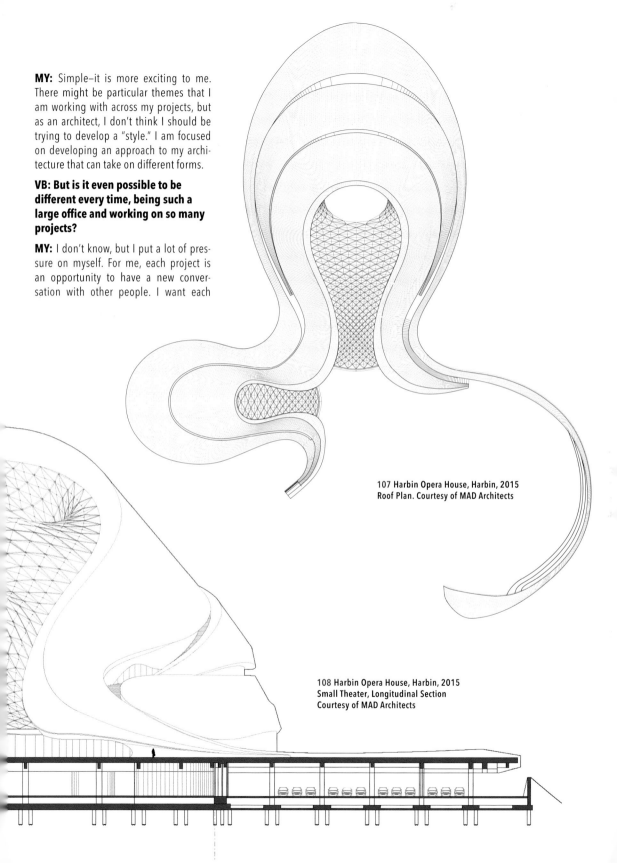

MY: Simple–it is more exciting to me. There might be particular themes that I am working with across my projects, but as an architect, I don't think I should be trying to develop a "style." I am focused on developing an approach to my architecture that can take on different forms.

VB: But is it even possible to be different every time, being such a large office and working on so many projects?

MY: I don't know, but I put a lot of pressure on myself. For me, each project is an opportunity to have a new conversation with other people. I want each

107 Harbin Opera House, Harbin, 2015
Roof Plan. Courtesy of MAD Architects

108 Harbin Opera House, Harbin, 2015
Small Theater, Longitudinal Section
Courtesy of MAD Architects

109 Harbin Opera House, Harbin, 2015 © Adam Mork

conversation to be meaningful and fresh. If I come to different places to say the same things, I am not interested. I am wasting my time. You are right; it can be challenging to have so many conversations at the same time. I didn't have many projects before, but now it is beginning to pressure me. I am constantly traveling and initiating new projects. But every time another project starts, I see new possibilities. I am curious, and my team always explores different typologies and scales. We often start projects that we have never done before.

VB: Would you say that architecture for you starts with a conversation?

MY: Architecture for me is a conversation, in which I look back to the past and project my ideas into the future. Architecture is art, attitude, and emotions. All these things need to be linked.

VB: You said once, "I treat my projects as art." Could you elaborate?

MY: Art is all about emotions. Art is about seeing things in a personal way. You can start a project with a site analysis or its function…

VB: But you don't do that.

MY: No, I don't. My emotions come from the cultural context. Each location represents a particular culture and brings out a different attitude, and mood in me. I look for different ways to respond to projects that are relevant to their particular context.

VB: One of your art installations, *Feelings are Facts,* was staged at Beijing's Ullens Center for Contemporary Art in 2010. What was that about?

MY: All reality is an illusion. I always doubt everything. I would rather make my own mistakes than accept someone's position without challenging it first. I want to discover my own reasons for everything. There are so many ways to look at things, which means there is no reality, in a way. Your own reaction and your own feelings should be what you believe in.

VB: You mean everything we see is an interpretation, which means everyone's perception is different, right?

110 Harbin Opera House, Harbin, 2015 © Hufton+Crow

MY: Yes, and therefore, as an architect, I am not creating realities or facts with my objects. I am creating illusions and atmospheres. The installation *Feelings are Facts* that I did with Olafur Eliasson is a space shaped by color, light, and fog with no clear boundaries. We agreed to make something together; something that no one would be able to identify who did what. I shaped the space and he designed the light, color, and fog. It is an experiential space where you must be alert with all your senses. The floor is all sculpted and curved. You can't see clearly, and you feel lost, off balance, and disoriented. You must learn how to navigate this unfamiliar reality and rely on senses that you normally do not pay much attention to. It was a good collaboration and we became good friends. Next time we may do a building together.

VB: When you talk about your architecture, you often refer to the idea of *Shan Shui*, which is a style of traditional Chinese brush and ink landscape paintings featuring mountains, rivers, and waterfalls…

MY: *Shan Shui* is a cultural typology. It is not just limited to paintings. You can come across *Shan Shui*

music, poems…even urban planning. It refers to both aesthetic and spiritual values.

VB: I read that *Shan Shui* paintings are not representative but rather contemplative. *Shan Shui* painting is not an open window for the viewer's eye, but rather a tool for the viewer's mind and a device for reflective thinking. Could you talk about the relationship between your work and *Shan Shui*?

MY: I grew up in the old Beijing, which is where we are now. The city was originally planned around lakes and gardens. They are all humanmade, but collectively, the interweaving aesthetics with functionality gave a feeling that we were immersed in a verdant landscape. So, what was created here was an illusion, an imaginary nature. That's what people perceived as nature, but not nature itself. There was an inner spirituality. That's what modern architecture is lacking. It is this inner spirituality that I want to bring into our urban centers. *Shan Shui* is a philosophy; it is about establishing emotional connections to nature. And this concept can be applied to projects on many different scales, even large urban scale in both our

111 Harbin Opera House, Harbin, 2015 © Hufton+Crow

existing cities and newly developing ones. This is what I am trying to do with my Shanshui City vision, as you can see in my project Huangshan Mountain Village in Anhui Province. The village blurs the boundaries between the geometries of architecture and nature; it is a part of the landscape, a part of geology.

I like how nature is a part of the city here in central Beijing, but I don't like that it is missing from new neighborhoods. So, as an architect, I want to take these key features of traditional architecture and translate them into new developments on a much bigger scale that we are building today. And I want to bring something unfamiliar into these new projects. I want to build buildings that no one has ever seen before. I don't want the middle ground. Some people may see my work as futuristic, but I see it as traditional because I carry old Eastern philosophy and use it to respond to new challenges.

VB: Your George Lucas Museum of Narrative Arts will be built in Los Angeles. Could you talk about your inspirations there?

MY: There is always this desire to create a connection between nature, architecture, and people. For the Lucas Museum, I had this vision of a cloud, and that is how the design evolved. You can see that it is almost floating above the ground, supporting a terraced rooftop garden, so that visitors and the public can experience both the museum's architecture and the surrounding park in a different way.

VB: By now you designed and built a number of commercial and cultural projects in the West. Do you see yourself as a Chinese or global architect?

MY: I don't actually care how people identify me, but the fact is that I am a Chinese architect. It is impossible for me not to be Chinese. Architecture is a part of one's culture and the language one speaks is the key. My architecture is shaped by the way I think, talk, express myself; it is shaped by my background.

VB: Would you say that developers and

architects in the West are more conservative than in China? What do you think Western architects could learn from the situation here?

MY: I would say that now many Chinese developers are more consciously searching for our cultural identity, which was not their concern before. We used to blindly copy whatever was coming from the West. Modernization was equated with the West. Now, we have an identity crisis because our cities no longer look like they are in China. And they look the same across the country. So now we have so many questions. Who are we? Where are we? Why are our cities so foreign and missing authentic characters? That's why now many developers are trying to explore and experiment more. Shanshui City proposal for Guiyang is one such project. We look at our past to better understand how to shape our future. Many of my clients don't want to repeat building that they know. They want something unique.

In the West, developers are more confident. They know what they want and that makes them much more conservative than here and much less open to experimentation. For example, developers in New York know exactly how to build their projects and they tell their architects what to do. It is a pity that there are so many talented architects in New York, and they don't have a project there. The possibility for expressing creativity there is very limited. The reason it was possible for us to realize Absolute Towers near Toronto is because the client was fresh, so he organized an international competition and a largely European jury picked our project. People in Canada love it and the project became very successful because there is nothing like it. Yet, if we talk about cultural projects, they are designed and managed much more thoughtfully in the West. There is a lot more experience there. But in China, we are producing so many cultural projects without a clear understanding of how to exploit them. So, for our office it is a double win—we are building very experimental commercial buildings

112 YueCheng Courtyard Kindergarten, Beijing, China, 2020. Photo by Hufton+Crow

in China and very innovative and sophisticated cultural projects in the West.

VB: If I asked you to describe your architecture in single words, what would they be?

MY: Natural, emotional, uncertain, undefined.

VB: What is your next exciting project?

MY: I am designing another opera house here in China. It is still being developed, but it will be very different from the one in Harbin, which was built at the time when many cities here were building iconic cultural projects. In Harbin, my intention was to build a more natural,

engaging, and inviting building. But for this one I want it to become almost a low-key building.

VB: Is that what your client agreed to? There must be another reason why they came to you, right?

MY: Well, it's true. So many clients want very iconic buildings. But I am trying to convince them that the building should reflect their confidence and that they don't need to show off their power, which would be a sign of their weakness, not strength. I think a good public building should be more about comfort and responding to the

113 Huangshan Mountain Village, Huangshan, Anhui Province 2017 © Hufton+Crow

urban context, not just project its image; a building that citizens can relate to. It will be a good challenge, for sure.

WANG Shuo
META-PROJECT

Beijing-based architect WANG Shuo (b. 1981, Beijing), the youngest of all architects interviewed for this book and the only one born in the 1980s, grew up in the family of neuroscientists. He was particularly good at math, wining the national math Olympics in high school. Yet, instead of going into computer science, as many of his classmates, he decided, intuitively, to study architecture. He earned his Bachelor of Architecture from Tsinghua University in 2004, followed by master's degree from Rice University in Houston in 2006. In his thesis, *Wild Beijing*, he focused on the emergence of spontaneous urbanism in his hometown. After completing his studies, Wang worked for one year at Peter Gluck's firm GLUCK+ in New York. The American practice is known for specializing in hands-on design-build projects and acting as general contractor, which gives the architects a lot of control over construction quality. Wang then relocated to Europe for two years, apprenticing at OMA in Rotterdam where he interacted with Rem Koolhaas firsthand. In late 2007, in anticipation of the 2008 Beijing Olympics and prospects of working on major projects in China, Wang went back home. He then spent two more years working at OMA Beijing with partner Ole Scheeren, the future founder of Büro Ole Scheeren. Working at OMA made an impact on Wang's interest in examining prevailing and emerging social patterns and tendencies in cities and the countryside. He started his new practice META-Project in Beijing in 2010 with his wife ZHANG Jing (b. 1981, Daqing), also a graduate of Tsinghua and then RISD, after which she worked for Hariri & Hariri in New York. The architects' work is guided by multidisciplinary, research-based approach, reflecting on situations, in which social, cultural, and everyday life interrelations overlap and create active, truly contemporary spaces. The architect's built works include House T/House by the Sea in Aranya in Qinghuangdao in Hebei Province (2018), two projects in Jilin Province – the Stage of Forest rest station (2016) and the New Youth Commune (2015), and two projects in Liaoning Province–the Water Tower Renovation in Shen Yang (2012) and the Beach Exhibit Center in Huludao (2011).

THE GOAL IS TO HARNESS QUALITIES THAT ARE SPONTANEOUS AND GENUINE

In conversation with **WANG Shuo** of META-Project, Beijing
META-Project studio in Beijing, November 4, 2019

Vladimir Belogolovsky: Before opening your own practice, you worked at GLUCK+ in New York and then at OMA in Rotterdam and Beijing. What was that experience like?

Wang Shuo: My experience with Peter Gluck was all about materiality and achieving good quality of construction. It prepared me well for China because architects here sometimes deal with contractors who don't have extensive knowledge of such things as, for example, what to add into concrete to achieve a good result. Architects often have to write a whole construction manual on how certain materials or details need to be done. Realization of projects is very important. I wanted to learn not only how to design beautiful buildings, but also how to construct wand craft them.

114 **WANG Shuo.** Courtesy of META-Project

My experience at OMA was very different. What I learned from them was that there is a process of knowledge production that you have to integrate into your design process. For example, right now we are working on a co-living project for young people here in Beijing. There are many Chinese people coming to cities for opportunities. Most of them can't afford to buy or even rent a decent place. What is the alternative? It is a form of collective living in the community. This model is not just about the economy, it is about socializing, living together, communal spaces, and hybrid programs. These are such projects

that you can't simply resolve by drawing abstract pretty shapes. You have to start with research. Ideas should be developed, not dreamed up. Otherwise, your project will be removed from reality and ineffective. We are not simply packaging spaces. We define and propose new kinds of spaces and programs. We think of architecture as a tool to make certain influences on the society based on our research. We believe our architecture can contribute to culture overall. There is always a reflection of what is happening within the society and understanding that

115 New Youth Commune, Songhua Lake in Jilin Province, 2015. Photo by Shengliang Su

design can be used to push, pull, and mediate the way the society functions.

VB: Could you talk about how your office operates and the kind of projects you work on?

WS: Our office is called META-Project, not Wang Shuo Architects or Office for "something" Architecture, and that's for a reason. We aim at launching different trajectories. Apart from the main focus of META-Project on realizing architectural projects there are two other divisions–META-Research and META-Prototype. META-Research is about interdisciplinary research such as hybrid living in the hutongs. We initiate round-table discussions with artists, architects, historians, sociologists, and other specialists. During these discussions the participants produce knowledge that we record, systematize, and then popularize through exhibitions, conferences, and publications. This research may not lead to any particular project. The point is to accumulate knowledge. These projects are funded through research grants. I call this exercise predesign homework that we need to do. During various discussions, my artist friends have

criticized how architects work because it is typical for architects to start projects superficially–without visiting the site, by just playing with maps, images, and information available. But going to the site and confronting people directly is very important. Otherwise, we are not working with the reality. This is why I called the studio META-, because it is about transcending the basic meaning, going beyond first impression. For example, data is just data, but meta-data is something that explains data.

The second division is META-Prototype. We produce prototypes that are not meant to be built. They are our recipes, so to speak. When clients approach us, we show them these prototypes. We often discuss them as ideas to better understand what kind of project our clients envision. We work with models that are proven by the real estate market and we push them further to see what else could be improved. We don't want to limit ourselves by simply doing the design. For example, if a client comes to us to design an apartment building, we want to discuss what kind of community will form in the space. We are not interested in just designing a bunch of apartments packed together. We want to create a total community by engaging residents, organizing various programs, proposing new ones, testing different ideas and evolving into something new. Perhaps in the end, our clients will not choose any of our prototypes, but they will get inspired and that may lead to another interesting solution. So, we constantly work with reality and insert something that we come across in our ongoing research.

VB: What would you say your architecture is about?

WS: First, we want to work on projects that can be built well and offer good experience. We overdetail all our drawings. We leave no space for mistakes. We want to go beyond expected building types. We want to reconsider the established types. We want to free ourselves from all preconceptions. I like studying urban behavior, how people tend to live together, what influences their decisions, and so on. These observations feed us with ideas. That's what helps us to propose a particular circulation, density patterns, new order, and leave space for spontaneous behaviors. There is beauty in chaotic, unregulated way of life. I was born and grew up in Beijing. In the 1990s, when I was a teenager it was a transformative time. For example, a street would be suddenly transformed into a book market with comics and all kinds of books, or music CDs. That made the city so alive and endlessly fascinating. Every neighborhood was so unique, specializing in different things. As an architect, I like such qualities of contemporary life. I look for them. I want to understand how these things work. Such phenomena cannot be reproduced, but certain qualities can be stimulated. In a way, I work like a scientist. I want to understand the DNA of a particulate place and use that to produce my own prototype. The goal is to harness qualities that are spontaneous and genuine. That's what our architecture is about—we try to recognize certain potential and invent a typology that would stimulate certain behavior or relationships. That's the intention. For sure, we are not just image designers, we brainstorm and develop programs. Clients always have ideas but, as an architect, I have to make a suggestion. We test ideas. Most importantly, we don't try to convince our clients based on aesthetics. We can actually

116 Water Tower Renovation, Shenyang
Liaoning Province, 2012. Photo by Su Chen

prove how our proposals would work based on our research and completed projects.

VB: What kind of architecture would you want to achieve?

WS: I would compare what we do to a prism, meaning information comes in, then it is reflected, reexamined, reorganized, and finally, projected and augmented. We use trial and error method, like a hypothesis. In other words, we want to be like a prism rather than a mirror. There are so many urban theories that are utopian because they are not based on real studies. They may be valuable, but not sustainable. A beautiful utopia may become a dystopia if realized. We are not just dreamers here.

VB: Could you talk about your design process?

WS: I never work on what buildings should look like. I am not sitting for hours sketching out my ideas and then handing them to my staff. That's not how we operate. As I said, we undertake research. We gather data as a team and then discuss what we find to move to the design stage. Once we start the discussions, we develop diagrams. Then we overlay them to see what can emerge out of that process. We work with satellite maps, site photos, urban conditions, all kinds of data and statistics. We work conceptually, not merely visually. We also work with the site very closely. We try to do as little damage as possible. For example, in the project Stage of Forest, we minimized the impact on the existing vegetation, considered the sun path, the views, and so on. In fact, we managed not to cut a single tree there. Our projects are very precise according the program and context.

VB: Here in China, I interviewed close to 30 leading independent architects, and almost none seem to be working this way. At least currently, this is not the Chinese model. I use the word model because so many local architects follow a very particular design methodology, which has to do with

117 Stage of Forest, Viewing platform and event space, Jilin Province, 2016. Photo by Shengliang Su

regionalism and image-driven nostalgia, as well as incorporating landscape and ruins. Your architecture does not fit that formula, which has become dominant here for at least a decade. For the most part, these architects don't forget for a moment that they are first and foremost– Chinese. You seem not to care about that at all.

WS: You know what it is? It is my age. I am much younger.

VB: This is very interesting. You are at least five-ten years younger than most of these architects. You are the new generation. Already I can see a rebel in you. What is it that you are rebelling against? By the way, those who were born in the '60s and '70s are also rebels. They are rebelling against what the foreigners have built in China, as well as the Local Design Institutes. So many of those projects are utterly out of place. These independent architects came up with their alternative way.

WS: I am not rebelling against these older architects. There is something heroic about their urge to resurrect Chinese culture. I don't have that in me. It is not an issue for me. I have traveled the world and I see myself a part of it. I don't see the world as East and West, or black and white. I want to direct my attention to addressing various issues. I don't have an image in front of me of what my architecture should look like. I am not trying to build something I know. I want to improve the situation and I have no idea how that is going to look like. I don't need to remind myself that I am Chinese. I am, but that's not what I am doing architecturally.

VB: I know some Chinese architects who also worked at OMA, but they disguise that. They don't seem to be contaminated by the methodology that you learned there and adopted so well.

WS: I agree, I was contaminated there. [Laughs.] I like it and I embrace that. The truth is that I get contaminated by a lot of things. I am contaminated by New York, Houston, LA, Rotterdam, Finland, Singapore, Bangkok, and so many other places where I worked and traveled to. That's what I think makes my work so interesting and rich. When I work on my designs, I don't have a burden of being Chinese. I don't even think about that at all. I am completely open to finding the best solution possible. I express in very straight forward and direct ways. Am I not Chinese enough? I don't think any of my clients have a problem with that. I don't think any of the people who use our buildings have any issues with that either.

VB: I was wondering what the reaction of the next generation of architects toward the current production would be. In the West it is typical for every new generation to bring new questions and issues. I thought–what will happen in China? And here you are–the new generation! Could you talk about your focus and views on preservation projects?

WS: While we do a lot of research and undertake various urban regeneration projects, we don't necessarily work with such notions as preservation and national or regional identity. Our focus is on stimulating and enhancing a spontaneous urban

118 Stage of Forest, Viewing platform and event space, Jilin Province, 2016. Sketch by Wang Shuo; Courtesy of META-Project

119 Stage of Forest, Viewing platform and event space, Jilin Province, 2016. Photo by Shengliang Su

mechanism to help regenerate various neighborhoods. For example, our META: HUTONGS multi-disciplinary research project was about revitalizing the hutongs. We have done several other renovation projects. Again, what we focus on are research and social studies. We are interested in social models and transformations, not just materials. That would be too narrow. We work with organizing spaces and circulations rather than images. We are not image-driven practice. We are not about reproducing certain looks. For example, recently it has become a phenomenon in China to reproduce certain aspects of Geoffrey Bawa's work. This Sri Lankan architect is considered to be the most influential architect that should be well studied by Chinese architects today. Many are obsessed with his ways of bringing nature into architecture.

VB: Carlo Scarpa is another influence for his inventive ways to interact with history and ruins. Both references have turned into a sort of following here in China. That's why I am happy to see some healthy opposition to that.

WS: I teach at Tsinghua and that's the most important thing I can teach my students–to encourage them to open their eyes and make an effort to observe what they see. I don't just ask them to collect data about the site. We have a reading list on urbanism and theory. We observe various phenomena right here in Beijing and we use them as sort of triggers in the design. The projects are as much about architecture as they are about inventing programs that are very complex, mixed, and layered.

Lyndon NERI & Rossana HU

NERI&HU

Architects Lyndon NERI (b. 1965, Philippines) and Rossana HU (b. 1968, Taiwan) established their research-based design studio, Neri&Hu in 2004 in Shanghai. The partners met while pursuing their undergraduate degrees at the University of California at Berkeley. Following that, Neri graduated from Harvard and Hu from Princeton. Before moving to China–their ancestral home–they both worked for a decade as partners at Michael Graves & Associates in Princeton. Over the last 15 years, the husband-and-wife team grew into a prolific, multidisciplinary practice of over 100 architects and designers, working on dozens of international projects at any given time. Among the architects' most renowned built works are Aranya Art Center in Qinhuangdao on the Bohai Sea (2019), The Brick Wall–the Tsingpu Yangzhou Retreat in Jiangsu Province (2017), the Suzhou Chapel (2016), the Sulwhasoo Flagship Store in Seoul (2016), and the Waterhouse at South Bund in Shanghai (2010). Apart from running an architectural practice the partners lead a retail store Design Republic and serve as creative directors of Stellar Works, a furniture brand. They both teach, most recently at Harvard and Yale. Their buildings are particularly known for their ambivalence about the time, in which they were created. The architects achieve that by preserving and archiving old buildings or their fragments, fusing remnants of history with materials and details of our own time to bring richness both in terms of history and textures of various materials. These projects interact delightfully with daylight, nature, and street life. People respond well to signs of wear and patina of time. Similar techniques are applied to how architects adjust and transform familiar programs and building types by playing with such opposite notions as closed and undefined, public and private, outside and inside, rough and sleek.

WE BELIEVE IN THE SUBTEXT OVER THE OBVIOUS AND THE POETIC OVER THE UTILITARIAN

In conversation with **Lyndon NERI** and **Rossana HU** of Neri&Hu, Shanghai
Neri&Hu office in Shanghai, March 11, 2019

120 Lyndon NERI and Rossana HU. Photo by Jiaxi Yang and Zhu Zhe

Vladimir Belogolovsky: I expect this conversation to be quite unusual here in China because you are far from a typical Chinese firm, as you were not brought up here. Could you tell me about your upbringings?

Rossana Hu: I grew up in Taiwan. My father is from the Mainland China and my mother from Taiwan. I was 12, when my family moved to America. My whole life completely changed. It was hard because I did not speak English, so being an intelligent child, as I was ahead in subjects related to science, it was hard to be treated as if I were this dumb kid. It took me about five years to fully adapt. First, we lived in

Chicago and then moved to California where I went to college.

Lyndon Neri: And I grew up in the Philippines in a Chinese family. My father was very traditional, so I went to a Chinese school in the Philippines and at home we only spoke Chinese. We went to the Chinese church, Chinese parties. It was like living in a bubble. Then, I moved to the U.S. for my last few years of high school in California. I was 15 then. Rossana and I met each other at the University of California at Berkeley.

VB: I understand that you never studied architecture in China. Does this circumstance

121 The Waterhouse at South Bund (The Vertical Lane House)
Shanghai, 2010. Photo by Pedro Pegenaute

LN: We actually relate more to the European architects. Partially because we have a similar tension and anxieties, such as—where are we going to get our next work from? The Europeans can't rely on their identity to get work. So many of them are not seen as Swiss, Portuguese, or Spanish architects. They want to be seen as good architects. We identify ourselves as diasporic Chinese and would often be seen as American architects in China, but I am not sure if we are truly American.

VB: I am surprised you say that because I am not sure there is such a thing as an American architect at all. Look at so many leading architects–both in the past, such as Mies, Gropius, Neutra, Kahn, and Saarinen–to now, such as Diller, Gehry, Libeskind, Safdie, and Viñoly, they are all first-generation immigrants. You can't group the Americans. They are very independent and individualistic, which is a healthy thing. On the other hand, it is very easy to group the Chinese. Very few stand out in the leading pack. You stand out, for sure.

give you a different perspective from other leading contemporary architects here?

LN: For sure this makes us different from the mainstream.

VB: I am not talking about the mainstream, I am referring to the leading independent, avant-garde architects who are all Chinese-born, mainly educated at the top Chinese universities–either at Tsinghua in Beijing or Tongji in Shanghai–and then continued their education in the U.S. There are very few exceptions from this trend, right?

RH: Absolutely. We had a different start, and we definitely see things differently. And we also see things differently from the American architects, even though, we were trained in the same schools. This is mainly because of our cultural background and interests.

LN: I agree to a certain extent, but you are only talking about a small group of American architects that are very independent in their thinking. These architects are quite global and are extremely critical with their projects and thinking. Even the smaller practices like So-IL, Johnston Marklee, and WorkAC, to name a few, also all run by first-generation immigrant partners, are all quite global in their mindset. But I am not referring to them. I am talking about the 95% of the architects and not the selected few. The construction industry in the U.S. has standardized most things, so it is hard to be different even if you want to. In terms of the Chinese architects, I am not sure if it is fair to generalize them as being all the same. China is a big country and someone like Liu Jiakun who practices in Chengdu deals with different issues from, say someone like Zhang Ke or Dong Gong who are in Beijing.

RH: You are talking about professional connection. But personally, it was important for both of us to come back home, even though we were not born here. It was important for me to come back to the city, which my father has left. He has left and then I came back, so there was no break. And then our kids grew up here. So that personal history has translated into our architectural identity. Because isn't personal identity always expressed in one's architecture?

VB: I am actually having a hard time to detect personal identities in the work of Chinese architects. But now that you are back to China and have been leading a successful practice here for 15 years, do you identify yourselves more as Chinese or American, or more broadly as Westerners?

LN: It is not just what we think, it is also about what we were told. Since as long as I can remember, my grandmother always told me, "You are Chinese, no matter what. When you are in a foreign land you need to protect your 'Chinese-ness' because your parents and grandparents are very afraid that you are going to lose it." Interestingly, some of the traditions that you may find in Chinese communities across the world are long gone in the Mainland China. So

being Chinese is very important. For example, when our kids tried to identify themselves as Americans it bothered me to the core. I would ask them, "Why are you acting so American?" So, who am I, really? [Laughs.]

RH: Personally, I can tell you that I identify myself as both Chinese and Taiwanese, more Chinese. And work-wise, I would say more Chinese and less international. Because here we are often seen as international and when we work abroad, we are identified as Chinese. So, we don't really see ourselves as either Chinese or American. We want to be seen as contemporary architects without this cultural identity label. We are very independent, and we don't belong to these groups of Chinese architects, so many of whom identify themselves with the leading schools–Tongji and Tsinghua. It is hard to be accepted as one of them if you are not a graduate of these elite schools

LN: So, we just focus on doing good work and we don't worry about our identity. When we started,

122 The Waterhouse at South Bund (The Vertical Lane House), Shanghai, 2010. Photo by Derryck Menere

123 The Commune Social, Shanghai, 2013. Photo by Pedro Pegenaute

we did not have any network. So, naturally, we are not part of a group, and we have no choice, but be independent. When we did our Waterhouse at South Bund here in Shanghai everyone noticed and so many, both Chinese and international critics and architects wrote about it. They realized that we have a serious pedagogy behind our work; that's what important. We addressed so many issues in this conversion of a 1930s Japanese army building into a boutique hotel–by exposing the building's historical layers that evoke the archival quality of a museum. There is a play with such polar notions as old and new, privacy and publicness, comfort and discomfort. This project brought attention to many of our other projects on all scales. This was about seven-eight years ago.

VB: Could you comment on the name of your office–Neri&Hu? This seems to be quite unusual and bold, here in China, to give an architectural practice your own names. In a way, you are held accountable for what you do, right?

RH: It is true, but we also have a name of our practice in Chinese, which is made up of syllables of our names and it is not obvious. So, for the Chinese architects if they don't know our names, they may take it for an abstract name, similarly to other Chinese architects. The meaning of our studio's name in Chinese is "as there is grace" or graceful. So, it is more abstracted and poetic.

LN: I guess, from a Western point of view, our firm's name does stand out. In that regard, we are different. We never really think about that.

VB: But it is hard to believe that the Chinese architects don't think about it because it is obvious that they follow each other very closely to become successful. They go to particular schools, as you mentioned, to belong to these two leading insider groups. They choose to continue their education in American leading universities. They name their firms in a particular way, in English. They go after certain kind of projects in the countryside, and there is now focus on preserving the existing

fabric. I am not criticizing these choices, but if you look at the work of architects in America or elsewhere you will not see such definitive patterns. There is greater diversity and focus on individual findings and distinctions. Architects do not repeat each other so closely. Chinese architecture is a collective project. You could almost confuse the production by the Chinese architects with the output of a single office. Of course, there are exceptions. Your practice is a glaring one.

LN: Interesting observation. It is hard to disagree with you.

VB: What would you say your work is about? What are the intentions of your architecture?

RH: Fundamentally, we are interested in the following issue—the identity and how do we represent it. Of course, we also need to respond to specifics of each project's program. But whatever that is, the question remains: What is the architectural identity of a project? We rely not only on forms, materials, colors, and finishes, but also on our experience, and how it has been evolving. So, the first years for us

124 Sulwhasoo Flagship Store (the Lantern), Seoul, South Korea, 2016. Photo by Pedro Pegenaute

were more about our personal journey together, but now we are more in search of representing China. We believe in architecture and design as a powerful cultural force. The functional aspects are less interesting for us, although they are prerequisite, of course—your design must WORK on a very pragmatic and realistic level. Yet, we believe in the subtext over the obvious and the poetic over the utilitarian. But we are still too young to have a distinctive language, so we flow in many directions, depending on the specificity of the project at hand

LN: We deal with a number of obsessions. In the first few years, it was more about personal obsessions and in the last five years, we became more interested in community-based obsessions. One of our obsessions is the notion of nostalgia. The fact that we both came out of Chinese diaspora has a lot to do with it. We had been unearthing this idea until we came across what is called "reflective nostalgia," a concept articulated by Russian-American late Harvard professor and novelist Svetlana Boym. In the context of the rapid growth of China's economy it resonated with us and since then it has become one of our guiding principles. We treat historical buildings as urban artifacts and for us they are never just about the past. Another obsession for our work deals with what we call total design, the idea of being able to see each project from the point of view of different disciplines and perspectives. Apart from architecture we get involved in doing interiors, furniture design, product design, and graphics. We find different ways of analyzing projects and solving problems.

VB: What you are saying is reflecting a common shift for so many architects around the world—the move from focusing on individual identity to giving it up in favor of this idea of

125 Aranya Art Center (the Void), Qinhuangdao, Hebei Province, 2019. Sketch by Lyndon Neri. Courtesy of Neri&Hu

solving problems at hand. This pragmatism converges so many ideas into so few. In 2012, David Chipperfield asked all architects: What is our common ground? We hardly knew what he was talking about because common ground was the last thing we wanted. But now common ground is so real. Architecture is dominated by problem-solving and tendency to reconcile with nature. In my view, 2012 was the peak of creativity for architects and look where we are now! The wings were cut. And what do architects do today–brick buildings, wood buildings, concrete buildings. Where are the ideas, dreams, metaphors? Look what happened to the iconic…

LN: Personally, I think this is healthy. Perhaps there are a few truly exceptional architectural talents that should be given space to create, but many of us are not in that category. So, hopefully, we can at least have the rigor to do good work. I think being grounded, being local, being contextual are not all bad. The problem is when there are no good ideas, not the lack of individual identities for the sake of being different.

VB: Are you saying that being "invisible" is fine?

LN: Being invisible perhaps in form making, but not invisible in terms of ideas.

VB: Sure, no one wants to be ahead of anyone else. No one wants to be a star. Everyone is looking around and trying to align with everybody else. That's the rhetoric I hear. I've been interviewing architects for a long time. If 15 years ago they told me–my work is my context, I am not a part of any group, I am an artist. Now they have entrenched themselves in solving problems, responding to the given context, and don't forget touching on social engagement and bringing in nature. There is a list. Please, tell me you are different.

LN: I don't know if we are different. In many ways we are who we are based on our background and that includes our educational background. I studied under Rafael Moneo at Harvard and he was my thesis advisor. That was a direct contrast to who I worked for, Michael Graves's. And as much as our work is very different from Graves, Michael taught us the importance of being interdisciplinary. Rafael Moneo, on the other hand, made a strong impression on how we approach architecture. I remember him telling me once that if a building stands out and becomes an icon, it can't be because that was the initial intent. If it becomes an icon because of the ideology behind it, then let it be. It can't be your decision; it should be the decision of the community that engages with that building. He insisted that architecture is valuable when the idea transcends time, not a shape. So, even if a building is not appreciated stylistically when it is built, time will pass, and people will look back and appreciate it if the idea is strong. That resonated with me and that's why we have a research component in our practice. Meaning and purpose is very important in a lot of our work. Overall, there is a certain degree of quietness that characterizes our work.

VB: Would you say your work is beautiful?

RH: I hope so. For us beauty is not the same as prettiness, though.

LN: Rem Koolhaas said, "Talk about beauty and you get boring answers, but talk about ugliness and things get interesting." Beauty is subjective…

VB: Do you realize that this is the biggest misconception about beauty? Real beauty is universal. People react to it. Let me give you an example. I talked to a number of architects here in China. As soon as we start talking about beauty they say, "Beauty? We are not interested. We work on solving issues–social, pragmatic, etc." Then they give you a list of projects that need to be visited to see them in person. So, I go there and meet with people who give you a whole list of things that don't work–this is too tight, that's too awkward, that's not practical, etc. Then they smile at you and say, "But this is so beautiful!" It is beauty that blinds everyone. It is beauty that saves architecture from being just a pile of bricks.

126 Aranya Art Center (the Void), Qinhuangdao, Hebei Province, 2019. Photo by Pedro Pegenaute

LN: Interesting. But this is not how we work here. We don't just do things that are practical. I can assure you.

RH: But nor do we do things that just look good. Of course, we bring our personal ideas to what we think is beautiful—whether by defining a thickness of a particular material, its color, its shape. These are all very personal decisions. But this is when theory comes in. Designers use theory as a crutch; they find reasons or famous quotes to support their choices. And there are examples of famous projects that if you don't know about theory or history behind them then they may not be perceived as beautiful. Projects are accompanied by stories that help a lot. If the story is not told the meaning and appreciation may be lost. There must be a clear idea and if it resonates, then details may vary. Apart from beauty we operate with ideas that are metaphoric, poetic, and again, nostalgic by referencing the past to move toward the future. We are looking for the poetic. There is a need for abstraction, to express the meaning without being obvious and literal. So, if we can bring poetry through space, light, form, and materials to a person who comes to our building then we will be happy.

VB: Lyndon, you said, "Have we really had breakthroughs in modern architecture? It's a period wherein people are somewhat lost, and in which we really have to be in search of ourselves, as architects." Were you talking about the current period? Could you talk about your own inspirations?

LN: A few years ago, we started making conscious efforts to visit real masterpieces that we still haven't been to. So, we visited Terragni's buildings in Como, buildings by Le Corbusier in India and France, the Bangladesh Parliament complex by Louis Kahn, works by Geoffrey Bawa in Sri Lanka, and churches by Sigurd Lewrentz in Sweden to name a few.

RH: This was quite an experience and we both agree that these buildings are so much more profound than anything built since. We are talking about works by all of our contemporaries.

VB: What do you think is missing?

LN: In those earlier projects we saw ideologies, deep thinking, real breakthroughs—conceptually, spatially, structurally, materially. So, we were thinking: What can we compare that's being built now to that? How far did we progress? Have we done any real breakthroughs as a profession? Nothing really happened in fifty years! We haven't done anything new! So, I got really depressed and feel like we should not even be practicing.

RH: All of us are just doing variations.

VB: What about Center Pompidou? Bilbao? Seattle Public Library, or Vitra Fire Station?

LN: But you are talking about a limited few.

VB: Are you planning to do something about it? You have over 100 people here. You have a research component, great resources. What holds you?

RH: We are asking this question ourselves.

LN: I am not sure if this is within our power. I think clients, be it the government or private sector, have all the information they need, but precisely because of this they are scared to go outside of what is accepted. We spend a lot of time persuading our clients.

VB: Interesting.

RH: Gehry and Hadid both created personal expressions. Their works are personalized sculptures in the form of architecture. Whereas Le Corbusier and Khan

127 Aranya Art Center (the Void), Qinhuangdao, Hebei Province, 2019. Photo by Pedro Pegenaute

have formulated ways to interpret architecture for generations and we are still relying on their findings to this day. So, for us the question is: Do we interpret them further to become something different or should their work be totally reinvented? We don't see real breakthroughs that happened in our time. Perhaps Hadid could be reinterpreted as a system, reformulated into something else, something not as personal. But still, this would be something form-driven. And Gehry, for sure does not engage other architects. It is his own thing. He is an artist which is great. But I don't believe that architecture is art. Art is about the self; if there is no self, there is no art. Architecture is not self-serving.

VB: Lyndon, what do you think?

LN: Well, I don't necessarily agree because art does not need to be self-serving. Some artists remove their self from their work, and it is all about social issues they choose to expose. And architecture can critique the society just as art can. Anyway, the difference between architecture and art may be another issue related to the difference between Neri and Hu. Rossana thinks before she draws, and I draw

128 Aranya Art Center (the Void), Qinhuangdao, Hebei Province, 2019. Photo by Pedro Pegenaute

before I think. I tend to add things and she tends to delete things. It is interesting how we intertwine, just like architecture intertwines with art. Perhaps it is this push-pull relationship that makes our work interesting.

VB: You said, "We absolutely hate projects that are purely decorative." What kind of projects do you like?

RH: Did you say that, Lyndon?

LN: Yes, I did. And I think lately we are struggling with some of the projects because that's what they have

become–decorative. Unfortunately, that's driven by some of our clients. But we try to design our projects holistically. One example that's exemplary for us is Maison de Verre in Paris by Pierre Chareau. Is it architecture, interior design, furniture design?

VB: You know, Yung Ho Chang told me that as Chinese architects, "We started to do a good work collectively. But, in a way, good work is not enough. These days, architects know how to do a good building. But it is also important to work in areas that are less explored in our discipline. It is important to work outside of one's own comfort zone. Maybe you fail. Maybe you are not going to produce something pretty. But it is necessary to challenge ourselves." Do you think this may apply to you? Can you honestly say we are risk-takers?

RH: Not enough.

LN: Perhaps we are stretching ourselves too thin–apart from taking on so many projects internationally, we teach in America, we design products for many brands in Europe, we lecture, judge competitions, and so on. Maybe it is time for us to be more focused. But all these involvements came out of the fact that we opened our firm late, we can't be too small because that will limit our ability of doing bigger projects. Still, we don't need to be as big as we are today.

VB: Is there a particular project built here in China over the last two decades that you admire most, either by Chinese or foreign architects?

RH: If I must pick one such project it would be Wang Shu's Ningbo History Museum [020]. There are moments about that building that are quite moving. And apart from architecture, what really moves me are the Chinese ancient gardens, particularly in Suzhou. The moments that the poetry of those gardens can offer are magical. I also love the fact that these places are anonymous; we don't know who built them by name.

LN: Personally, I like many of Wang Shu's explorations at the new Xiangshan Campus [005-008, 029-033] he built at China Academy of Art in Hangzhou.

LI Hu
OPEN ARCHITECTURE

Beijing-based architect LI Hu (b. 1973, Fushun, Liaoning Province) received his Bachelor of Architecture from Tsinghua University in Beijing in 1996 and Master of Architecture from Rice University in Houston in 1998. He joined Steven Holl Architects in 2000 and became a partner in 2005. Since 2006, he led SHA's Beijing office with projects across Asia. Together with Holl and Yung Ho Chang, Li cofounded an architectural journal *32: Beijing/New York* in 2002. The same year, Li and his partner-wife, HUANG Wenjing (b. 1973, Anyang, Henan Province) setup OPEN Architecture in New York, an experimental design and research studio; it was established as a formal practice in Beijing in 2008. Li served as director of Studio-X Beijing, operated by Columbia University's GSAPP, and he is a visiting professor at his alma mater and Central Academy of Fine Arts (CAFA), also in Beijing. In 2017, the architects' book *Towards Openness* was published by ORO Editions with testimonies by Kenneth Frampton and Steven Holl. OPEN Architecture's realized projects include the Chapel of Sound near Beijing (2020), an art center Tank Shanghai (2019), the Pingshan Performing Arts Center in Shenzhen (2019), a minimal housing prototype MARS Case for House Vision Exhibition in Beijing (2018), a laboratory and office building for Tsinghua Ocean Center in Shenzhen (2016), the Garden School/Beijing No.4 High School Fangshan Campus in Beijing (2014), and the Gehua Youth and Cultural Center in Beidaihe District in Qinhuangdao, Hebei Province (2012). Arguably, OPEN Architecture's most artistic creation is UCCA Dune Art Museum in Aranya near Qinhuangdao (2018). Inspired by children playing and digging in the sand, the building is conceived as a system of interconnected galleries embedded into the dunes, just meters away from the Bohai Sea. The galleries' concrete shells were literally shaped by the hands of the local workers and shipbuilders who used linear strips of wood to construct the formwork, leaving irregular texture, all painted white. Organic oculus-like skylights, each different size and pointing to its own direction, flood the cavernous spaces with natural light that renders the interiors in such delightful ways that they seem to come alive. The following conversation with Li Hu took place during his visit to New York where he and Huang Wenjing came to deliver their lecture OPEN Questions at Syracuse University's Fisher Center in Manhattan.

ARCHITECTURE IS AN EXPRESSION OF HOPE

In conversation with **LI Hu** of OPEN Architecture, Beijing
Conrad Hotel, Battery Park City, New York, February 17, 2019

Vladimir Belogolovsky: After graduating from Tsinghua University and then from Rice, you worked with Steven Holl for a decade–first in New York and then as director of his Beijing office, collaborating on several major projects. Could you talk about the influences he had on you?

LH: There are many influences, but I intentionally avoid any formal similarities with Steven's work. [Laughs]. First, any project needs to be driven by a clear and strong concept from the very beginning, in order not to be compromised as easily. There is always a compromise–budget, time, and so on. But if your idea is strong it will survive to the end. I am talking about real ideas, not mere beautification. Steven taught me this–start with strong, original idea and end with details that bring a human touch and, in a way, spiritual quality to the project by focusing on the textures, materials, and key details. He said, "Skip the middle step," such as dressing facades.

The second lesson I learned from Steven is the importance of being an idealist. To survive this very tough profession you must be an idealist, meaning, not making any compromises to your values. You can say "no" to a project, but do not compromise your values. And the third influence–he always works like an artist.

VB: Is that how you work? Do you see yourself as an artist?

LH: Not literally. We work differently. I don't start every project with watercolors. But to me an artist is someone who does what he truly believes in. Architecture is a means of expression. You are saying something with your work. To me that's art. Every

129 LI Hu. Courtesy of OPEN Architecture

project must resonate with the architect's ideas and intentions.

VB: During your lecture here in New York, you said that your Chapel of Sound project was inspired by a souvenir stone that you brought from India. To me this insight is quite refreshing because architects no longer openly admit of having inspirations that may be spontaneous, irrational, and random. Is it a typical process for you?

LH: Inspirations come from different directions. Any design process is a search for ideas. And ideas must work with forms. The stone from India is not a souvenir. I brought it from the site of our very first project, the Metro Valley Business Park, that we did there in

130 Beijing No. 4 High School, Fangshan Campus, Beijing, 2014. Photo by Shengliang Su

2008; it has not yet been realized. I always collect something from sites where we work–rocks, shells, driftwood. I just pick up things that may be strange or special for no particular purpose. I may use them for something, or I may not. They are just memory pieces. So that piece of rock was among many other objects that sit on shelves in our office. Sometimes you glance at something and it sparks an idea.

VB: This example proves that architectural design is quite spontaneous and can go into many directions.

LH: It proves that architecture is about both intentional and unintentional, rational and irrational. It is never as simple as one plus one equals two. So sometimes, the design process can take a long time; other times, it can be very fast. Still, even when ideas come quickly, we may need to spend months developing them.

VB: So, if you look at that stone from India and the final form of the Chapel of Sound you can still recognize that form, right?

LH: Yes. [Laughs.]

VB: Let's talk more about your inspirations. For example, you said that your Dune Museum was inspired by children digging in the sand. How was that concept developed?

LH: Well, there were so many things there. Yet, when you decide to design in the dunes your choices are limited. In the case of that museum, I woke up one morning and did a sketch that very accurately resembles what ultimately was built. One of the inspirations was Louis Kahn's phrase that a building is a society of rooms. The Pantheon with its oculus was another idea, as were natural grottos and caves, such as Benagil Beach Sea Cave in Portugal. Nature, as an inspiration, can be found in all of our work. And all these things were researched before I did the sketch that I mentioned. So, there are multiple inspirations in that project–digging into the sand, the feeling of sand's softness and formlessness, the exploration of forms that are optimal to withhold the sand's pressure all around, and so on.

VB: And there was no particular program, right?

LH: Well, initially, there was a fuzzy program with no operator, which is the nature of many Chinese projects, unlike in the West where everything is run by huge boards of directors who hand you a very detailed brief that needs to be followed with little space for reinventing it. In China, you work on fuzzy programs, with fuzzy budgets, and often with no operator. So, you start with an interesting idea and you use your imagination all the time. That kind of freedom is very critical for the work. This project was approved right away. It is important to be able to convince your client with a kind of unbound idealism. Then it took us a year just to develop the forms. And if we didn't have the deadline, we would be still working on it, because you can keep improving things endlessly. That's the nature of architecture.

VB: You said that contemporary cities should offer "a space of joy." And you added that your work "tries to inject pleasure and poetry into space." Could you elaborate on that?

LH: We always try to create space with an expression. Architecture is not just buildings and objects. It could be, if we are talking about mediocre architecture. But good architecture radiates with emotions, poetry, joy, spirituality, inclusiveness, connectiveness. I just came back from Brazil where I visited many modernist projects by Lina Bo Bardi, Oscar Niemeyer, Paulo Mendes da Rocha; I find these works to be very poetic, inclusive, and spiritual. These buildings are about many things; I really connected with them emotionally. They are very beautiful and spatially generous. I want to do architecture of generosity,

which is missing today. Architects used to be very idealistic and now they are more opportunistic.

VB: Since you opened your practice with Huang Wenjing a decade ago you completed a variety of projects. Could you summarize what your architecture is about and what are your main intentions?

LH: Architecture is an expression of hope. In our projects we examine such issues as how we live together and our relationship with nature. In every one of our projects, no matter what's the scale, program, or location, we address these issues. With our architecture we try to inspire people to act responsibly. Architecture should be a sanctuary. It should protect everything that's vulnerable–nature in particular, as well as relationships among people. Architecture should accentuate our feelings about nature and each other.

VB: You said, "We seek to use architecture to express our emotions and reactions in the simplest, yet most powerful way–to create a kind of spectacle, a delightful, and touching experience." Is this the ultimate goal of your architecture–to create "a kind of spectacle, a delightful, and touching experience?"

LH: Yes, and in the most idealistic way. A building should become a spectacle–not for its strange form, but for raising itself to the level of art. If you look

131 Chapel of Sound, Chengde, Hebei Province, Concept Sketch, 2017. Courtesy of OPEN Architecture

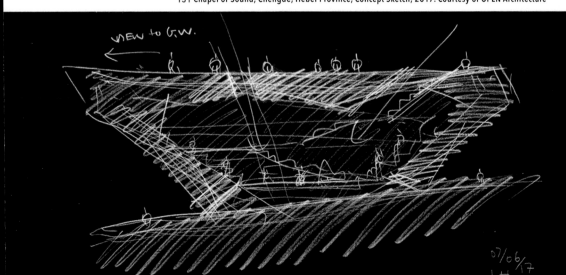

132 **UCCA Dune Art Museum, Aranya, Qinhuangdao, Hebei Province, 2018. Photo by Wu Qingshan © OPEN Architecture**

at the Dune Art Space, in a way, it disappears and becomes a humble background for the art. At the same time, it is a spectacle in itself. So, a good building should be both–at once a kind of shelf or platform to anticipate many things which will happen there, and a meaningful, special place that stands on its own. Architecture is so complex; it can't be summarized in a word.

VB: Still, when you try to pick the right words, it forces you to examine your work in the most fundamental ways. You often use such words as openness, connectiveness, and reaching out. What other single-term words would you use to describe your work and the kind of architecture that you try to achieve?

LH: I would use the word hope. Architecture is hope. No matter how angry we get about our world, when we work, we express our hope. We inject it into everything we do. We work as artists; we express in our architecture everything we believe in.

VB: You believe that architecture is art and architects are artists, right?

LH: Sincerely so. There is different art and there are different artists. Like the works of artists, the works of architects are all different and individual. Being an artist means being true to yourself. Just like art, your architecture represents who you are. You are your architecture. Your architecture is what you believe in. And I may spend my whole life searching for my expression in architecture. Our architecture evolves because every opportunity is different. And not only do we choose to do things differently, we choose to do different things. For example, in 2014, we finished Beijing No. 4 High School. That project attracted so much attention that we were asked to do similar schools all over China.

VB: But you didn't want to turn into school architects.

LH: No, we only take on projects that offer new possibilities. I don't want to become a specialist and I don't want to become a stylist. I don't believe in singular style as a solution for everything. It is a good business model but that is not architecture. I look for different opportunities that require different architectural solutions. Every time we start a project, we have no idea where to begin. [Laughs.] We are now working on a new urban center project in Shenzhen. It is a competition and an opportunity to reinvent the city. I want to design a kind of city that would be different from what is built everywhere. I don't like massive, chunky, solid towers that dominate many city centers now. We want to do something that will grow from a very small scale and footprint into a high-rise. That hasn't quite been done yet. So, every time I don't know what to do, but at the same time I know what to do–something different. To do something that the place is calling for. I am trying to be very observant and listen to the sounds and voices of the site to seek opportunities to build something responsive and unique.

VB: This attention to the particularities of each site reminds me the approaches of such architects as Renzo Piano and Glenn Murcutt, who are very meticulous about their responses to each place. Whereas, for example, Alvaro Siza told me that he can't help himself. He has an urge to sketch something right away, as soon as he gets the project, before going to the site. This approach manifests in the expression of a language that not only has become his own, but a kind of modern vernacular for the entire region; there is Siza in every contemporary Portuguese architect today. It has become an unsurmountable challenge for many local architects to overcome the weight of his influence.

LH: I try to break away from my own influences and find something new.

VB: Critiquing the current situation in China, or perhaps around the world in general, you made this comment: "We build too much, too fast." What do you think about this–construction and design process time only going to compress further, how should architects adapt to that reality?

LH: This is true, we build too much, too fast. Architecture has become a commodity, political propaganda, engine for economy rather than a work of art to serve the public by bringing people closer together. Particularly in China, architects are not ready to take on this challenge, the building industry is not ready, our politicians and developers are not ready. We have created projects that already have become our regrets for the future. We can't easily rebuild what we accumulated in the last couple of decades. We are going to live with that for a very long time. We have built not only stupid architecture but stupid cities. We didn't have time to plan something smart. We have amassed a mindless production of junk.

VB: And it seems that so many of the Chinese independent architects who are doing good projects, completely gave up on the idea that they could be relevant in cities. So many have retreated to the countryside to work on tiny projects. This trend is encouraged and celebrated by the international press. In the meantime, the mainstream architects keep destroying Chinese cities.

133 UCCA Dune Art Museum, Aranya, Qinhuangdao, Hebei Province, 2018
Photo by Wu Qingshan © OPEN Architecture

LH: I agree. It's an unfortunate reality that the opportunities to build in urban centers are, for the most part, given to larger corporate firms and design institutes rather than to young independent Chinese architects who are often denied the chance to make full use of their talents by working on more relevant urban projects. We try to work in cities despite all the struggle involved. I believe in celebrating public architecture.

VB: You mentioned that you often rewrite briefs and programs given to you by clients. Could you touch on that? This is something that also must have come from Holl, right? He is a utopian and idealist. The word idealism must be his favorite.

LH: Well, Steven is one of many influences. There are a number of architects who are well known for this. Rem Koolhaas is one. And it goes back to Louis Kahn and Le Corbusier. I think that every great architect must be able to redefine the mission with his own interpretation. Every project is about imagining the future. It has to do with the rebellious nature of great, searching architects—you must find ways for doing things differently. But it is not about distrusting the client. It is about working with the client. Because in most cases, I am not even given a clear brief. Sometimes, I wish I would be given a good program to work around it. But in most cases, there is no program, whatsoever. Often our clients just tell us, "You are going to do a great job." Our client for the Tank Shanghai public art park simply said to us, "Make something interesting." [Laughs.] That was the brief. So, the programming was in our contract. We were completely responsible for it.

VB: You said that you always tell your students to challenge conventional thinking. You said, "Challenge what your teachers tell you. Why trust them?" At the same time, you noticed in one of your interviews that it used to be that school was ahead of practice, meaning new ideas used to come from schools. But now it is the opposite. The practice is ahead because as a practitioner you deal with more issues and need to come up with new strategies. My own teaching experience confirms this. When students are challenged with assignments, they are looking for answers in projects that are already built, which means that they are working with ideas that may be 10 years old. They are not inventing something that does not yet exist. Teaching has become more pragmatic and less idealistic. What do you think? How do you bring excitement and inspirations to your students?

LH: This is very interesting. Before answering that I would like to note that very often, when we are given a project, we can't refer to something that was done before because we are challenged with completely new, unprecedented programs. So, we go ahead and invent something new. Now, about teaching, I can't teach people how to design. I don't think design can be taught in school. These ideas were expressed by Le Corbusier, way back. But what I can show my students is how to think differently. Students often need to be shaken up. We need to teach them how to think and how to break away from the norm, routine, and any expectations. Teaching is also very important for me personally. I like having a dialogue to bounce ideas. I like teaching fundamental ways of observation and curiosity. It is also important to do research, not just design.

VB: For anyone who spent time in China in recent years it is apparent now that the best architecture there is now produced by local architects. What advice would you give to foreign architects who are working on projects in China?

LH: Spend more time on design and spend more time on construction site. Projects that I did with Steven Holl that were built 7-10 years ago were of better quality than what foreign architects are building there today. Now it is more about business operation. Many architects are not serious about achieving good results in China. They don't follow up. I believe in architecture on the ground. I can achieve the most idealistic result if I am committed and going to the site every day. I often design on site. I talk to the workers to better understand the problems. I draw my details on the site. Finding relevant solutions is

134 Tank Shanghai, Shanghai, 2019. Photo by INSAW Image

the only way, more so in China. This is how architects such as Carlo Scarpa or Lina Bo Bardi worked. I can see their ghosts when I visit their buildings. The idea of global architecture needs to be revisited. Architecture needs to be hands-on. In some countries, it is easier to achieve results with less efforts, but in China, you need to be present on site.

VB: Chinese architects told me that to produce good work you need to follow one of the two models. You either open a successful business unrelated to architecture such as a restaurant or hotel. Or you prioritize by breaking projects into two groups—large, mediocre, and profitable ones to subsidize those that are small, experimental, and losing money. How do you organize your projects?

LH: Well, I can name many examples of those two types; some of these architects are quite famous now. But I don't believe in that. I am not a very good businessman. [Laughs.] I heard Henry Cobb once told Frank Gehry, who was actually following the second model you are referring to, "You have the front door and the back door. You close one of them or you will end up doing something that's not important your whole life." Since then Gehry closed the back door. This is how I started from day one. To me everything must be idealistic. Architecture to me is not business. You are either a good businessman or a good architect. I want to do what I know and love best.

ZHU Pei
STUDIO ZHU-PEI

Beijing-based architect ZHU Pei (b. 1962, Beijing) stands out for his diverse and expressive forms. This must explain why his commissions almost exclusively constitute art museums all over the country. Yet, Zhu insists that architecture is not sculpture; his work is about experience and history that has been in a precarious state of transformation. Zhu received his first Master of Architecture at Tsinghua University in 1991 and his second Master of Architecture at the University of California at Berkley in 2000. He worked at RTKL Associates (now CallisonRTKL) in Los Angeles from 1994 to 1999, the year when he became one of four founding partners of Shenzhen-based URBANUS, which he left in 2004 to start his own practice in 2005. Zhu has been teaching at leading universities, including his alma mater, Harvard's GSD, and Columbia University in New York. In 2018, the architect was named the new dean of School of Architecture at CAFA, the Central Academy of Fine Arts in Beijing. Zhu's inspirations may not be surprising or unique—nature and history—but his daring, yet, non-signature solutions are remarkable and enlightening. Just two years after establishing his studio, the architect was commissioned by the Guggenheim Foundation to design the Guggenheim Art Pavilion in Saadiyar Island Cultural District in Abu Dhabi and the Guggenheim Museum in Beijing (both unrealized). His built works include the Jingdezhen Imperial Kiln Museum in Jingdezhen, Jiangxi (2020); the Shou County Culture and Art Center in Anhui (2020); the Yang Liping Performing Arts Center in Dali, Yunnan (under construction); the Minsheng Museum of Modern Art in Beijing (2015); the OCT Design Museum in Shenzhen (2012); Digital Beijing, Olympics Control Center (2008); and Courtyard House renovation for artist Cai Guo-Qiang in Beijing (2007).

FOR ME NATURE IS ATTITUDE

In conversation with **ZHU Pei** of Studio Zhu-Pei, Beijing
Studio Zhu-Pei in Beijing, April 17, 2017 & November 27, 2018

Zhu Pei: More than half of all the models that are usually on display, in my studio here, are currently being shown at Aedes gallery in Berlin; the show is called *Mind Landscapes*. There are five projects on display: the Jingdezhen Imperial Kiln Museum, the Yang Liping Performing Arts Center, the Dali Museum of Contemporary Art, the Shou County Culture and Art Center, and the Shijingshan Cultural Center. All projects are under construction because I wanted to show my current thinking and design process, and a range of interests based on place, climate, culture, lifestyles, local materials, history, and most of all, nature. I want my architecture to reflect all these particular conditions, to learn from them, and create a new experience, which would be very specific for every place.

Vladimir Belogolovsky: You just said that nature is the most important of all of your inspirations. But when I look at the photos of your exhibition in Berlin, the layout is very geometric and abstract. And almost everything there is represented in white color. Even your landscape drawings are shown in black and white. Your nature is nonrepresentational, right?

ZP: Sure, people typically associate nature with green color, with mountains and the forest. But today most people live in cities. In my work, I don't emphasize physical nature, unlike so many other architects who try to mimic nature literally, with greenery that covers their architecture, which is a counter-Chinese idea. That is not real nature. I never try to make my architecture look like nature. It is impossible anyway. No architecture can be like nature. The idea is to respond to nature, not to copy it. For example, many good ideas can be learned from traditional houses

135 ZHU Pei. Courtesy of Studio Zhu-Pei

with tall courtyards, solid walls, and small windows as a response to a hot and humid climate. So, for me nature is attitude; it is all about our attitude toward how we respond to the climate. Architecture should be our direct response to nature and about how we want to build our relationship with it. Also, I don't like buildings that express technology or cover themselves in expensive, shiny materials. That's very pretentious.

VB: Just by looking at your works such as currently under construction projects–the Imperial Kiln Museum and Yang Liping Performing Arts Center, or your other well-known earlier works–Digital Beijing or OCT Design Museum, it is hard to believe that all

181

136 Caiguoqiang Courtyard House Renovation, Beijing, 2007 © Studio Zhu-Pei

of these works were designed by one architect. Why are they so different? What are the main intentions behind your architecture?

ZP: I strongly believe in specificity of each project. Climate is one of the key reasons for finding very different solutions and expressions. So, you can't apply one standard stylistic approach. This is my approach and I hate to use the same kind of architecture everywhere. Some architects developed their signature styles. I am not interested in that. I am modest in that respect and I would rather design architecture that's specific and not personified or recognized. So, the materials and forms I use are always different. What never changes is my attitude–I always aim at creating something beautiful to complement nature. My favorite architect is Le Corbusier, and he changed all the time. His monastery La Tourette and Ronchamp chapel were designed around the same time, but you can't find buildings that are more different. It is because the sites, programs, and scales all contribute to the resultant forms being very different. But if you go beyond these buildings' forms you can find similarities in the materials, colors, or the way the light is treated, and in how these buildings relate to nature.

VB: Well, let's not idealize Le Corbusier who may be many architects' favorite. Still, to say that he was interested in site specificity more than in projecting his own ideas is a bit of a stretch. He was a fountainhead of ideas and he used opportunities that came his way to implement them. Ronchamp is a wonderful building, but I can perfectly picture it in another location. There is nothing specific about it and being a brilliant architect, he could have come up with a number of other solutions for that site. Or he could have Ronchamp built elsewhere and we would love it just as much.

ZP: I may disagree with your idea. Ronchamp works so well with its site.

VB: Of course, it does. He was a genius. All I am saying is that the design came from his mind and heart, not primarily from the site… You know, so many of contemporary architects are so hung up on deriving ideas from the site that there is no way they would ever come up with something as liberating as Ronchamp. For that to occur you need to look for ideas beyond the site. When an architect has something to say the site may be just as well a mere blank canvas. There is nothing consequential about great architecture. It comes from the architect. A number of architects told me that they didn't like their site to the point that they would create their own site and literally put a fence around it. What's a traditional Chinese courtyard house if not a world within itself?

ZP: You are right. Innovation is always the key for architecture. In my case, I am very much inspired by different local conditions, and then create new experience for the specific place.

VB: There is a bit of a contradiction in the idea of bringing well-known architects to other places to express something local, don't you think? There is nothing modest about that. For centuries, it was all about inviting accomplished architects from overseas, so they could bring with them something new,

personal, and iconic. Bernini's invitation to Paris by Louis XIV is a famous example. Today, just like every museum wants to own a Picasso, every city wants to build a building by Hadid...

ZP: That's not true...Not anymore!

VB: But Beijing already has two huge built works by Hadid–two commercial centers, and two more are in the making–an airport and a skyscraper.

ZP: There must be a balance. As an architect, you need to create the experience that people know; then you need to try to create the experience that people don't know. That is perfect architecture. Architecture is not about creating something strange. Architecture is not sculpture. It is all about the experience, about going inside, exploring, getting excited. So many new cities are built based on the latest fashion or like theme parks rather than real cities. But I believe in architecture that's rooted. If you build in China, you have

137 Minsheng Museum of Modern Art, Beijing, 2015 © Qingzhu Photography

138 Shou County Culture and Art Center, Anhui Province, 2019 © schranimage

to connect it with local Chinese culture. Architecture should be based on two fundamental principles—one is the root and the other one is innovation and new experience. I think you need to combine revolutionary thinking and respect for local culture and conditions. Architects coming from a different place have an advantage of seeing things differently. That is very important.

VB: You once said, "I seek a new definition for architecture, exploring traditional ideas with a futuristic mindset." What words would you use to describe your work or the kind of architecture you want to achieve?

ZP: Two words that I already used—root and innovation. The root is associated with nature and culture, and innovation is all about the new experience.

VB: You called your approach to architecture a non-architecture style.

ZP: Because I hate the idea of having a style. I don't have a style. I want to be different every time. I want to be more experimental. I want to forget what I have done in the past.

VB: Do you see architecture as art, and do you believe in the concept of architect as artist?

ZP: Yes, I strongly believe that architecture is art. And if architecture is art this means that architects are artists. Why do we call some people artists and others designers? Artists create something that didn't exist before. They create new perspectives, new experiences, new ideas. But there is a difference between architecture and art. Architecture is not only about space but also about function and experience. Art is created for everyone. But architecture is very specific. Architects create buildings for a specific people, place, culture, and climate.

VB: I would like to ask you to comment on some of your own quotes. You said, "The most

important moment for architecture is not the completion of the building, but when the spaces intersect with people."

ZP: This is correct. When you look at a traditional Chinese painting, it looks incomplete. It is the job of the observer to complete the painting in his or her mind. Just like Chinese scholars' landscape paintings, they have never sat down in front of the mountains to sketch them. They would travel for months in the mountains to experience them. When they came home, they would try to recapture those moods by putting together all the accumulated memories into their paintings. Chinese gardens and architecture are also focused on the experience to create spaces to walk, to view, to live, and to roam. No building should be completely finished. There should always be some space left for peoples' interpretation. Architecture should be just like a Chinese painting; it should strive for exploring possibilities beyond the immediate function. A building that's created just to perform a particular function is a dead building. Look at the traditional hutong with its courtyard in the middle. There is no particular function for that. It is just emptiness, but it also means everything. People eat in the courtyard, socialize, get married there. We call it the incomplete space. But this is the most important space in the house, its heart. When we work on our buildings, we try to avoid providing finished solutions; we leave space for interpretations, so different functions can be imagined beyond our own expectations. A building should be like a sponge; there should be many incomplete spaces in between.

VB: Another quote, "We seek natural logic using great contradictions. Creating ambiguous spaces is one of my signatures."

ZP: For example, when I did a courtyard house for artist Cai Guo-Qiang here in Beijing, it was mostly a renovation of a historical hutong, but the part that was damaged beyond restoration I rebuilt as a new pavilion without trying to copy anything. I used new, even futuristic materials and forms to contrast with the old ones. It was a very ambitious project; some would call it ambiguous, but to me this way of juxtaposing old and new is about respecting the past, while moving into the future. Most people would see this example as contradictory, but for me this is how I search for a new harmony. In every project, I look for opportunities to express my work in the most contemporary ways.

VB: You also said, "You cannot just use traditional tiles and then claim that this is traditional architecture." Was this a particular criticism aimed at your colleague Wang Shu?

ZP: Not really. Different architects have different approaches. I admire Wang Shu's work very much and we share many ideas. He is looking for the root; I am also looking for the root. What I was criticizing in that quote was the way to build traditional architecture

139 Jingdezhen Imperial Kiln Museum, Jingdezhen, Jiangxi Province, 2016-20. Watercolor by Zhu Pei; Courtesy of Studio Zhu-Pei

140 Jingdezhen Imperial Kiln Museum, Jingdezhen, Jiangxi Province, 2020 © schranimage

today by using new materials to copy traditional imagery. Wang Shu's work has a deep soul. He uses recycled material, which I like and, in fact, I am now working on the Imperial Kiln Museum in Jingdezhen where I am also recycling local bricks, which was a local tradition; the kiln structures needed to be rebuilt very often and the workers recycled the old bricks to build their houses. So, there is a strong culture in China to recycle and repurpose building materials.

VB: And the final quote, "Our studio has always been geared toward the future."

ZP: Yes, I am always looking for ways to create new experiences, something that did not exist in the past.

VB: What are your favorite buildings?

ZP: The Acropolis in Athens. Also, some traditional villages in China. I like getting inspiration from buildings that were built based on collective thinking and not driven by one person's ideas. There is something natural about how these structures were developed. And in our attempts to build the future we have to study and know the past. Also, unlike many traditional structures in the West such as Neoclassical palaces or the Forbidden City here in Beijing, I prefer to avoid primary axis and symmetry. I like the approach of adapting architecture to the place. Then I feel that this kind of architecture was done as a careful collaboration with nature.

VB: If you had a chance to have a conversation with any one architect, who would that be?

ZP: Le Corbusier. He was so great. I love his very artistic mind and dynamic, innovative architecture.

141 Jingdezhen Imperial Kiln Museum, Jingdezhen, Jiangxi Province, 2020 © Studio Zhu-Pei

142 Jingdezhen Imperial Kiln Museum, Jingdezhen, Jiangxi Province, 2020 © schranimage

HUA Li
TRACE ARCHITECTURE OFFICE

Beijing-based architect HUA Li (b. 1972, Gansu Province) received his bachelor's (1994) and master's (1997) degrees from the Architecture School at Tsinghua University, and then graduated from Yale University with his second Master of Architecture in 1999. Hua apprenticed in New York at the office of Herbert Beckhard Frank Richlan & Associates. The firm's founders were former partners at Marcel Breuer office before starting their own practice in early 1980s. This experience introduced Hua to dealing with masonry and precast concrete, while working on cultural and educational projects in New York City area. Returning to Beijing in 2003, Hua established Universal Architecture Studio (UAS) with his former classmate at Tsinghua. Parallel to that he started his teaching career—first at the Central Academy of Fine Arts, CAFA and then at his alma mater. In 2009, Hua left the partnership and established his own practice, Trace Architecture Office, TAO. His studio currently consists of about 20 architects. TAO's built projects include the Xiadi Paddy Field Bookstore of Librairie Avant-Garde in Fujian Province (2019); the Xinzhai Coffee Manor in Yunnan Province (2018); the Swan Lake Bridge House and Viewing Tower in Shandong Province (2018); the Rocknave Teahouse in Weihai, Shandong Province (2015); the Forest Building at Grand Canal Forest Park in Beijing (2014); the Xiaoquan Elementary School in Deyang, Sichuan Province (2010); and the Gaoligong Museum of Handcraft Paper in Baoshan City, Yunnan Province (2010), for which the architect was short-listed for 2013 Aga Kahn Award for Architecture, the only nominee from China that year. Our interview was conducted at TAO's bureau, which is located at a courtyard artists' studios compound designed by Ai Weiwei's FAKE Design in Caochangdi Village, a thriving arts and cultural hub on the outskirts of Beijing. The architect discussed what could be learned from the past, about bringing ideas from literature into architecture to ignite imagination, the need for questioning conventions and fundamentals, and what would make architecture his own.

WHAT IS THE FUTURE
IF NOT A TRANSFORMATION OF THE PAST?

In conversation with **HUA Li** of Trace Architecture Office, TAO, Beijing
Trace Architecture Office, TAO studio in Beijing, October 30, 2019

Vladimir Belogolovsky: Your practice is called Trace Architecture Office. Could you elaborate on this name? Is there a hint at your desire to find inspiration in the past, rather than the future?

Hua Li: To a certain extent, you may say so. Although, I never thought about this that way. [Laughs.]

VB: Is that so? Wouldn't you agree that to trace means to reproduce something that already exists?

HL: Not exactly. To me the word trace has to do with many layers. It is associated with the process rather than the result. Because architecture is more about complexity and about making it. To me architecture never refers to a single layer, be it theory, history, aesthetics, or functionality. It is about interweaving all these layers in each project that defines the foundation of my work. I would disagree with you that trace only refers to the past because, in a way, the future is also based on the past. What is the future if not a transformation of the past?

VB: Could you talk more about these notions of evolution and transformation in your work? You use traditional materials such as brick a lot. But how do you move into the future by insisting on using the brick? So much of today's architecture is about the past. It is about warmth, comfort, and safety that's associated with the past. So many new buildings look intentionally, as if they have been around for a long time. There seems to be a certain fear of the future.

143 HUA Li. Courtesy of Trace Architecture Office

HL: There may be some connections with the past through brick, but I don't agree with your assumption that a particular material is identified with the past. The materials themselves shouldn't be labeled as either nostalgic or futuristic. The meaning of a material depends on how it is used and what needs to be expressed.

VB: What you are saying is that any material has the future.

HL: Sure. Brick does not belong to the past only. Brick is a kind of material that can be used in any era.

144 Xiaoquan Elementary School, Xiaoquan Town, Sichuan Province, 2010 © Yao Li

It is a traditional material, but why can't it be used in the future? What matters is how you use it.

VB: What I like about the future is that we know little about it. We try reinventing what we already know. What I often see in contemporary Chinese architecture is that the future is seen as a mere reinterpretation of the past. I don't see a commitment to inventing something entirely new.

HL: Perhaps we have different definitions of the future! [Laughs.] Again, to me the past has its place in the future as well. There is no future without the past. It is grounded in the past. History is important here in China, but so much of it was ruined in recent years, so it is natural for us to try to preserve as much as we can. I am not giving up on looking at history, but, in the meantime, I want to achieve something that has never been done before. Future incorporates the past; you never lose the connection with the past. Future evolves and transforms from the past, and that's what makes history.

VB: I think this says a lot about our time. For example, the fathers of the modern movement threw all stylistic references of the past into the dustbin of history. Now we seem to be very interested about what's in that dustbin. There is no urge for inventing something entirely new. Currently, there seems to be more satisfaction with unearthing something that we are already familiar with.

HL: I don't fully agree. I think every era has an urge for something new. But I would use the word evolution, rather than revolution to describe architecture in our own time. Architecture has many dimensions, connections, and limitations. You never invent architecture out of nothing. The modern movement to me is an attitude rather than a style. "Modern" is an action instead of a result. You may say that my work is affiliated with the heritage of modern architecture, but I don't really care how my work is termed or labeled. I believe that architecture that's valuable always belongs to its time, but also goes beyond its time.

VB: After graduating from Tsinghua here in Beijing you studied architecture at Yale. Could you talk about your experience there?

HL: Studying at Tsinghua gave me solid design skills and artistic touch. In contrast, Yale was about how to propose a question, how to interpret ideas in architecture. One of my professors was visionary Austrian-born American architect Raimund Abraham. That studio motivated many intriguing ideas. The objective was to translate what you encounter in literature into architecture. That was inspiring. Abraham would remove all real-life constraints for us. That kind of exercise helps to ignite imagination and explore fundamentals. It is important to discuss architecture more fundamentally, not just pragmatically. Architecture can be so much more!

VB: What would you say are the main intentions of your architecture?

HL: Architecture to me is about solving real problems, while creating poetry. The title of my first monograph is *Origin and Gravity*. Origin is about the essence, fundamentals, and the starting point. In other words, every project starts with a question: What is my project about? Gravity is about how to work with reality and specific conditions. Every project has a unique situation. That's what I want to address most. I don't start my designs with preconceptions. It is all about questioning and testing. Every project requires this kind of investigative process, like fermentation, so to speak.

VB: It says on your website that you are critical at contemporary architecture as an obsession to produce fashionable forms. It says that you "Envision architecture as an evolving organism, being an inseparable whole with its environment, rather than just a formal object." Could you elaborate on this view?

HL: I see architecture as a part of an overall environment, rather than isolated objects. Architecture is always about connecting with its site, surroundings, and people. Each project is site-specific and therefore, unique.

VB: You said, "Architecture should solve concrete problems of location, scale, material, relation with people." This is all very clear, but how do you bring subjectivity into your work? Do you at all try to make architecture your own?

145 Bridge House, Swan Lake Park, Shandong Province, 2019 © Chen Hao

146 Forest Building, Grand Canal Forest Park, Beijing, 2014 © Xia Zhi

I am developing my own perspective, questions, and answers in my practice all the time. But I don't pose these identity-searching kinds of questions consciously.

VB: What I am saying is that there is a kind of common ground among the Chinese architects that would be very unusual to encounter in other countries. For example, Russia went through somewhat similar recent history and opened up to the world around the same time as China. Yet, architecture there is wildly different from one architect to another. There is a range of ideas–from following historical examples, neo-modernist and neo-constructivist models to versions of post-modernist models, deconstructivist and parametric tendencies. There is no consensus about Russia's regional or national architecture. And just like in China the entire architectural production during the Soviet times was in the hands of the design institutes. There was just one kind of architecture, one prevailing view. But once the system collapsed a whole range of ideas emerged. Here, on the other hand, leading independent architects have no disagreement; all of you are moving in one direction. I am not saying this is good or bad, I am simply bringing attention to this phenomenon.

HL: Honestly, I did not see it that way. I think independent architects in China today are also very different. There are no prevailing values, which reflects China's fast-paced and chaotic development. The way I see my work is autobiographical. I try to find my own path, to establish my own history.

VB: This is actually exacerbated by the fact that so many architects around the world are now giving up on the idea of personal authorship; many prefer to work as a group, collaboratively. Still, there is a tendency in the West for architects to see something published and reject it, thinking: "let me tweak it, let me find my own way." But here the tendency is to incorporate various tricks. Architects here seem to be fine with sharing ideas. There is no

HL: Subjectivity is carried in design thinking and expressed through a particular form. A form is always subjective and that's what distinguishes one architecture from another. Every project is expressed through its own unique form and that's what makes architecture my own.

VB: The current architectural production in China, coming from the offices of leading independent architects, appears to have strong similarities, as far as focusing on projects located in the countryside, similar building types, typically done on a small scale, predominantly out of traditional materials, trying to reconcile architecture with nature, and insistence on preserving ruins, just to list a few key features. Do you agree with this observation?

HL: Not really. From social and cultural perspectives, there is certainly some common ground that these architects share. But how to make architecture, is still up to each architect's own vision and approach.

147 Rocknave Teahouse, Weihai, Shandong Province, 2015 © Hua Li

competition for authorship. Once a particular solution is introduced it is up for grabs for everyone.

HL: I think you are exaggerating this. Honestly, I don't see that much difference between here and the West. Some architects claim that their work is not referential and entirely inventive, but the reality is that no one can create in a vacuum and everyone is influenced either by history or by what other contemporaries are doing, at least to a certain degree. I don't think that here architects don't care about authorship, but it seems true that it's more difficult to be original today everywhere. Nevertheless, I don't think architects can always invent. You can't come up with an invention in every single project.

VB: Here in China, are there architects who you would consider your model figures? Who are your authorities? What kind of practice are you trying to build?

HL: I don't have authorities. But talking about model figures, I would want to mention Yung Ho Chang, who was the first in the country to start an independent practice in 1993. He served as a strong example showing that it is important to create alternative models and reflect on how architecture could be practiced independently. That was hugely influential on young architects all over China.

VB: What do you think are the most pressing issues for Chinese architects today?

HL: Clearly, to ask more questions. I am listening to your questions and I wonder: Do I know how to answer them? But I want to address these issues. Over the last two decades, China had gone through so much development. For sure there is not enough debate and how to balance between modernization and preserving traditions. Architects should challenge the mainstream and even their own past. We do need this critical thinking and questioning. It is healthy to avoid ever becoming too satisfied with your own success. I think it is important for young architects to think about what else can be achieved, rather than just follow a path that's already accepted.

VB: That's exactly right and my feeling is that a certain level of idealism and success, already has been achieved. If you look at the production of the Chinese leading studios, you will see a certain balance between modernization and preservation, there is a social purpose, beauty, I will even say seductive beauty. Are we satisfied? Many critics are celebrating and even suggesting that this kind of regional architecture could be adapted beyond China. So many projects are resolved as if they were beautiful paintings; there is nothing to add,

nothing to take away, a perfect harmony has been achieved, or so it seems. How would you progress from here? What new questions would you raise?

HL: Perhaps at this stage it is the right time to ask all these questions. I believe certain qualities were achieved and they should be carried on. For me new question is always this: Then what? What is next? What are our limits? What else could we do to set ourselves free in architecture? We can only progress if we ask questions. That's clear.

VB: You apprenticed at the office of Herbert Beckhard Frank Richlan & Associates in New York whose founders worked for Marcel Breuer. His work was always somewhat out of balance. For example, he pushed his cantilevers to

148 Xinzhai Coffee Manor, Bawan Village, Baoshan, Yunnan Province, 2014-18. Sketch by Hua Li. Courtesy of Trace Architecture Office

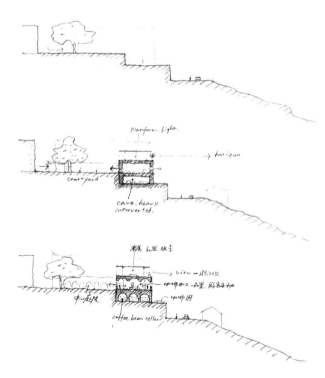

the absolute extremes. There is something awkward about his buildings, pushing for new juxtapositions, contrasts, revisiting what we have accustomed to, constantly pushing the limits. I don't see that in China today. There seems to be a strive for perfection and with every new project something is rearranged ever so slightly.

HL: That's not how I feel. There is some truth to that, but I can assure you that I am not like that. I have my own anxieties each time I start a new project. I would not be satisfied by repeating something that I have done before. I would search something different. Architecture is a dialogue between what has been always there and what needs to change. You just talked about ruins. It is important to develop a position about ruins conceptually, not merely aesthetically. For example, for Louis Kahn ruins were an inspiration to evoke eternity. Whereas, for Arata Isozaki a ruin is a metaphor of mortality. These are opposing concepts. How to achieve the quality of timeless in architecture is important. Yet, the tension between the unchanged and what's new makes architecture fascinating. How do you see this?

VB: I seem to be more interested in posing questions. And one question I would ask now is this: What will the next generation, the generation of your students want? What will be their reaction against this balance and strive for perfection? What will be there left for them to do? I don't know in what way they will react, but I guarantee you that they will smash this accumulation of beautifully composed buildings fundamentally. Simply because traditionally, every new generation wants to revolt against the previous one. The sons kill their fathers, so to speak. It is inevitable. How will they be dissatisfied with the current situation? I think their key reason for dissatisfaction will be anonymity and impersonal qualities of today's architecture. China is such a vast and diverse country. But if you look at the current production here, who do we have that stands out? Perhaps Ma Yansong, Atelier Deshaus... Who else? Don't you think that this situation is asking for revolution?

194

149 Xinzhai Coffee Manor, Bawan Village, Baoshan, Yunnan Province, 2018 © Chen Hao

There will come a moment when younger architects will ask these questions. They will say: "I am fed up; I want to find my own way." That's what I think.

HL: Well, whether they will rebel or not, new technologies will arrive and point to many new directions. In any case, aesthetics and beauty are subjective notions. Perhaps the emergence of artificial intelligence will transform architecture entirely and maybe aesthetics will go away as an issue because architecture will be the result of all kinds of codes and algorithms, not defined by subjective intentions coming from architects. I think the idea of a good project is not about celebrating something, but to generate a debate. In that sense we will never be satisfied because there will always be new questions and new alternatives.

ZHANG Li
ATELIER TEAMMINUS

ZHANG Li (b. 1970, Beijing) earned his Bachelor and Master of Architecture degrees from Tsinghua University in Beijing. He has been heading Atelier TeamMinus since 2001. The 50-person practice operates within Architectural Design & Research Institute (THAD) of Tsinghua University. In 2020, after our interview that follows, he became dean of the School of Architecture, his alma mater. And if that's not enough, since 2012, the architect and educator has been serving as the editor-in-chief of *World Architecture*, China's leading architectural magazine. Zhang was selected as the curator of the Chinese Pavilion at the 2021 Venice Architecture Biennale. In addition to actively teaching at Tsinghua he taught at Harvard's GSD, Berlage Institute (now the Berlage Center for Advanced Studies in Architecture and Urban Design at Delft University of Technology in the Netherlands), the National University of Singapore, and other prestigious universities around the world. Among his most notable built works are the Gujiaying Horticulture Village Visitor Center in Jiangsu Province (2019), the Aranya Qixing Youth Camp near Qinhuangdao in Hebei Province (2016), the Roof Gardens at China Pavilion 2010 Expo in Shanghai, and Ningbo Hefeng Creative Plaza (2007). Zhang headed Venue Planning and Sustainability in Beijing's bid for the Olympic Winter Games 2022, for which he designed two large sports projects: Big Air ramp at Shougang Park (2019) and Zhangjiakou Zone (2019), both at *Zhangjiakou* Olympic Village, about 200 kilometers northwest of Beijing. My favorite of Zhang's projects is the Janamani Visitor Center in Yushu, Tibetan Autonomous Prefecture in Qinghai Province (2013). The city is famous for Jianamani, the world's largest Tibetan Buddhist cairn–or a pile of stones–where over the course of three centuries more than 250 million pieces of Mani stones were brought by pilgrims. Jianamani was damaged by the 2010 earthquake; its rebuilding started before local houses were repaired. The Visitor Center was built out of recycled stone and wood. Its 11 viewing platforms point to the surrounding historical sites directly visible from the center's roof.

IF YOU CAN'T DO BEAUTIFUL THINGS YOU ARE DOOMED

In conversation with **ZHANG Li** of Atelier TeamMinus, Beijing
Atelier TeamMinus in Beijing, January 2, 2019

Vladimir Belogolovsky: You are the editor-in-chief of *World Architecture* magazine, a practicing architect, and professor and chair of the Architecture Department at Tsinghua University here in Beijing. How do you combine such different, if not conflicting roles, particularly being both practitioner and critic?

Zhang Li: You are right about this conflict. Being a critic, you need to be very open; you don't want your mind to follow any particular beliefs. As we know, architects have their own ideas and we try to find ways to spread them around. But, in any case, if you look at the history of the 20th century it was not that rare to have editors or critics as practicing architects at the same time. Famous examples would include Aldo Rossi who was the editor of *Casabella* in Italy and Aldo van Eyck who was the editor of *Forum* in the Netherlands, both in the 1950s-'60s. And another Italian architect and designer Gio Ponti was the founder and director of *Domus* magazine for much of his life. As far as teaching, one may argue that it is essential for architects because it has to do with exercising our curiosity. So, combining these three roles–being a critic, a teacher, and a practicing architect–helps to open up one's mind. And I can feel a certain transformation in my practicing experience since I took the role of the critic. I have become more critical and more open to possibilities. As an editor, I pay more attention to the debate and I avoid any kind of repetition in my work.

VB: Many architects told me that they see their practice as a single project. This implies repetition. They revisit certain ideas and try to improve their line of inquiry.

ZL: I am not interested in repeating anything. I see architecture as a process leading toward

150 ZHANG Li. Courtesy of TeamMinus

understanding the architecture's knowledge. Let's call that an inquiry into what may constitute truth in architecture. I am very curious about this process and architecture is only the means to that, not the end. So, for me repeating the same means is not the right way to my architecture's inquiry. I need to reach to different results to discover something new.

VB: *World Architecture* is a bilingual magazine, in Chinese and English. Who is your key audience and what is your vision for it?

ZL: It is actually not entirely bilingual. By law that would require the magazine to be registered. So, we have certain material, which is not translated into English. About two thirds of our readers are Chinese and the magazine is available overseas. Our vision is to facilitate mainly Chinese architects with a platform for real debate. We cover issues and projects worldwide, but our focus is on projects right here in China. We believe that architecture can be fully understood and debated only through its relevance to a particular community. Both architecture and publications are meaningless without its context.

VB: As a critic, how do you assess the current creative climate in China and opportunities here for Chinese architects to innovate?

ZL: Opportunities are growing, but we need to participate more openly in a critical debate. Chinese culture, of course, is dominated by Confucianism, which is not necessarily conducive to a debate.

VB: I agree. There is so much of the good work, but the debate seems to be absent. Can there be any architecture without a debate?

ZL: I believe debates make architecture. The current debate in Chinese architecture is, let's say, shallow. There are people who are willing to debate and there are architects who believe their practices are driven by discussions. But in reality, on a bigger scale, the real debate is not there yet.

VB: And the global turn toward pragmatics, away from developing personal identities

151 Jianamani Visitor Center, Yushu, Qinghai Province, 2013 Courtesy of TeamMinus

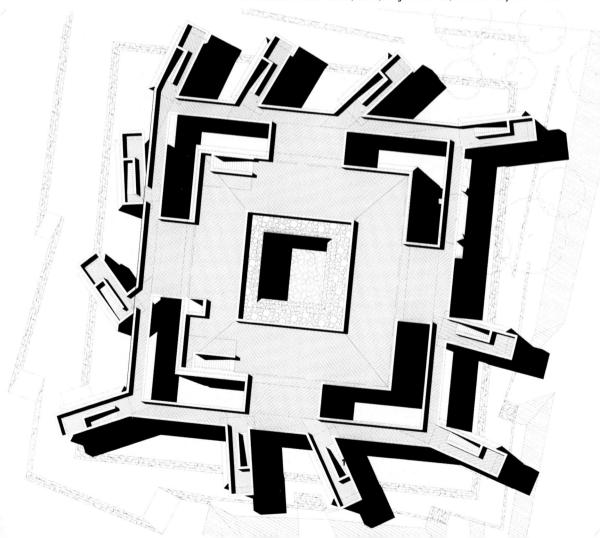

is not very helpful. Still, globally, there are stronger traditions for debates and developing individual positions. But let me ask you very directly. Would you be able to name, let's say, a leading figure in architecture here in China? By name, one person? And would you say your opinion is shared by others?

ZL: Yes, a very straight forward question. Very hard. You have to understand that the greatest majority of Chinese architects were trained for very specific tasks. There are very few architects who were trained outside of this system. So, one breed is this newly defined group of independent architects who are leading non state-owned and state-funded ateliers. Yung Ho Chang was the first of this breed of architects. He is the big-brother-like figure to these independentlyminded practitioners. His work is not easy to categorize. Most importantly, his way of practice is academic and experimental.

And the opposite of this breed is a big stream of thousands of architects who are working at the enormous system of state-owned Local Design Institutes (LDIs). If you visit any city in China, the great majority of all buildings that you see, surely are designed by these LDIs. They are the ones that are truly shaping the Chinese cities. They are actually working better and better. Though, the design institute system is not necessarily fostering debates and criticism. Out of this breed the big-brother-like figure would have to be Cui Kai, the chief architect of China Architecture Design & Research Group (CADG) here in Beijing.

VB: And you are so carefully avoiding naming one figure that we can't imagine contemporary Chinese architecture without and that is Wang Shu.

ZL: Probably because he is one of a kind and does not constitute a prime example to most architects, despite his high-profile status.

VB: OK, let's stop this right there because some of the architects I interviewed did not want me to publish our interviews because they felt they said too much about him. You conducted many interviews with China's leading architects. What

where your most interesting discoveries?

ZL: The most interesting discoveries had to do with their personalities, not their work. I also find fascinating to talk about what they want to achieve in contrast to what they actually achieved. So, I like these discrepancies between what is the goal and what is achieved. I want to know why is there this discrepancy?

VB: Out of all the architects you interviewed what conversation would you say was the most rewarding.

ZL: I interviewed Yung Ho Chang and Cui Kai, and the Tsinghua Dean Zhuang Weimin [since our interview Zhang Li replaced Zhuang Weimin as the dean at Tsinghua's Architecture School], all of whom are dominant figures. But to answer your question, I would like to mention one very special name: Li Xiaodong. He is somewhat unique in China. There is an ancient Chinese proverb, "One needs to step outside of a mountain in order to see it." I think he is the only architect in China who somehow can distance himself from architecture's immediacy. He is both serious and not very serious. He is like a guru to many young architects here and he is equally dedicated to teaching and practicing. He is not just about practicing architecture but breathing it, fully engaging in teaching, critiquing, and searching for its identity. His practice is very small, and all of his projects are very special.

VB: Let me ask you something. I have visited a number of projects here in China. They are generally praised by international critics and portrayed by the architects themselves as pragmatic and about addressing real issues. They insist that their work is based primarily on a particular context, site, budget, program, and so on. They are not at all about making beautiful objects. But...

ZL: There is always a but, isn't there? [Laughs.]

VB: Well, what I am getting at is this. When you visit these places and talk to people who actually work there, the first thing they tell you is that nothing makes sense! This is too tight,

152 a), b) Jianamani Visitor Center, Yushu, Qinghai Province, 2013
Courtesy of TeamMinus

that's too awkward, that's too impractical, or even dangerous, such as a sharp door handle aligned with kids' eye level at a kindergarten, and so on. And then at the very end of the tour they smile and say with such joy, "But, this place is so beautiful!" What do you think about this discrepancy and why are architects fooling us?

ZL: Very interesting observation. Architects want to see themselves more liberal than conservative, and, if possible, on the intellectual side. And, of course, we want to see ourselves as very ethical. So, there is always an abuse of the ethical line. We deliberately try to mix the line of ethics with the line of aesthetics. But great architecture is always about this line of aesthetics. No matter how moral, how ethical, how correct you are, if you can't do beautiful things you are doomed. Don't you ever forget that architecture is about beauty. We have a visiting professor at Tsinghua, Terrence Curry, who proposed to have a seminar on beauty. He was opposed by most of our faculty. Another member of the faculty asked, "What age are you living in, if you propose to talk about beauty?"

VB: Sure, beauty may be quite subjective and hard to talk about in concrete terms. On the other hand, if you say that you want your architecture to do good for the society, there is this immediate connection and legitimate approval. The problem is that they don't do what they say. And then there is this emphasis on social benefits. Is there architecture that's not social? How is an expensive hotel for tourists more social than an opera house or an exclusive teahouse more social than an art museum?

ZL: I would say that one of the most blatant lies that has been told by architects today is that architecture is not only beautiful, but it is also right. It is a lie because architecture is great because it is beautiful.

VB: You have a very diverse portfolio in terms of scale, program, geography, and even visual language. Your current projects include two ski jumps for the 2022 Beijing Winter Olympics

153 Jianamani Visitor Center, Yushu, Qinghai Province, 2013. Courtesy of TeamMinus

in Chongli and two history museums, among other projects. What would you say your architecture is about?

ZL: My architecture is about my understanding of the people I work with–everyone, from my team to the client, to consultants. My architecture is about design as a positive intervention in the real world.

VB: But there are so many projects that you work on at the same time. Do you try to understand everyone involved?

ZL: But the good projects constitute only a very small part. Because there are other projects that I maybe not even aware of. [Laughs.] I don't work on every project, as there are other partners here. I am involved with about half of the projects.

VB: So why do you even take those projects? Why don't you focus on the ones that you really like?

ZL: Well, here in China, if you want to do good work you have to support yourself somehow. Big-scale projects are always more economically viable. I am sorry to say it, but that is the hard truth. Some architects take on projects that are not that good, to support the good ones. And some architects even own other businesses such as a restaurant or hotel to support their practice. And some architects, not to

be mentioned here, do projects for fun because their spouses or business partners can afford that.

VB: Interesting. Based on my observations, since early 2000s, Chinese architects succeeded in forming, if I can call it, a collective identity in architecture that can't be confused with any other identity. Architecture being built here is distinctly Chinese. And despite the fact that many leading international architects are building in China today, I would argue that the best work here is now being produced by the Chinese. Yet, if we look at this production it is somewhat formulaic. So many architects seem to ask very similar questions. I want to talk about the lack of variety and not enough of risk-taking.

ZL: You are correct. The term collective is worrying. You and I were raised in our respective collective societies. And it is hard for us to distance ourselves from that kind of thinking so quickly. We need some time, maybe another decade before we can go deeper, and become more diversified.

VB: Let me paint to you a portrait of a typical successful, independent Chinese architect today. He is a male. His choice of profession was suggested by his parents. He was educated abroad, at a prestigious American university.

As an extension to that he comes from a family that's independently wealthy, to the point that he can afford to sponsor or co-own his initial projects. His practice has a catchy name in English and does not include his own name. He favors traditional materials, humble building techniques, and he prefers to build in the countryside. His work is small in scale and building types are limited to projects that tend to entertain the tourists. And these buildings often feature ambiguity between what's old and what's new. Is this an accurate picture? Don't you think it is a very particular path for such a diverse country as China? Or is it really that diverse?

ZL: Well, I would agree with you for the most part. I wouldn't agree only with the part about wealthy families because before late 1970s China was a very poor country. But you are right, some architects come from families that have become quite wealthy very quickly.

But the rest is very precise. I think you already answered your own question. I agree the picture you painted is not very diverse. We can do better. We need to expect something better, more diverse and closer to real life than these poetic portraitures of tourism-friendly, image-oriented, consumerist architecture. I am glad that you are not satisfied with the constantly updated stream of seductive images. But that's why I mentioned the work of Li Xiaodong. His work is beyond the surface, beyond the first impression. He both cares and he doesn't care about his details at the same time. His architecture is not calculated. If you visit his works, of which there are very few, you will discover things that seem to be left there as an error or unfinished. His work is not about perfection. Yet, there is this platonic order, symmetry, hierarchy. But nothing is forced.

VB: When I look at even some of the best projects by the Chinese architects, I see that

154 Aranya Qixing Yuth Center, Qinghuangdao, Hebei Province, 2016. Courtesy of TeamMinus

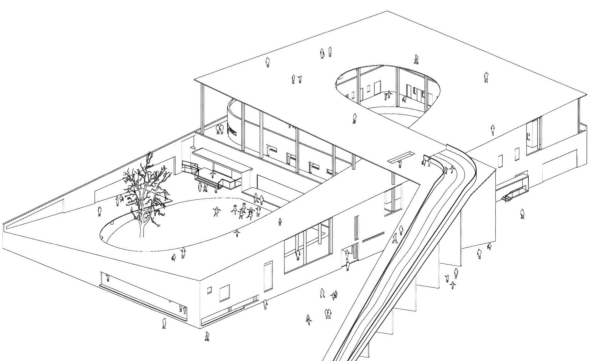

155 Aranya Qixing Yuth Center, Qinghuangdao, Hebei Province, 2016. Courtesy of TeamMinus

they are concerned with historical continuity, questions of identity, materiality. What do you think are the most critical issues that Chinese architects face today?

ZL: I will paint this picture with a very broad brush. All issues related to anthropology here in China–space, meanings, people–are very important. Chinese architects have gone through so many influences in the 20th century. These were the trends that people very closely followed collectively–from modernism to art deco, Soviet style architecture, to American post-modernism, and now to rural, regionalist works. But you are right, the architects' thinking is still very collective. And many of these rural projects are quite oppressive, even if beautiful. Oppressive because of their prescriptive tone. They force a certain behavior or attitude. We are in short of openness, curiosity. Many architects have become satisfied with their image-making, but this satisfaction is fake. We need to keep asking many questions, constantly.

VB: Wouldn't you say that architects can only be diverse if they become themselves? If everyone starts searching for their own individuality,

ideas will no longer be collective. They may be shared, but not copied uncritically.

ZL: That's the way to remain authentic and truthful. Each project is different and specific for a certain group of people for a specific place, and a specific program.

VB: Do you have role models?

ZL: I would name two figures: Carlo Scarpa and Jacob Bakema. I like Scarpa for his talent to develop ideas right on the site. His architecture reminds me of traditional Chinese gardens. And I like Bakema for blurring and interplay of horizontal and vertical elements in his modernist and very rational buildings.

VB: What single-term words would you use to describe your architecture?

ZL: Situation, anthropological, non-calculated. I don't mean careless, but not very careful, not too precise. I care not to be very careful.

TONG Ming

TM STUDIO

TONG Ming (b. 1968, Nanjing) received his bachelor's (1990) and master's (1993) degrees in architecture from Southeast University in Nanjing. He then applied to American universities, but despite being accepted by some of them, he could not get a student visa, as they were very limited in those days. So, he decided to continue his studies in China. In 1995, Tong moved to Shanghai to pursue his PhD in Urban Planning at Tongji University, which he obtained in 1999. He then worked at Suzhou Design Institute until establishing his own independent University-based practice, TM Studio in 2004. Tong is the chief planner of Shanghai Tongji Urban Planning and Design Institute. The architect also maintains his studio, called UNO, Urban Network Office in the West Bund, specializing in organizing seminars, workshops, exhibitions, and lectures. Tong is a professor at the School of Architecture at Southeast University. The architect translated two important books that were not available in Chinese before: Colin Rowe's *Collage City* and *Cities of Tomorrow* by Peter Hall. He wrote his own book *From Mythology to Fairy Tales* and worked on publishing an updated Chinese version of *Glimpses of Gardens in Eastern China*, a book written by his grandfather TONG Jun (also known internationally as TUNG Chuin, 1900-83) who was one of China's first modern architects and one of the first Chinese graduates of the University of Pennsylvania under Paul Cret. Tong's projects include several interventions in Shanghai–Changli Garden, a 350-meter-long curved green space on the edge of a large housing community (2020), improvements at the intersection of Jinjing Road and Jiahong Road in Pudong (2019), URBANCROSS Gallery (2017), the TM Studio West Bund (2015), and "A Courtyard with Lotus" (2011), as well as Park Block Renovation in Taizhou, Zhejiang Province (2007) and Dong's House Teahouse on Pingjiang Road in Suzhou (2004). We spoke about Tong's role in commissioning Wang Shu's first major building, his grandfather's research on Chinese classical gardens, and his frustrations with uncertainties of his own buildings that often unexpectedly change their intended use or even get abandoned altogether.

A BUILDING CAN FEEL LIKE A GARDEN

Interview with **TONG Ming** of TM Studio, Shanghai
WeChat video call between New York and Shanghai, August 5, 2020

Vladimir Belogolovsky: Your grandfather, Tong Jun was one of China's first modern architects. Did you consider studying anything else but architecture?

Tong Ming: Definitely, that fact alone was the most important reason for me to go into architecture. But when the time came to choose my major at the university, I initially picked mathematics, which was quite random. [Laughs.] I was interested in that a lot. In fact, in the 1980s such subjects as mathematics, physics, and science in general, were all very popular. But then my mother went to the university with me, and we had a talk with people at the administration. She convinced me that I should pursue architecture. She insisted that it was important to continue our family's tradition, even though my parents did not study architecture. That's how it started. But I have to say that the first time I felt something special about architecture was some years after I graduated. That was in 1998, when I finally had an opportunity to work on my first real project, the campus of Wenzheng College in Suzhou. Even though it was a very large project, at the time, I had no prior experience of designing a real building. It was during that project that I invited Wang Shu to take over the design of Wenzheng College Library at Suzhou University [018], the most important building on campus. I am very proud of that building because it became our first major realized project for both of us.

VB: Why did you choose him to be the architect if he did not have the experience needed at that time? How did you know you could count on him?

TM: I knew Wang Shu well because we were classmates at Tongji University. I worked on urban planning projects and he worked on architectural

156 TONG Ming. Courtesy of TM Studio

projects. Also, we lived next to each other at the dormitory. I went to work with a Local Design Institute in Suzhou, specifically to head the design of that project. I was invited there through a friend of my wife who studied architecture with me in Nanjing and we worked at the Institute in Suzhou together. Since then she left architecture. In 2004, I was asked to do another job–Dong's House Restaurant on Pingjiang Road–a small renovation project in historical district in Suzhou. That commission led directly to starting my own independent practice, which I opened that year in Shanghai. The project was a conversion of a traditional residential courtyard. It was launched by the local government as an exemplary renovation project to transform the declined residential and industrial block into restaurants and bars to promote the riverfront street as an attractive tourist area. I used traditional materials in contemporary ways to create a series of indoor and outdoor terraces. The main facade facing the river was clad in dark hollow brick that allowed visitors to view the surroundings from within. Yet, the wall shielded the interiors from being viewed from outside during the day. This device made the entire structure look like a lantern at night and helped to create a special atmosphere.

VB: TM Studio is Tongji University-based design and research practice. Could you talk about this model?

TM: I started my career as a teacher. Chinese universities encourage their professors to start practicing, and they assist in many ways. It makes sense both for them and for professors because architecture is both theoretical and practical. It is hard to teach without practicing experience. That's why schools help us

157 Park Block Renovation, Taizhou, Zhejiang Province, 2007
© Lv Hengzhong

with starting our own studios. For example, they let us use their resources. In fact, most professors at our university are practicing architects. The difficult part about that is that less than half of my time is left to practice. Still, I like teaching because of the creative environment, a possibility to discuss ideas and projects with colleagues and students, and not only within architecture school but from other disciplines as well. It enriches my experience and gives many inspirations to my work.

VB: What are some of the assignments that you give to your students?

TM: They are very much related to particular urban sites and conditions. For example, last semester I asked them to analyze the Bund area here in Shanghai and develop projects for its improvement. Everyone knows about the magnificent facades of the banks, hotels, and clubs built along the Bund in the 1930s but if you go into the area a little deeper you will discover very poor living conditions for many residents there. There are communal apartments with shared basic amenities where people live in very crowded places. We visited this neighborhood with students to see people's living conditions firsthand. Then I encouraged my students to propose alternative sociological and economic models, and redefine existing programs, not just propose an abstract formal design, however beautiful.

VB: Speaking of specific urban initiatives, your office in the West Bund is situated in a special Culture and Art Pilot Zone. There is now a whole cluster of museums, galleries, studios, and showrooms. For example, there are several architectural studios such as Atelier Deshaus and Atelier Z+ right next to your office. Other cultural spaces include Long Museum, West Bund Art Center, Yuz Museum, Tank Shanghai, Shanghai Center of Photography, and Fab-Union Space among others. How was this art cluster planned and what were the incentives given by the local government to you and other participants to bring new studios and galleries there?

TM: We were invited to participate in this program, but I did not take part in the planning process. The idea was promoted by Shanghai's Xuhui District Mayor Sun Jiwei who was trained as an architect at Tongji University. Dozens of cultural and art institutions were invited to build our spaces on free land and we all were offered very favorable five-year lease contract, even though we had to pay for construction of our spaces. This was done to regenerate the area's former industrial zone into a world-class urban waterfront public space with a potential to grow into the largest art zone in Asia. We were invited along several other architects such as Atelier Deshaus and Philip F. Yuan, and a number of artists, collectors, and art institutions that you mentioned. Yet, the space we built on the West Bund is not our main space, as we decided to stay at the university and develop the new West Bund space into a cultural hub to host seminars, exhibitions, lectures, and workshops. We were invited in early 2015 and finished our space by the end of that year. Starting the West Bund space led to building another similar space in a historical part of the same district.

158 A Courtyard with Lotus, Yuanxiang Lake, Jiading District, Shanghai, 2011
© TM Studio

VB: You are talking about URBANCROSS Gallery, right? What was the reason for initiating another cultural space and running two of them at the same time?

TM: Yes, URBANCROSS is a very small but centrally-located space. The reason for embarking on both projects was to go beyond a mere architectural design. To be honest, over the years, I became very frustrated by the fact that here in China, so many projects change their programs halfway through or soon after they are completed. Projects change hands or owners change their minds. I have done some projects that were simply abandoned. So, naturally, I wanted to take on projects that I would have control over—not only in terms of design, but also program and operation. We consciously started looking for such opportunities to turn them into a kind of laboratories to test our ideas. So, when we were invited to refurbish a space for a local community, we proposed the idea that became known as URBANCROSS, a multifunctional gallery space. It is just 20 square meters, but it unfolds onto the sidewalk and becomes a part of the street around

it to engage people who live in the neighborhood or even those who just happen to pass by to encourage them to take part in cultural exchanges. The project is an idea incubator, an urban cultural hub on the street corner, which is a gateway into its neighborhood. There are a number of places like this in the city and they are supported by local government to improve the street atmosphere. This space operated from 2017, but unfortunately, it was forced to close a year later. It was due to an exhibition by a group of artists whose sculptures offended the public. After that event, the local authorities lost their control over such hubs and their future operation will depend on the city government. In the meantime, these cultural hubs remain shut down.

VB: Do you think they will be reopened?

TM: We hope this situation is temporary. But it is very frustrating for now.

VB: You translated Colin Rowe's *Collage City* and *Cities of Tomorrow* by Peter Hall. Why did you decide to undertake these projects and did this experience make a particular influence on your own work as an architect?

TM: These books are very critical for me personally. I still go back to these texts regularly because they are so fundamental. It is funny, I came across *Collage City* by accident, simply by browsing books at the university library when I was an undergraduate student. There were very few books in the English-language section, so it stood out. I could not read it at the time, but I was quite curious. So, I decided to translate it for my own studies, but also for those students who otherwise would not be able to read this important book. One of the key influences on me personally was that you cannot reduce design to purely formal exercises. Architecture is not about designing buildings as objects, but about creating an urban fabric, continuity, knowledge, understanding and appreciating history, feelings, emotions, and so much more. This book expanded my mind and allowed me to do my designs differently, depending on very specific situations. And as far as *Cities of Tomorrow*, it was important for me to study modern urban models and precedents. And what is a better way of exploring a subject than translating it into your own language!? But I will also tell you that I will not engage in any

more translations. [Laughs.] It is a lot of work, but I am happy I translated very important books that were not available in Chinese before.

VB: You said that when your practice consisted of just you and no one else you enjoyed that the most and that designing alone is the best way for an architect to design. Then there is no communication issue and the architect can handle everything on their own. Do you still believe that?

TM: Well, that's what I said, and I still think it is true. [Laughs.] But now we have two offices–TM Studio and UNO, Urban Network Office, each consisting of several people. TM Studio is focused on architectural projects and UNO on organizing and running cultural events such as seminars, workshops, exhibitions, and lectures. Well, to address your question, in my opinion, architectural design is something very personal. The whole process of architecture making depends on good communication–from the moment you put your ideas on paper you must convey them to people at your office, your engineer, your client,

end-users, and the public at large. Inevitably, something gets lost in all of these steps. To keep your idea pure, you need to reduce these steps and limit the number of players involved. This is why I resisted expanding my office for 15 years. We are still small, but before I was working with even fewer people.

I decided to expand when I was working on "A Courtyard with Lotus" project. I would say it changed my attitude toward architecture and even my character. It was a rural site, on Yuanxiang Lake, which was quickly being absorbed by the city of Shanghai. The original program was a tourist center and public restrooms. The project was designed and constructed according to my idea. But once it was finished it remained abandoned for three years. Then it was taken over by a restaurant. They changed everything, so you can imagine my frustration. But then I let it go, as I had a revelation—architecture should not be merely a personal vision—untouched by real life. That's not enough. Now, I am convinced that architecture should be used as a social tool. In other words, it should serve a purpose. And if you can accept this basic idea, you can accept any result. Changes are inevitable and they are necessary. I can feel sad about my personal vision, but I should be grateful that my building can be useful. So, after that project I started to be much more engaging with people instead of simply working out my original idealist visions. It is a mature way of working and I feel more relevant.

VB: What was the main concept and inspiration for your Lotus project?

TM: It was quite challenging because that parcel of land was in the middle of nowhere. You can say there was no context whatsoever. So, originally, it started as a project with a good view, a scenic exercise. Today, I would refuse to do a project without any context. The initial idea was to create a garden because a garden is a self-contained entity within opaque walls around its perimeter. First, I wanted to plant young trees to create an instant garden with a structure at the center. But then I found an easier solution—instead of a garden with trees I planned a pond because waterlilies could be planted much quicker and cheaper than trees that would take years to grow. All necessary rooms—a tearoom, management offices, public spaces, restrooms, and so on—were expressed as a series of linked structures with low-placed windows to focus on water. It may seem contradictory that the whole idea of a scenic place became so cut off from the surrounding context and entirely self-contained and self-centered. The whole structure was conceived like an artificial nature. And each room looked similar—you could not tell which one is a tearoom, a management office, or a toilet.

VB: You repeatedly said that architecture must have a purpose and be driven by a program. Yet, again and again, for whatever reason, projects change hands, new clients come, and they bring their new visions along that impact your original intentions. So, wouldn't it be logical to focus on the building itself, the shell, and produce such a beautiful building that no one would want to make any changes to its appearance? The use could change, but architecture would be untouchable. Wouldn't a beautiful shell, autonomous of its intended purpose, be a proper solution? Then, if the program changes, the architecture would remain. No one would want to add or take away anything.

TM: No, that's not my position…Well, I am fine that I, as an architect, cannot control the situation. I think there is a fundamental contradiction in architectural design. On the one hand, architecture is art, but on the other a social tool. I am not just an artistic architect. I am an urban planner and I want to be a responsible architect. I can't simply focus on crafting my own object as an artwork and not care about its use. At the same time, I often think about my first independent project since I opened my practice, on Pingjiang Road in Suzhou. It now sits there empty, waiting for its new use. I want to address the issues of use ahead of time. A beautiful building that has no use and can't be adapted is not the answer. I think we should work on producing real buildings that work and that have a purpose. Architecture should be able to evolve. I can't change anything about it. What I can change, however, is my attitude. I should not insist on seeing architecture as a complete thing.

It is never complete, never finished. The most beautiful moment for architecture is when it is occupied by people. With this understanding I have become much more open-minded. And I think this personal revelation has to do with some of the ideas expressed in *Collage City*, which is a critique of utopian modern architecture and the idea of the heroic architect. How do we resolve this conflict and learn to generate beautiful architecture that responses to each situation in very particular, local, and specific ways. To achieve that you need good cooperation. That's where I see the real power of architecture.

VB: You said, "Architecture could be the medium through which people can share ideas and experiences." Could you elaborate on this idea?

TM: Absolutely. I see architecture as a process of assembling people's feelings, memories, and desires.

VB: You also said, "Inventing something from scratch is not as useful or meaningful as to discovering and interpreting something that is already a part of our environment." Could you touch on your design process, which you compared to looking through a fog, meaning you can't see what's coming. Destination is unclear. You said you prefer to call this process a research instead of design.

TM: Again, architecture could be inspired by an initial conversation with people who I am going to do the design for, by a site visit, or often by my own experience that may not be directly related to the project. What's important is not how you start, but how you address real issues. What's important is that the design should not be thought of as something settled and finished. It has to be able to react and adapt. So, I try to see the project from as many different points of views as possible. I want to test different ideas.

VB: We discussed the importance of program and use. But apart from functional and pragmatic aspects you address other phenomena, which are quite immaterial. For example, in one of your talks you devoted some

160 J-Homesquare, Rest and Play Area at Intersection of Jinjing Road and Jiahong Road, Pudong District, Shanghai, 2019 © Fangfang Tian

time to the importance of shadows and sunlight in your work. How would you summarize what your architecture is about?

TM: Yes, early on, I could spend a whole afternoon paying close attention to such things as moving shadows and analyze how architecture could respond to that. But I changed. You can tell very touching stories, but these stories may not be truthful. I try to make my architecture in a very truthful way. Yes, in my heart, I still think about the sunlight and shadow patterns, but in my mind, I think of issues that are more tangible and relevant.

VB: Would you say that you are moving from being very observant, poetic, and idealistic to becoming more grounded, engaging, and ultimately pragmatic?

TM: I would say so. This may have to do with my personal character. When I was younger, I was more solitary, contemplative, and, as you said, idealistic.

VB: What words or short phrases would you use to describe your work or the kind of architecture that you try to achieve?

TM: Urban society, follow changes, memories, social meanings. Architecture should be for people and shared by people.

VB: I wonder what you think about the issue of expressing artistic authorship. Let me read a passage from Wang Shu. He said, "I tried to build a diverse world as a resistance to the uniform world. But I also wanted to avoid the kind of singularity that comes from a design of a single architect... Anonymous diversity might be designed by time; no human being could do that. I tried anyhow." Do you share his intention to achieve a kind of anonymity without expressing personal authorship, which can be felt in the work of many leading independent architects in China? What is your position?

TM: I agree with his idea of anonymity, but I would not use the word "resistance." That is associated with Wang Shu. To him architecture is a tool to resist and to present an argument. For me architecture is about absorption of ideas and circumstances.

VB: Your grandfather Tong Jun was a well-known modern architect. You recently published an updated Chinese version of his book *Glimpses of Gardens in Eastern China* and Wang Shu wrote an introduction to it because he considers your grandfather one of the key influences on his work. Could you talk about the importance of Tong Jun's contribution?

TM: The first time my grandfather's book was published was in the 1930s. It appeared in English in a

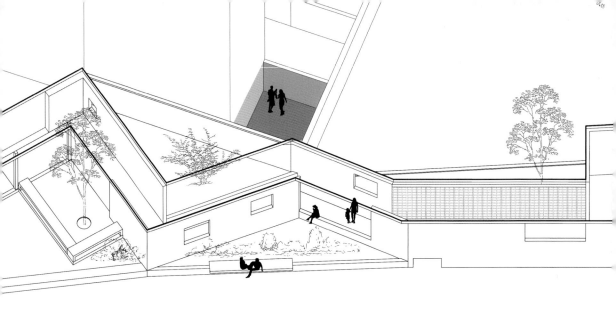

161 Changli Garden, Shanghai, 2020. Courtesy of TM Studio

Chinese journal *T'ien Hsia Monthly*. Since then he continued working on the manuscript throughout his life. In 1997, a bilingual book came out, for which I contributed as an editor. I was working on my PhD. The recent book you are referring to was published in Chinese in 2018. Wang Shu wrote an introduction because he felt indebted to this book. Tong Jun believed that a garden is a world. Similarly, in Wang Shu's words, architecture is a world; meaning, it is about creating a new world, not merely another building or a city of buildings. Another important point is that a garden is a system of fragments. It is not planned as a whole design or an image. Gardens are created over long periods of time and they are made up of the roots of different plants. And as they die out, they get replaced one fragment at a time. He compared a garden to a ruin, which is cultivated, regenerated, and kept alive.

VB: You are saying that a garden is an organic thing and it is a continuously evolving organism, right?

TM: Yes, you can say that. A garden does not start from scratch; it is an ongoing process. So, for Wang Shu a building is like a living thing or being a part of nature. In other words, it is an environment, not a thing. When a tree dies another tree will replace

it. That's the basic idea and that's what Wang Shu learned and used as the key principle in his own work. For example, he uses reclaimed materials to add to his own buildings. His architecture is a cycle of adding, reusing, rethinking, and transforming.

VB: Is there one particular quote that stands out in your memory from your grandfather's texts?

TM: The book is not a theory. It is a historical account that describes the history of Chinese classical gardens. It is an analysis–how they originated, evolved, and transformed. Gardens in Eastern China are unlike any other gardens in the world. They are very organic, and they change continuously. A garden is a living creature.

VB: One of the phrases that your grandfather said in the book is a wonderful aphorism, "Even without flowers and trees it would still make a garden." How would you interpret it?

TM: Here is my understanding of it. Normally, a garden is understood as a container of nature or scenery–the plants, flowers, trees. But you can create a garden without living organisms. So, what he was really saying is that it is not the things, but the relationships between them that's important.

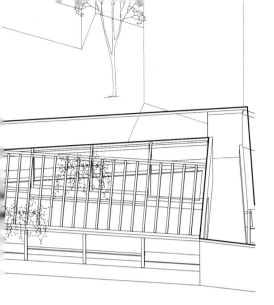

became the first architect in China who clearly conceptualized how architecture could be practiced as a conceptual and autonomous project. We don't really know where the design ideas come from. What is clear is that an architectural design could be guided by intuition. We can theorize about it, but the process is quite spontaneous. We can't explain logically something that is quite illogical. For me it was Yung Ho Chang who was first to demonstrate a rational way of developing architecture, and that gave a lot of inspiration to younger architects.

The relationship between elements is more important than the elements themselves. In other words, a building can feel like a garden. And now you can see what inspired my Lotus project.

VB: Which building built in China in the last 20 years, would you nominate as the most significant achievement?

TM: Instead of citing a single building, I would name one architect whose work I consider quite important and influential to me. That is Yung Ho Chang. He

VB: So, perhaps the most significant building built in China since the turn of the century would be one of his buildings?

TM: In that case I would suggest his recent Jishou Art Museum in Xiangxi in western Hunan [056]. The Museum is situated in the center of this historical city and is designed as a bridge that connects two riverbanks over Wanrong River. The Museum doubles as a gallery on the upper level and a pedestrian walkway on the lower level, which is always accessible to anyone. So, this museum acts as a covered bridge and true public space. It inserts art into the very heart of urban life where regular people may encounter it by pure chance.

162 Changli Garden, Shanghai, 2020 © TM Studio

WANG Hui

URBANUS

Architect WANG Hui (b. 1967, Beijing) co-founded URBANUS in 1999 in Shenzhen with his partners LIU Xiaodu (b. 1962, Beijing), MENG Yan (b. 1965, Beijing), and Zhu Pei who left in 2004 to start his own practice, Studio Zhu-Pei in Beijing. The architect received his bachelor's and master's degrees from the Architecture School at Tsinghua University in Beijing where he studied from 1985 to 1993. It was while being a student at Tsinghua that he met both of his current partners—Liu was his teaching assistant, while Meng studied two years ahead. After graduation, following the examples of both Liu and Meng, Wang acquired his Master of Architecture from Miami University in Oxford, Ohio in 1997. He then apprenticed in New York until 2002, while also moonlighting for URBANUS remotely. Wang heads the company's Beijing office, which he set up in 2003, overseeing projects in Beijing-Tianjin-Tangshan triangle, the Yangtze River Delta region, and other parts of China. He combines that with teaching at his alma mater and at Beijing University of Civil Engineering and Architecture. The firm has established a strong reputation among the largest independent architectural practices in China. Over the last two decades they have amassed a diverse portfolio—from hutong interventions to large urban complexes, mainly built in Shenzhen. URBANUS has become recognized for such projects as the Pingshan Cultural Complex (2019), SHUM YIP UpperHills LOFT (2018), the CGN Headquarters (2015), the Maillen Hotel & Apartment (2011), and the Daffen Art Museum (2007)—all in Shenzhen. Projects designed by Wang Hui include the Botanic Garden of International Horticultural Expo in Beijing (2019), the Holy Fire Lit Place for the 2nd National Youth 2019 Games at Xihoudu Archaeological Site in Shanxi Province, the Environmental Improvement for the Five Dragon Temple in Ruicheng City in Shanxi Province (2016), the Tangshan Urban Planning Museum and Park in Hebei Province (2008), and Maritime Art Museum in Dalian in Liaoning province (2008). In 2017, together with curator Hou Hanru, partners Liu and Meng served as co-curators of the Urbanism\Architecture Bi-City Biennale (UABB) of Shenzhen and Hong Kong, the world's only Biennial exhibition focused on urbanism.

EVERY GENERATION HAS A RESPONSIBILITY TO DESIGN A BETTER LIFE

In conversation with **WANG Hui** of URBANUS, Beijing, Shenzhen
WeChat video call between New York and Beijing, July 7, 2020

Vladimir Belogolovsky: What was it that triggered your initial interest in architecture?

Wang Hui: You know, I consider my generation quite lucky because we have experienced China's dramatic transformation–from a poor agrarian country to economic powerhouse that can compete on the world stage with some of the most advanced countries. Incidentally, today is July 7. It is the day when all Chinese students are taking the annual university entrance exam called *gaokao*. It is usually held in June, but this year it was delayed due to the coronavirus pandemic. So, I remember my own exam in 1985, when I was applying to Tsinghua University. Higher education was still very rare at that point. It was the beginning of political and economic reforms when we just started catching up with the progressive world. That was a very optimistic time and naturally, many young people wanted to contribute positively to the success of our country, to build a better tomorrow, so to speak. The question was: How can I be useful to the society? Now the times are very different. For example, this year my son is going to college and he selected the discipline that he liked, which is computer science, that he will be studying in America. I didn't push him into architecture; it was entirely his choice. But for me it was about what was needed for my country, not what I liked. And I was prepared for my studies, as I took art classes since I was a little boy. So, my main idea was about becoming an architect to be able to change the physical environment around me, to transform the look of my country quite literally.

You know, I was born in the Hutong area in central Beijing where my family lived along with several other households in *siheyuan*, a traditional courtyard

163 WANG Hui. Courtesy of URBANUS

house where we all had to share basic utilities such as running water for cooking. We didn't even have a toilet or a shower there. We had to rely on public facilities in the hutong. Imagine, going there every morning! So, living in the hutong you would know all your neighbors. You know, well preserved traditional Chinese architecture is very beautiful, but not when everything starts to get subdivided and added haphazardly. So, one can say that we lived in a slum. Okay, so now you know why I wanted to become an architect. [Laughs.]

VB: I am trying to imagine whether living conditions alone would be enough as a driving force for a young person to want to become an architect and to do something about it.

164 Maritime Art Museum, Dalian, Liaoning Province, 2008
Courtesy of URBANUS

Have you seen any examples of other types of buildings that you liked? If your lifestyle is the only way you know how to live, there is no reason to change anything. To want to change that you have to know that another lifestyle is possible.

WH: You are right, there were no places where I could see something else. But we had these beautiful poster-size wall calendars. Every month page featured one photo. These calendars were very popular because they would be just about the only decoration in the house. And some of these calendars had buildings. Otherwise, we had cement floor and painted walls, and maybe a small bookshelf. Imagine, living

in such a poor environment! Of course, I would be inspired by an image of a beautiful modern building. But also, I remember watching TV programs about foreign countries and modern buildings. It was modernity that was attractive and inspiring. It was such a shocking contrast to what we were accustomed to here. I remember when I was a high school student, we went on a tour to Tsinghua University. And when we visited the School of Architecture, we were shown architectural drawings framed and hung in the corridors. That was something totally new and very impressive. I had no idea about the difference between architecture, civil engineering, structure, design, and so on. I just remember being very impressed because everything looked brand new. So, that's what I wanted to study and change everything that was around us then.

VB: After Tsinghua, you and your partners were educated at Miami University, a small school in Oxford, Ohio. What was the reason for studying there?

WH: At that time Miami University was one of very few schools in the U.S. that offered full scholarship to foreign students. Xiaodu studied there first and established a good reputation as a Tsinghua student. Then Yan went there a couple of years later, and then I followed him a couple of years after that. To get a full scholarship was the only way to get a student visa from the Chinese government. Miami University made us very close and we became good friends.

VB: Did you go to the States right after graduating from Tsinghua?

WH: Because of the 1989 student protests, the government initiated a new policy. Students had to work inside the country for five years before applying for a student visa. So, right after my graduation I started teaching at the Central Academy of Fine Arts (CAFA) and after two years the policy was reversed. So, I applied for Miami University and my visa as soon as I could, which was in 1995, graduating in 1997. Then I moved to New York where Yan was already living. Once there I started working—first at Gruzen Samton, then Gensler, and finally at Handel Architects. I stayed in New York for five years. I got married in

165 Tangshan Urban Planning Museum and Park, Tangshan, Hebei Province, 2008. Courtesy of URBANUS

New York. My wife and I experienced the September 11th attacks, and my son was born there in 2002, the year we came back to China. Living in New York City, a great urban encyclopedia, has shaped my worldview a lot and I consider it to be fundamental for my subsequent career and practice.

VB: But URBANUS was started in 1999 in Shenzhen, right?

WH: Yes, in 1999, we founded our firm in New York City and Xiaodu went back to Beijing first, while Yan and I collaborated with him from America. As we were still working for other companies in New York, we moonlighted for URBANUS. [Laughs.] Beijing is a very conservative city, so Xiaodu headed for Shenzhen, a fast-paced city and the right place for young entrepreneurs. There is a huge market for young people. Even many developers there are very young. What's important is that the local government developed confidence and trust in young people, which is very important and unusual in China overall. We were not experienced, but we were still invited to take part in the most important competitions. For example, the headquarters of the

Urban Planning Bureau of Shenzhen. Our first successful project in Shenzhen was a landscape design. Then the Bureau chief told us, "Let's see whether you can do architecture." He had a lot of confidence in us and allowed us to try many innovative construction methods, such as exposed concrete and a T-shaped steel curtain wall system. We developed our own experimental construction methods directly with the manufacturer. It was this sort of freedom for young architects that inspired us to express the spirit of our age. This uniqueness of Shenzhen was and still is very rare in other cities.

VB: And you still had to collaborate with Local Design Institute there, right? Could you touch on that?

WH: There is a catch. We, independent architects, here in China, always work on small parts of very large projects. Only if the developers want something special, something eye-catching such as a sales office or museum, they would commission us. So, good architecture is a niche market. Typically, large institutes do very repetitive projects. To them it is profitable to work on large projects even for low fees.

But for us it is all about doing something interesting and new with very marginal profits.

This is a general background in China. Even a licensed individual architect cannot legally practice independently. Only an enterprise or a company with a license granted to the office can do that. Besides, it is not rewarding to take over the whole job because the lump sum budget is set. The fees for good design architects are squeezed out from all the support work such as mechanical or structural services. It makes financial sense only if you just do schematic and design development, which may amount to 60 percent of the total fee. Although, it may seem profitable not to furnish the full service, indeed the design architect still has to collaborate with the Local Design Institutes, and therefore, their profits can be eaten up by extra work, unspecified in the contract.

VB: URBANUS is a very unusual independent practice in China for at least three reasons. One, you are focused on working on large-scale urban projects. Two, you have two offices–in Shenzhen and Beijing. And three, you have three partners. Could you comment on this observation? Did you model your practice on a particular global corporate firm such as SOM, KPF, or Gensler?

WH: Yes, of course, we always wanted to build a very professional, you may even say, corporate firm. But the truth is that none of us is good at management. [Laughs.] And seriously, we never treat our design practice as a business enterprise. Yes, we are unique in many ways here in China. But our model is a hybrid. We are all doing a bit of everything–marketing, management, design, research, presentation, and so on. We are not only focused on design, and we don't have clear divisions between our responsibilities. This doesn't mean that we are not professional. But we are a little messy. In a way, we operate as a small design practice. And that's what limits our capacity to grow. Each of the partners leads a number of projects and we are not able to manage more than about 30 people each. So, the company maintains around 100 people–two thirds in Shenzhen and one third here in Beijing. Again, from the very beginning, we have decided not to be corporate, but design-oriented

firm. Or, even beyond that, we are determined to be a design firm based on research in making architecture more socially engaging. We have developed our own research department for that.

VB: You position your firm in the following way, "URBANUS is more than a design practice, it is a think-tank, an urban curator, and mediator. It aims to formulate architectural strategy from the complexities and uncertainties in contemporary Chinese urbanism." This was stated in one of your lectures. Could you talk about the key intentions of your work? How would you define your focus?

WH: This is exactly right; these are our intentions. [Laughs.] Well, China has many great designers, but there is a lack of diversity. What sets us apart is that URBANUS is really focused on addressing social issues. We are not at all about making the next architectural statement or achieving the most beautiful space. We do believe that architecture's main intention is to address social issues. Also, if you look at many architects around the world, such as in the U.S. or Europe, of course, there are many social issues there too. But here in China, they are more acute, and we have to address them more attentively. So many fundamental issues are in flux. The situation is not stable. So, in China the role of architects has a bigger meaning. We can help to distribute good quality of life to those who otherwise don't have access to it. We can deliver social justice. For example, public space is very important. Our architecture tries to create opportunities for creating public spaces as much as possible. So, when my partners curated the Urbanism\Architecture Bi-City Biennale, they changed the previous trend of always picking a popular or even fashionable space to do an exhibition that would showcase sleek international projects. Instead, they brought their biennale right into the heart of an urban village to be directly engaged with real issues of a real neighborhood where ordinary people live. More than that, it is the neighborhood where URBANUS is situated, the place we know from inside out. That was a very strong social action, not just a design statement.

So, every time we get a project, I always ask: What is it that I really want to say? We don't have any pressure to accept projects just to occupy our people for the sake of business. We only work on projects that we think are valuable and would allow us to address social issues. We already made many statements and interesting projects. Now we are focused on community making, not merely form making. We love to work on projects that improve daily lives of ordinary people. For example, in our Botanic Garden Pavilion for the 2019 Horticultural Expo I cared more about how to create public amenity by using the greenhouse space as an active agent of shaping a community than simply to design an attractive form. Such community centers are very useful in making people to become familiar and friendly with one another. Developers are preoccupied with how to make their developments profitable, but they never invest in how to build communities. That's what we try to offer with our projects. Architecture is not virtual, it is real. It can offer a real link between people.

VB: What I find very interesting is that in Shenzhen developers seem to be quite naïve and willing to learn from architects who have little experience, but a lot of imagination. For example, in New York, architects would be the last people developers listen to. In fact, architects often get hired a couple of years after the projects would be in full development. Even such starchitects as Herzog & de Meuron would be hired to design the type and shape of windows after the typology and even plans would be all worked out. You seem to enjoy a lot more freedom to shape your projects not only physically, but even programmatically, which is rare in the West, at least when architects team up with developers.

WH: Well, it seems like that. Still, the reality is not always that rosy. We have earned our reputation and trust. Of course, we have to listen to our clients not only because they have the money, but also because they may have more experience. For example, if they ask us to design a villa, they know more about that

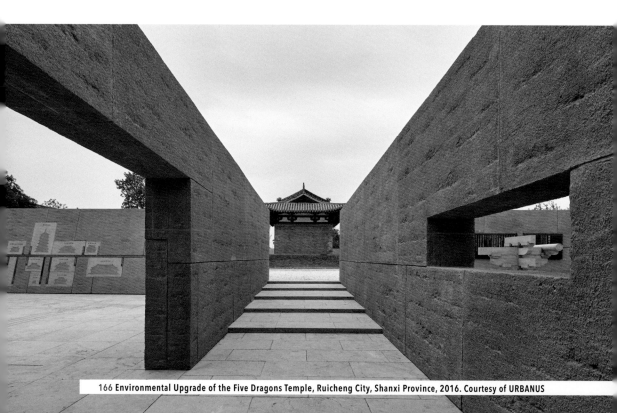

kind of lifestyle because they live it, while we can only observe it from a distance. At the same time, as an architect, you have to propose a vision and push it beyond what you have ever seen, and beyond what your client could imagine. We are more imaginative, more utopian, and more broadminded.

VB: You said that urban situation in China often erodes social and communal bonds found in urban villages and other traditional settings. Is there a particular project that URBANUS built that you could call successful in preserving these qualities?

WH: One such project would be Shum Yip Upper Hills LOFT built in Shenzhen in 2018. It is a giant superblock project with towers designed by SOM and shopping mall by Arquitectonica. We were asked to design a residential component situated on top of the mall. We introduced a village typology with loft apartments with private courtyards where neighbors can interact and socialize. The project is shaped as a system of small villages with public and private courtyards to promote multi-dimensional lifestyles. We succeeded in bringing a good diversity and density with a real community sense. This was a result of many years of research and experimenting with our other projects. Well, not just research, but love for urban lifestyle. Clearly, this project was approved because people like when they have many choices and when living places are emotionally charged, not simply based on dry profit-based calculations. It is a social network, a social connection that we try to build. So, in China we do have certain advantages in some projects and architects may lead projects. Don't forget that China is a socialist country. So, when architects appeal to the government or developers not in terms of mere design, but people's living conditions, they will be listened to. It is a moral issue.

Originally, we were expected to just build three large buildings on top of that shopping mall. Then my partner Meng Yan analyzed the situation and proposed a much more nuanced solution. Everyone

167 Botanic Garden of International Horticultural Expo, Beijing, 2019. Sketch by Wang Hui; Courtesy of URBANUS

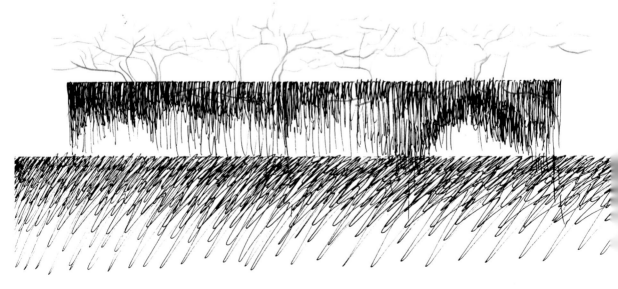

loved it right away. But the developer said, "If you can do all that for the same original fee, go ahead." [Laughs.] So, we do have power to persuade people, but, as I told you, we are not good businessmen. Another architect could simply develop one floor and then repeat the same thing again and again. Financially, that's what would make sense. But we would never do that. For us, finding the urban village analogy was the right approach.

VB: Alberti compared a city to a big house and a house to a small city. Similarly, this project and a number of your other projects evoke typologies of a whole city or a small village. What was your inspiration for that project?

WH: I like this quote by Alberti very much. The topic for both of my master's degrees was how to create a building as a group of buildings. In other words, the idea is to avoid designing a building as a singular object. Back then I was particularly inspired by such projects as Léon Krier's Atlantis Hotel [1986, unbuilt], a building like an island and Aldo Rossi's Quartier Schützenstrasse [1998], a collage-like urban residential block in Berlin. Apart from the fact that these examples are expressed in post-modernist language, I do believe in the idea of architecture as a city or a group of buildings, not a singular mono-lithic object or image. Architecture is a mixture of many things, just like Venturi was advocating in his *Complexity and Contradiction* book for architecture of complexity, vitality, ambiguity, diversity of mean-ings, and coexistence of apparent contradictions.

However, the model for China's urbanization seems to be a city composed of similar buildings without complexity. For example, a huge housing devel-opment typically relies on a very limited number of housing unit types. There are very few proven models that are repeated again and again all over the country. This has resulted in the banality of urban landscape and life. That's why we need to propose creative solutions to restore our cities. That's what our projects try to do – to regenerate urban vitality. Therefore, this idea of imagining a house as a small city is very relevant and that's how we try to approach all our buildings.

VB: I understand that you view Shenzhen development as successful. Could it serve as a model for other parts of China?

WH: Shenzhen is a very atypical Chinese city. It was one of the three original Special Economic Zones (SEZ) that were established in 1979–80 open policy during the transition from a centrally planned system to a socialist market economy. The other two SEZ, Zhuhai and Shantou in Guangdong Province are not as successful as Shenzhen because they are lacking that sort of unprecedented outpouring of in-vestments from all over the country and the world. Shenzhen's entrepreneurial spirit is unique and very attractive to young people. That's why it is very hard to replicate Shenzhen. Whenever we have a project in a less advanced area, we always warn our clients not to mimic Shenzhen superficially. We deeply believe that locality is the key aspect of each project in terms of its social, cultural, and economic dimensions.

VB: Yet, in 2003, you opened your second office in Beijing. Why?

WH: Beijing is both political and cultural capital of China. Coming to Beijing was a strategic move because here we can address many political, cultural, and economic issues. So, we decided to open another office here, as it could present us with opportunities all over the country. Also, all three of us were born and raised here. We want to do something meaning-ful in the city. And Beijing has a better position to reach our missions all over China and hence to better implement our holistic approach toward China's ur-banization. We are not focusing on a particular place. And we want to be challenged by a variety of differ-ent issues. We don't want to specialize in anything. We probably did more different types of buildings than any other independent architectural studio in the country. We deal with different scales and issues. And we don't have our own recognizable architectur-al language.

VB: It is interesting that most of the leading independent architects are also Tsinghua graduates and are based in Beijing, as opposed to other cities. Yet, most of their works are either far from the capital or so small that you

have to look for them. In fact, if you come to Beijing or other parts of China, to look for these projects, they are so hidden that you may miss them entirely. Their production is indeed a subculture. Your work is right in the center and highly visible, right?

WH: Sure, but I would not call us the mainstream. We are also a part of this subculture. What we do is marginal. But you are right, we are not hiding. We try to face all kinds of challenges. We want to be where we are most needed. We have to be responsible and take opportunities. Still, we want to use our opportunities in very different situations and locations. Whenever we go to other places, our clients always expect us to do something that belongs to Tier-1 cities—Beijing, Shanghai, Guangzhou, and Shenzhen. [Laughs.] So, I always try to convince them to do something particular to their own place and situation. I love to study what the third or fourth tier of China's cities should be like, as the levels of urbanization in the country are not equally spread out, and there should be a pragmatic strategy to achieve a good balance between the ambition of the development and the affordability of investment.

VB: Could you give an example?

WH: Let's take a look at our Tangshan Urban Planning Museum and Park built in Tangshan, Hebei Province in 2008. In 1976, Tangshan suffered a devastating earthquake. Hundreds of thousands of people died and 85% of buildings were destroyed. When we were asked to design that planning museum, the city told us to clear the site first. But our idea was to preserve the old flour mill structures that were left there. The original four warehouses were built during the Second World War and two more were added after the earthquake. In recent years, the urbanization movement in Tangshan has been as devastating as the 1976 earthquake itself, as it has eradicated the city's architectural and therefore tangible history. Taking the advantage of transforming this group of buildings into a new urban planning museum, our idea was to preserve that little history of the place that was left. We introduced something fresh, but not terribly shocking, and definitely not from scratch. So, the existing buildings were recycled as showrooms

to house the presentation of new designs for the new city. This is a clear statement–to emphasize visually that the new respects the old. Another appropriate example would be my teaching assignments at Tsinghua. Dealing with the issue that such a big city like Beijing is becoming less and less affordable for young professionals, I asked my students to repurpose an existing bus terminal site in downtown area into a miniature city for the youth. I am interested in these research topics because they could influence real policies. When you have case studies you can present them to the authorities and, sometimes, a study may become a real project. It is important to work on ideas that may seem utopian, but that could be turned into reality, if they have real potential. To us cities are not just abstractions, they are very real. Architects should exercise real visions. Today, young architects have to be very active. They need to look for opportunities in real life much more than we did because our generation enjoyed so much development, we didn't have to look for work. It was everywhere. We simply had to make a choice between working on either good projects or bad projects. But my students' future is totally different as they will live in the world without the pressure to keep adding more and more buildings. So, what I want to teach them is how to propose projects that could address social issues and present useful, interesting, and valuable typologies to resolve them. Architecture is always necessary. I believe every generation has a responsibility to design a better life. I am optimistic– every generation has its own mission.

VB: Speaking of your Dalian Art Museum built in 2008, you said, "The biggest deficiency of contemporary architecture is that it has become the antithesis of the landscape." In that project you achieved an unusual unity between architecture and landscape. Then in 2010, you explored a similar idea, but on a much grander scale in your Beijing CBD Core Area Urban Plan and Building design. Could you talk about this idea of architecture as landscape?

WH: Yes, in some of the projects you can find this tendency–to merge architecture and landscape. But in the case of the Dalian Art Museum, the site

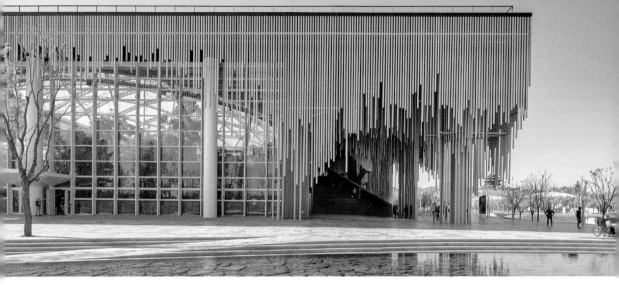

168 Botanic Garden of International Horticultural Expo, Beijing, 2019. Courtesy of URBANUS

is entirely new and flat. In fact, it is a landfill. So, the idea there was to create something very artificial. I mentioned before the need for something eye-catching. That's all. It was about folding a building into this artificial landscape because there is nothing natural in that entire area and the only thing that could be identified with something natural was to design a building that would behave as if it were a landscape, a small gesture to bring something lively there. But in the Beijing CBD project the idea was much more determined–to bring architecture and landscape into a single entity and to propose a different kind of urban setting on a grand urban scale. The project was about re-defining the street blocks with skyscrapers; to propose an alternative model to a generic grid layout of urban high-rises. We tried to reimagine a mixed-use urban complex, a new kind of city for the future. We collaborated with experts on infrastructure services, traffic interchanges, landscape design, urban management, and sustainable development. We attempted to bring singular skyscrapers into a whole system of ground-level circulation, and underground spaces. Imagine, buildings' podiums would form a whole network of urban public infrastructure system! So, we are talking about entirely artificial, humanmade landscape merging with the city. Unfortunately, our, perhaps utopian vision, was not realized.

VB: The CBD is dominated by Rem Koolhaas's CCTV building [001]. What is your view of it?

WH: Although it looks like a weird building, I would say that this may be the most important building built in China in recent decades. It was designed by a foreigner who, I think, understands China better than any Chinese. He reads Chinese leaders' and people's minds very well. That was a very particular time in history when the country's place in the new world history was to be redefined. Koolhaas had to make a decision between two important competition invitations: CCTV and the redevelopment of the World Trade Center in New York. He selected the CCTV competition as he believed that China was on the ascending track. What he came up with is a building with a spiral circulation, which meant to turn a government-controlled propaganda institution into a space of open urban promenade in the shape of a vertical loop. Such a program was arbitrarily invented by the architect. It was not given to him by the client. However, such a delirious idea was accepted both by

169 Holy Fire Lit Place for the Second China National Youth Games 2019, Ruicheng, Shanxi Province, 2019
© Tianpei Zeng; Courtesy of URBANUS

the government and the public. It was celebrated and promoted. This could only happen at that moment in history. It was the time when the country wanted to assert a new image of openness that would be recognized by the West. So, CCTV is an iconic building in terms of an image of new open China. It is not an icon simply for the sake of being iconic. Many architects have entered that competition with creditable buildings, but Koolhaas presented a meaning of a building. Although it does not represent the zeitgeist, it fulfilled an illusion of what the Chinese government and this entire country wanted upon that moment in history. So, my admiration for CCTV is not based on how successfully it works as a building, but how important architecture has become in China.

VB: What you are saying is that this building has a great potential, which one day may be fulfilled. It is a kind of spiritual object because it is promising something that may still happen. It is a building for the future. Yet, today, you can't even come close to it because of the security, so it is seen only as an image. Also, the building became a closure of his own iconic period in his career, as he reached a certain limitation on the iconic, achieving perhaps the most iconic image that architecture could offer. He topped his mission of designing the

most original, as opposed to merely the tallest building in Beijing. And by doing that he lost interest in doing that ever again. He sensed that such opportunity would never present itself again, anyway. So, his mission was fulfilled, and new chapters of his career would then follow–generic, preservation, countryside, and so on.

WH: Absolutely. CCTV was a perfect situation for using an ultimate icon in the iconic period. But iconic is not simply about form making. Any student can do an interesting form. But a good icon is always about its time and place. It was a totally new image, without any burden of history to attract public attention and to galvanize public support. It was very particular for that moment–not a hutong, not the Forbidden City, not Tiananmen Square, not the tallest tower, but a modern and open loop. Peter Eisenman would argue that his proposed skyscraper for Berlin [Max Reinhardt Haus, 1992, project] was also a vertical loop. But that was a formal exercise, while CCTV became an icon with an appropriate identity.

VB: Yet, interestingly enough, both projects were shaped by ideals and forces that are quite independent of their internal functions. Koolhaas must be an important figure for you, as a number of projects designed by URBANUS evoke OMA's ideas. For example, their Louisville Museum Plaza seems to inspire some of your mixed-use projects. I already compared your firm to SOM of China, but perhaps, more appropriately, URBANUS could be associated as the OMA of China. You also collaborated with OMA on Shenzhen Central Plaza competition that you won as a team. What do you think about that?

WH: Although OMA's methodology has lots of influences on us, and our Shenzhen office has collaborated with them on some projects, I would not draw a definitive conclusion that we are the OMA of China. We have dissimilar approaches and very different status standings. The scope of our works is quite different, as our projects are more about everyday struggle to pursue certain urban scenarios. But OMA, let's face it, is one of the top starchitects. They are invited to undertake high profile landmark commissions. Also, we have totally different scales of humanpower and project resources. I think each office is unique and our designs are characterized by our respective leaders. Drawing any parallels here is just an illusion.

VB: How would you describe a good city or a building?

WH: You have to have tolerance. You know, cities and buildings are not designed, they are used. They are developed by the usage. Design is only the birth of the building. A building is not just about a sleek image. The media often cares about a single photogenic, Instagramable image on the screen, something that's perfectly balanced and close to perfection. But I think a good building is something that can absorb changes and transform into something new in the future. It is important for others to add their own scenarios as well. That's what I think good architecture is.

VB: What would you say about the state of architecture in China right now and what are your main concerns in architecture today?

WH: Diversity is my big concern. Although China has plenty of good practices, to come across strong personal identity is still rare. Just a decade ago, if you showed me ten buildings and asked me to identify leading architects behind them, I would say that it could be anyone. But now, when I see Chinese projects published, I can tell who the architect is. I think this is a good sign of maturity of China's architectural practice. Now we have quite a few good architects who have their unique identities, even signatures. I think achieving unique qualities of individual architecture is a good thing rather than anonymity, which makes cities and urban experience very similar. I think China should look for good examples in other countries. Look at Japan, for example, where there are so many unique architects. What I think contributed to that were such major events as the Olympics in 1964 and 1972, and the World Expo in 1970. These major events gave Japanese architects of that generation opportunities to express their dreams. That's what produced such creative architects as

170 Holy Fire Lit Place for the Second China National Youth Games 2019, Ruicheng, Shanxi Province, 2019
© Baiqiang Cao; Courtesy of URBANUS

171 Holy Fire Lit Place for the Second China National Youth Games 2019, Ruicheng, Shanxi Province, 2019
© Tianpei Zeng; Courtesy of URBANUS

Kenzo Tange, Kisho Kurokawa, Arata Isozaki, and the subsequent generations of architects.

VB: Kengo Kuma told me that visiting Tange's Olympic structures sparked his dream of becoming an architect. And similarly, China had its own Olympics and World Expo, right?

WH: You are right, but, unfortunately, the most important projects such as the Bird's Nest, Watercube, or the Capital Airport were all awarded to foreign designers. Nonetheless, it is good to have great examples by the best architects in the world in your hometown. Our design institutes received invaluable experience because all of those projects were drawn by Chinese architects working at the Local Design Institutes. These designers are now much more skilled. So, the most important thing for our architects now is to achieve their own identities. We talked about solving social issues before. Of course, that's very important. But now we also have to look at the next step: How do we develop diversity and unique architectural languages, rather than finding solutions with generic answers. How do we contribute to the body of knowledge of world architecture? You know, the ultimate goal for any architect is to achieve a place in history. And to do that you need to have a unique language that cannot be imagined or even replicated by others. And it is important not only to express individual qualities, but also regional ones. If you look at the work in South America, for example, you immediately recognize that. And it is not simply traditional, it is very modern. Yet, it is not placeless. They use the same concrete, but we know that it is their concrete.

VB: Some of the key venues for the 2022 Beijing Winter Olympics were designed by local architects. And your own pavilion for the 2019 Beijing International Horticultural Expo, also makes a strong case that Chinese architects will have more chances to exercise their visions.

WH: Indeed, there are some good signs that our government will trust our own designers in commissioning them prestigious projects that used to be given to foreigners. And in fact, the 2019 Horticultural Expo employed Chinese architects for the design of the master plan and all important pavilions. With the fortune of designing the Botanic Garden Pavilion, I received the experience of a world class challenge. I think similar opportunities will encourage my fellow Chinese architects to jump out of the trap of daily chores to work on elaborating their personal language, while thinking both locally and globally.

DONG Gong
VECTOR ARCHITECTS

Beijing-based DONG Gong's (b. 1972, Beijing) path to becoming a practicing architect was long and consequential. The idea to study architecture at China's top school, Tsinghua University in his hometown was the suggestion of his parents, engineering professors, both teaching at Tsinghua. He admits that he practically grew up on campus. After receiving his bachelor's in 1994, Dong taught for two years at his alma mater and then proceeded to earn his master's there from 1996 to 1999. He told me that architects of his generation are remarkably ambitious and even obsessed about achieving relevance and success. So, there is no surprise that Dong then went for another Master of Architecture at the University of Illinois at Urbana-Champaign, which he acquired in 2001. He stayed in the U.S. to get a solid experience from some of the top American practices: SCB in Chicago and at the offices of Richard Meier and Steven Holl in New York. He returned to China in 2008 to establish his atelier, Vector Architects in Beijing. Dong's work is very special, it has a great range–it is quite mature and both familiar and exotic. Yet, Dong's projects are not easily achieved, as he readily admits that architecture is a struggle for him. The architect's most renowned built works include the Seashore Chapel (2015), the Seashore Library (2015), and the Seashore Restaurant (2018), the trilogy of small, strikingly beautiful structures within a short walk from each other. Collectively, they have gained an iconic identity to the Aranya Community in the Beidaihe District, a popular beach resort in Qinhuangdao on China's Bohai Sea coast. His Yangshuo Sugar House Hotel (2017), a resort complex on the Li River near Guilin has become a reference model for many architects on how to find harmony in coexistence of architecture that appears to be archaic and authentic on the one hand and sleek and contemporary, on the other. The following interview was recorded during our initial meeting at Dong Gong's studio in Beijing and expanded based on two subsequent conversations, both in person and over Skype.

I BELIEVE IN QUESTIONS THAT ARE ETERNAL

In conversation with **DONG Gong** of Vector Architects, Beijing
Vector Architects' studio in Beijing, December 11, 2018, September 29, 2019 & November 30, 2019

Vladimir Belogolovsky: Could you talk about some of now well-known architects who studied with you at Tsinghua University? I think this would provide an important background to the current architectural scene in China.

Dong Gong: I studied in parallel classes with Hua Li of TAO during my undergraduate studies and one year under Zhang Ke of ZAO/standardarchitecture. Li Hu of Open Architecture was two years behind. Xu Tiantian of DnA was three years behind me. And Wang Hui, one of the three partners of URBANUS was four years ahead of me. All of us interacted and our studies overlapped. For example, we all took a painting class, in which our professor combined the best students from different years. So, there were many opportunities for our interaction. I think it was a very intense period of about six or seven years at Tsinghua, where many students have grown into very strong architects. There are now quite a few very good architects who were trained at Tsinghua during that time. And for sure, we all influenced each other. There was a strong urge to become good architects, and if you look at the younger architects that came into practice since that period, they don't stand out as much. For whatever reason that moment of forging talented architects is gone. I think the mindset then was very different from today. The main goal then for us was to become very good architects and to be recognized in our time. We were very ambitious, selfish, and trying hard to become successful. Now not all students aim at being strong practicing architects. The situation is more diverse. Some want to go into development, others into teaching. There is less focus on the success as a practicing architect, unlike in the early 1990s. There was a lot of pressure to succeed. Now the focus is dispersed.

172 DONG Gong. Courtesy of Vector Architects

VB: Speaking of the most profound influence on you as an architect you mentioned your professor at the University of Illinois, Henry Plummer. Could you talk about his influence, especially regarding your fascination with natural light and ways of capturing it?

DG: Plummer wrote about natural light as a fundamental element of architecture. I have one of his books, a special issue of *A+U* on the poetics of light in Japanese architecture. I always keep this book on my desk. He discussed with me the phenomenon of light as something ephemeral and metaphysical. Yet, light can decisively impact the way buildings are experienced. He talked about daylight as an inexhaustible source of miracles. He is an educator,

173 Seashore Library, Aranya, Qinghuangdao, Hebei Province, 2015 © Shengliang Su

writer, and photographer. I took his design studio in my first year and he was my thesis advisor in the second year. He taught me things that are hard to put into words, such as the importance of ambiance and atmosphere. You can never handle light by itself, without considering such aspects as weight, gravity, air, materiality, texture, transparency, and so on. I never heard of this kind of approach to architecture before. At Tsinghua, we were preoccupied with composing very physical and concrete forms, and spaces where programs and circulation were more important. We were learning more about engineering of architecture and less about its artistic dimension. I graduated from Tsinghua and I could immediately go into practice. But was I ready? Now I understand the difference and I appreciate what I learned from Plummer. It was the first time I discovered ambiance, atmosphere, and intangibles, metaphysics. It became a new window for me. Form and appearance became secondary. I try to discover the most inner dimension of architecture. I was also an exchange student in Munich and Plummer gave me a whole list of buildings to visit specifically to better understand the quality of light. These were not just modern buildings, but also historical structures such as churches and train stations. He introduced me to such texts as by Juhani Pallasmaa who helped me to understand architecture on a phenomenological level as a kind of environmental psychology.

VB: You mentioned that you were teaching about light at Tsinghua. Could you talk about that?

DG: Light is a multifaceted phenomenon. When I had a chance to teach, I focused on light immediately and I literally translated Plummer's teachings into Chinese. But in my second year of teaching, I started personalizing this course. I brought examples from Chinese history rather than universal cases. I wanted to be more specific and contextual about the qualities of light. And recently, I was invited to teach about light at Illinois. So, we keep in touch with Plummer.

VB: Apart from your discoveries and experiments with the sunlight, where do you derive your inspirations from?

DG: Light is very important. Anything I draw I start by capturing light first. Then it is mostly about testing ideas. I don't get distracted with inspirations. It is really about being together with yourself. When I am not designing, I am spending a lot of time with artists, visiting exhibitions, traveling. But during the design process it is very intense. It is very personal, and I don't want to discuss it or talk about it to anyone. This process is felt not only in my brain but in my entire body.

VB: You said, "Architecture is neither the beginning nor the end. Instead, it is a medium,

a medium to connect and reveal." Could you elaborate on that?

DG: It is easy to think about architecture, as a result of creating physical objects. But, in a way, there is no end in architecture. You cannot finish architecture. Architects are not capable of that. Architecture will keep growing by itself–it will age, change use, and so on. Architecture never simply reveals itself, something else is always reveled through it. The most powerful architecture is not about itself, but what you can see through it or what you can observe. What does space allow you to see? What can space connect you to? The spirit, the power, it should be felt. The meaning of architecture should not be described by scholars or architects, but it should be felt by people. Space has the power to connect people.

VB: You started your practice just a little over a decade ago, but already you have accumulated a diverse body of work. Could you go over this experience and how would you define your current focus?

DG: The first few years were about digesting what I learned at school and professional practice, mostly in New York at the offices of Richard Meier and Steven Holl. It was all about grasping the right scale, choosing the right materials, forms. Now I am asking deeper questions and I try to stretch my abilities to create architecture. So, every day I feel more and more challenging. I pay a lot of attention to architects such as Alvaro Siza and Eduardo Souto de Moura whose works are wrapped in many layers of deep architectural thinking. I particularly like the aura of Souto de Moura's works. I also like how he tries to break away from the influence of his mentor and friend Siza. He is not relying on any formulas or easy effects. He is not about pleasing anyone. He embraces the heritage, but still wants to be independent and go further. I am intrigued by both their similarities and contradictions. I enjoy the process. Architecture is a struggle; I am struggling. I don't have confidence to say that my work is progressing but for sure it will be different. I can promise you

174 Vector Architects, Seashore Chapel, Aranya, Qinhuangdao, Hebei Province, 2015 © Chen Hao

175 Yangshuo Sugar House Hotel on the Li River near Guilin, 2017 © Chen Hao

that. I am trying to engage with deeper layers of architectural thinking and culture. I want to throw away what I know well. I want to engage with something new and different. I am not interested in doing what I have done before. I know one thing—it takes me more time to do a conceptual design than before. I want to discover new territories, otherwise, what's the point? To me architecture is not about producing, not about productivity. Being too comfortable and sure of what you do is dangerous. I think artists do their best work when they are searching, when they are struggling.

VB: Could you summarize what your architecture is about?

DG: It is actually quite hard because I feel that my work keeps changing. My understanding and interpretations of architecture are changing. What is the ultimate goal? Is it a personal expression of an artist or is it about giving back something to the people who will ultimately occupy your spaces?

VB: Did you solve this dilemma for yourself? Do you treat architecture more as an artform or a tool to respond to society's pragmatic needs?

DG: More and more I am becoming convinced that there is no contradiction between these two. Before, I had to find my place between these two extreme positions—being an artist by focusing on my own agenda and addressing the needs of the clients and users. Now I feel that first, you need to be a good architect.

You need to be confident in your knowledge and experience. But then you need to realize that the only way to achieve high-level architecture is by taking it very personally and emotionally. Architecture should be treated as art. An artist by definition has a social value because of what she or he brings to the society. An architect has a responsibility, but he has to elevate his work to the level of art. Of course, many people criticize this position. But that is what I believe in. Because the only way to be able to communicate with the society and universe is to be true to yourself. Architecture can be very superficial if you simply address all the immediate needs and pragmatics.

VB: You compare your design process to a chemical reaction. What are the key ingredients that you rely on from project to project?

DG: Every project is a painful process to me. Because when you just start there are so many unknowns: you don't know enough about the site, program, and you don't have enough imagination about the potential spatial qualities. So, it is bits and pieces of issues that are in front of you. For me the only way to find a solution is to spend time by sketching and modeling one option after another. There is no shortcut for this. I have to spend at least four to eight weeks warming up. I never had a project when I would come up with a satisfying solution after just one week of work.

VB: I am going over your works and the works of some other leading Chinese architects,

and what I see is that collectively, you pursue very similar notions in very similar ways, especially, when it comes to focusing on projects in the countryside, using traditional materials, interacting with history, and capturing light. Some critics even tend to describe these attitudes as a singular approach called "pragmatic regionalism." Do you see this attempt in Chinese architects to align with each other? What do you think about this observation?

DG: Interesting. I agree that there is a certain Chinese canon. Yet, I try to resist putting my so-called "Chinese-ness" on display. So many Chinese architects develop a particular Chinese way of designing their buildings. I am against that. I think culture is important, but it should not be translated literally. I want to discover who I am. I don't want to scream about the fact that I am Chinese. That is clear. I want to reveal what is not clear. We are often criticized for being anonymous and not local or regional. So, I am not aligned, and I don't think there is a group that I would want to be aligned with. This has to do with Chinese culture and how the Chinese treat authorities. There is an obedience of certain rules and ways of doing things. There is no protest or will for reinvention. Not enough. We don't have a natural confrontation between generations the way you have in the West. If you are just one year older, I will tend to respect you just for that. There is a strong culture for regarding established traditions. It is unusual to question things. That's true.

VB: Yet, there is a clear emergence of a unique architectural identity here that features very common regional characteristics. Interestingly, this new architecture is quite different from both traditional Chinese architecture and from contemporary architecture in the West where most of the leading independent Chinese architects were trained. The result here is a kind of fusion. Do you see its roots?

DG: Clearly, it was the Cultural Revolution here that disconnected us from history. We cut all the roots. The last 20 years we are preoccupied with rediscovering our own history. We don't have a burden of history, in a way. And what you also have to consider

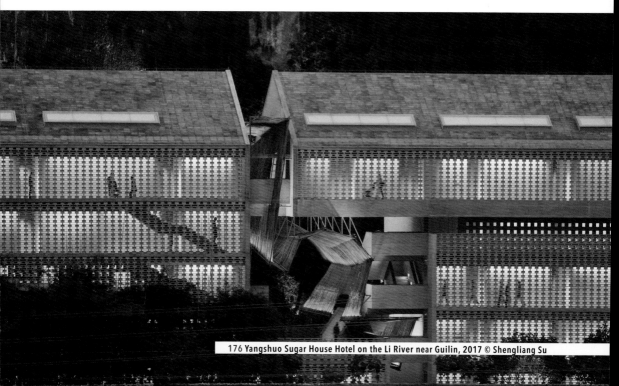

176 Yangshuo Sugar House Hotel on the Li River near Guilin, 2017 © Shengliang Su

177 Yangshuo Sugar House Hotel on the Li River near Guilin, 2017 © Shengliang Su

is the fact that we have many more opportunities for construction here than in the West.

VB: Your Seashore Chapel project seems so simple. Is this simplicity deceptive?

DG: Yes, it was very hard to achieve. We did three distinctly different schemes–complete with many sketches and models. But usually, after these many weeks of struggling there is a moment when all questions and issues dissipate, and one particular design emerges. When that happens, that's what I call that chemical reaction. Then I know that I found my solution. This has become a standard process for me. When this happens, you know–from now on, this is the direction. And then my team joins me to test more minor variations.

VB: I see this chapel as a very poetic, almost living and breathing thing, the kind of creature that, for example, John Hejduk could have designed. What happens when the water level rises?

DG: It turns into a boat. It intrigues me. It may have to do with the religious experience. It is not just an object, absolutely. It is anchored to the ground in one moment and it gets loose and liberated in another. The chapel is facing Bohai Bay where the level of water does not fluctuate much. But in summertime, the water comes to the lower half of the columns. I like to think of it as a vessel.

VB: The scale of your works tends to be small.

Building types seem to be limited, so far, to a particular range: small hotels, libraries, community centers, sales offices, showrooms, an elementary school, and a chapel, among others. How do you see the mission of your practice? What do you focus on?

DG: Here in China, there is one building type that I purposely avoid working on and that is a multistory apartment building. That is because these buildings are not defined by architects, but instead, are shaped by market forces that are set by developers. These high-rises are not designed for a great living environment but simply provide a commercial product. So, besides that, I am willing to do anything. But unfortunately, the building types you just mentioned were not chosen by us. The truth is that my office, and other similar independent practices, don't have too many chances to work on bigger scale public projects because most of that work is taken by the huge system of Local Design Institutes. Only by accumulating a number of small projects it is possible to increase the scale and variety of projects. This is a gradual path. The more architects become known the more chances they get to be invited to work on bigger projects. So, I can predict that in the next few years we will see an increase of scale for avant-garde Chinese architects.

VB: I stayed at your Yangshuo Sugar House Hotel. Unquestionably, it is a seductively beautiful place. But to me the result is

234

somewhat ambiguous about what was there before and what was added. The whole place seems to be frozen in time and it is not clear whether the time is in the past or present. There seems to be a lack of tension between the old and the new. Disagree?

DG: I like the word "ambiguous." For me the ultimate design goal of this architectural intervention was to pursue an atmospheric harmony with the existing industrial structures, as well as the surrounding characteristic karst peaks and the Li River. I think of all of them together, as a new place, not frozen in time. There were two conditions: the natural beauty of the site, very sublime, almost too perfect to even touch; and the second – the existing industrial building. It had a very strong character on its own.

In terms of program the new structures had to bring about 13,000 square meters of space, while the existing was less than a quarter of that. That's why I didn't want it to be overwhelming. So, let me take your criticism for being ambiguous by not distinguishing clearly what is new and what is old, as a compliment. [Laughs.] It was actually very difficult to achieve because I didn't want to just copy anything. What I did, I connected various pieces and complimented them. There is no competition between the old and the new.

VB: Would you say that this intention of erasing the distinctions between the old and the new is the main motive in this project?

DG: Yes, the main issue was all about how to bring together the old and the new. I went through several very different masterplan strategies. The one that was ultimately chosen was the humblest, most appropriate, and, in my opinion, most successful. It was clear that we had to use similar geometry, tectonics, and materiality to create the right balance and harmony. The decision to keep the original structures was made by the client, two brothers. The original sugar mill complex was built on the Li River in late 1960s and by early 1980s it was already abandoned due to the government's new policy to protect rivers from industrial usage. This site is also right next to a major road, so when these two brothers saw it a few years ago by chance they liked its cathedral-like silhouette.

That's how their initial interest was sparked–by the quality of the old building.

VB: Interestingly, every evening there was a film screening. When I asked for the program, I was told that there was just one film–Andrey Tarkovsky's *Nostalgia*. The final scene in the film has a famous image inside of the ruined and partially flooded cathedral, which seems to be a strong reference to your hotel's preserved sugar cane loading dock with a swimming pool in the middle. Did the inspiration come from the film?

DG: Absolutely! This is the image that the elder brother brought to the project. He studied at the Beijing Academy of Film and it is his favorite work. So, for him, that final scene from the film is like a spiritual icon for the entire project. That was in fact the reason for buying the site in the first place, as he fell in love with that frame of the loading dock. So, this became an important reference for me as well. I always appreciate when clients share their intentions and even visions with me. I like working with such clients because I don't need to try completely different schemes.

VB: Many of your projects fall into the category of adaptive reuse. Do you have a particular position toward these renovation projects? Do you see them differently from your ground up buildings?

DG: Here in China, we have a unique situation and that is the pressure of building many new buildings in a very short period of time. That means that until recently very little attention was payed to the existing buildings. It was easier and cheaper to take old structures down and replace them with the new ones. This attitude has changed over the last decade. Now the society raises many questions about historical buildings. We suddenly realized that not many are left. For me personally, whether I design a building from scratch or incorporate an existing structure, I would not say if it makes a fundamental difference on how I approach the design. My approach is rooted in a particular condition. If I have an existing building in front of me, I examine it first. If I have to build a new building, I examine the local condition before making my decision. My architecture is specific and responsive. Of course, technically, my responses will be very different, but not from the design strategy point of view.

VB: You just said that the attitude toward preserving older buildings is a recent phenomenon in China, barely a decade old. Was there a particular project, demolition, or other events that made an effect on this shift?

DG: It happened gradually. I wouldn't emphasize one particular building or event. It became very clear to many people that we have gone too far with the new developments that were built right over the preexisting ones. For too long our people valued the brand new over the old, no matter how unique. That attitude led to the loss of too many important historical buildings. Over the last decade, finally, we have realized that we have been losing our history and

178 Captain's House, Fuzhou, Fujian Province, 2017
Sketch by Dong Gong. Courtesy by Vector Architects

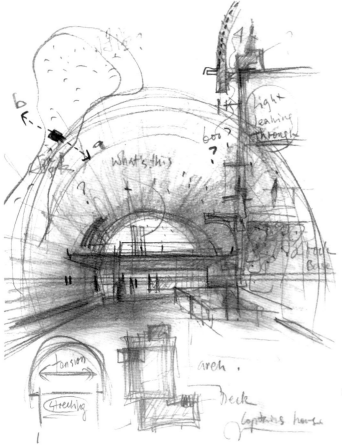

roots. So many new cities were built from scratch or in place of historical neighborhoods that were completely erased.

VB: Are there any limitations that Chinese architects have to deal with when working on historical projects?

DG: Let me mention one relevant story. Before the founding of the People's Republic of China 70 years ago, Beijing used to have an ancient inner-city wall where the second city ring road is situated today. Liang Sicheng, the Father of Modern Chinese architecture was particularly known for his interest in preserving historical architecture. He had a talk with Chairman Mao about his proposal to take new administrative center for government buildings outside of the historical center and he wanted to preserve most of the center and the wall. He also proposed to turn the top of the wall into an elevated public park. Every time I recall this story, I think about the High Line Park in New York that made an effect on so many cities around the world. Imagine, we could have built it decades before, but we failed to recognize the unique qualities of the structures that we had and lost since then. Through the process of modernizing Beijing from the imperial city to the contemporary metropolis it has become today, so much has been lost. So, over the years, there were so many unfortunate demolitions that it is hard to pinpoint any one, which is more important than others, but it is all these cases combined that finally, about a decade ago, raised the awareness of so many people who realized enough is enough. They understood that these barbaric demolitions must stop.

VB: What do you think about Wang Shu's Ningbo History Museum [020] where he used reclaimed bricks and tiles on the building's facade? It was finished precisely ten years ago. Did his building play a certain role in this sudden revelation about the significance of history?

DG: As far as the role of Wang Shu, yes, it is very critical. But the important thing for him was in preserving a historical atmosphere, the value of older buildings, and their emotional impact. Yet, it is not about preserving a specific building or site in a literal sense. In Ningbo, he used bricks and tiles recycled from buildings demolished in the area. He brought the awareness of the issue, but the idea was not to save a particular building. He also did it in a very poetic and beautiful way, so it is very persuasive. You don't need to be a specialist to appreciate the beauty of his work. But our work is very different, we deal with specific conditions head on, whether related to preservation or not.

179 Captain's House, Fuzhou, Fujian Province, 2017 © Chen Hao

VB: So many buildings in China are not landmarked or protected. Are there any particular regulations that architects need to observe? Who decides on whether certain historical buildings should stay or be demolished?

DG: Everything is very specific. In China, we have a code that tells you whether something is landmarked. If a particular building is classified as a landmark, then it is the law. But in most cases buildings are not protected and then it is up to the client. And in that case, the role of an architect is very important because for the most part, the client will listen to what the architect may suggest.

VB: How do you see historical buildings in your work, is it a kind of foundation for expressing your own ideas? There is never a literal preservation, always an opportunity to add something entirely new, right?

DG: Pure preservation projects are typically done by LDIs that specialize in that type of work. For us it is more about evolution than preservation. It is always clear that there is a new life in the old building.

VB: What is a good building for you?

DG: A good building should provide a feeling of intimacy. No matter how gorgeous a building may be, if you don't feel being a part of it, it is very cold. And within this intimacy some space should be left to allow for a kind of spiritual connection to the place. If that balance is achieved, for me that is a good building. It is important not to go too far and not to turn a building into a spectacle. Two examples that immediately come to mind are the Pantheon in Rome and the Kunsthaus Bregenz in Austria by Peter Zumthor. They were built in different times, but I don't think

that matters. Architecture needs to deal with the limitations of technology of its time. I think the important question is this: What is the problem? I believe in questions that are eternal. I believe the issues we need to address are fundamental–it is about our body, scale, physical limitations, and senses. Look at all the changes around us. Our way of life changed so much over time, but our body is still basically the same. So, there are some constant values that don't change. There are certain permanent relations of our body to the outside world. You always have to answer these questions: How do you live? What makes us human? What is the relationship between the human and the world around us? When I go to spaces that resonate with me, it seems that I can talk to the architect in person. The message is there. To create a good building means to consider many issues, many intangibles.

VB: What words would you use to describe your architecture?

DG: Boundary–beyond boundary. Limitation–beyond limitation. Dark – light. Time and timeless. Weight and weightless. I am intrigued by such paradoxical opposites. This is what ultimately humanity is about. But I get lost when I am looking for the right words. Feelings are very imprecise.

ZHANG Ke
ZAO/STANDARDARCHITECTURE

Beijing-based architect ZHANG Ke (b. 1970, Beijing) started his education at Tsinghua University and then became the first Chinese student to be accepted to Harvard's GSD in recent years, graduating in 1998. While Tsinghua equipped Zhang with technical know-how, Harvard encouraged him to raise questions, such as why we build in the first place. After working for three years in Boston and New York, he returned to Beijing to open his practice, ZAO/standardarchitecture in 2001. Naming one's practice standardarchitecture in a single word hints that Zhang's architecture is anything but standard. With every project the architect revisits the fundamentals. Zhang represents a new generation of ambitious independent Chinese architects who spent years abroad, mainly in the U.S. Along with other independent architects, he has been reexamining both traditional ways of building in China and contemporary visions that were imposed on major Chinese cities by Western architects and planners. Understandably, his works tend to be on a small scale, and he stays away from challenging local builders using foreign materials and techniques. He deals with what is possible, and he finds pleasure in it. Yet, being rooted in history does not mean to be grounded. One of Zhang's most intriguing projects is Micro Hutong built in the center of Beijing in 2013. It occupies a rectangular plot of mere 70 square meters that the architect divided into two equal rectangles–a gallery/living room space at the front and shared live/workspace, arranged around a courtyard, in the back. The courtyard part is a kind of micro-urban model where tiny rooms–a study, bedroom, teahouse, and toilet–are expressed as separate volumes, suspended at various heights over the courtyard. The place recalls a playground for kids and excludes anyone who is unfit or too big to pass through tight corridors, doorways, or climb ladders. The project is not a real house, but a provocative idea for shared living that could function as an artist residence, hostel, or dormitory unit. Other well-known built works–all in Linzhi, Tibet–include the Niang'ou Boat Terminal (2013), the Yarluntzangbu Boat Terminal (2008), the Niyang River Visitor Centre (2008), and the Namcha Barwa Visitor Centre (2008).

IS A NEW REVOLUTION POSSIBLE TODAY?

In conversation with **ZHANG Ke** of ZAO/standardarchitecture, Beijing
ZAO/standardarchitecture studio in Beijing, December 20, 2018

Vladimir Belogolovsky: Let me start with the name of your practice, ZAO/standardarchitecture. Could you say a few words about it?

Zhang Ke: ZAO stands for Zhang Architectural Office. In Chinese zao means to build, to make, to put things together. It is also the last character of "标 (Biao) 准 (Zhun) 营 (Ying) 造 (Zao)," the Chinese translation of standardarchitecture.

VB: And stadardarchitecture is all written in lowercase letters in one word.

ZK: Just by writing it in such an unusual way we wanted to underline the fact that our architecture is not standard at all. And the other thing, I wanted to emphasize was that it is our own work that becomes the standard for us. With every project we revisit the fundamentals. So, there are no standards, no stereotypes. We put together two words to create a new one–standardarchitecture. We are very ambitious, we want to be the standard ourselves, for ourselves, and, hopefully, for others as well, every time, with every project.

VB: I read this on your website, "Although standardarchitecture's built works often take exceptionally provocative visual results, their buildings and landscapes are always rooted in the historical and cultural settings with a degree of intellectual debate." Does this mean that with every project you tend to make a particular point?

ZK: Definitely. Just think about it—every year millions of buildings are being built all over the world. We could just build our share of so many of these expedient things. But I think it is important to inquire this: What is the essence of building in our time? We

180 ZHANG Ke © ZAO/standardarchitecture

raise questions. We try to provoke and inspire people with our architecture.

VB: That's how you see the mission of your practice–to provoke and inspire.

ZK: Of course! For example, one of the questions that we raise is about our attitude toward heritage. What is our interpretation of history? For us it is important to come up with unambiguously contemporary solution. And each time the solution must be our own. So many architects copy what they have seen published. But for us architecture is not about copying, it is about thinking. Can we investigate our roots and reconnect them to our own contemporary culture?

VB: What I find very attractive in your work is that there is both: there is this connection to the roots, meaning history, and there is this striking contemporaneity that is not passive but very active.

ZK: I think the work should be active and it may be striking. But my question is: Is there anything behind it? I try to push this first impression further. I am interested in achieving sensual qualities. I want to go beyond the visual effects. Architecture should be intelligent, and we should ask such questions as: How can we relate to the place where we build? How can we address the local community and all people that will use our buildings? Is it possible to be innovative and inventive, and yet, respective of history when dealing with historical buildings? I say all of these are possible. We need overlaps of histories, programs, materials, spaces; this is where we will discover many new possibilities. That's what

181 Great Wall Watch House, Outside of Beijing (project)
Sketch by Zhang Ke. Courtesy by ZAO/standardarchitecture

architecture is about–discovering, reinterpreting, and inventing new possibilities.

VB: A couple of years ago you had an exhibition at Aedes in Berlin called "Contemplating with the Basics." What was the main idea for that show and why did you choose such a basic title?

ZK: We exhibited several of our projects, in which we combined living and working models. We contemplated what is possible. I think that every new generation of architects needs to revisit this very basic question about architecture: Why do we build? Of course, we need housing, offices, cultural buildings, infrastructure. But beyond that, how do we mark our time? By asking these fundamental questions we will achieve different results and enrich architecture. Bauhaus architecture was a great revolution against historical styles. Architects then needed to create a radical shift to reflect on the revolution in their own technological age of the machine. Is a new revolution possible today?

VB: In your advice to young architects you said that it is never too early to start your own practice. You yourself graduated from Harvard's GSD in 1998 and opened your office here in Beijing in 2001. Who did you work for in those in-between three years, and was that experience enough for you to strike on your own?

ZK: Yes, because you can never be ready. I think 30 is a good age to start your own independent, alternative studio; definitely before you settle down with a family life. This is what I am telling all my talented students. [Laughs.] I worked at various places: a bit in Boston, in New York for a big commercial firm, and then for a small studio in SoHo. And in my last year there I worked part-time, so I could start my own practice. This is when I won my very first competition in Beijing, a conservation project to preserve the last remaining fragment of Ming dynasty city wall as part of an urban park.

VB: You said that while studying at Harvard what you learned most is to doubt everything you are told and look for your own ways and solutions. Could you talk about that?

ZK: What this refers to is about being always subconscious of what we do and whether it is relative to our time. We were taught about what was done in the past, but now I am much more interested in what my contemporaries are doing. I studied for eight years at Tsinghua before GSD. There was little information exchange at the time, and we were always told what was right and what was not. There was no place for questioning. We had to believe our professors. The GSD was different. Of course, we also had to believe quite a few dogmas, but we were given reasons for believing in them. What I tell my students at the GSD now is that they should never accept anything they are told without question. The most important thing is to question everything and develop a position.

VB: About the time when you just started your practice you said, "When I returned home, I was quite rebellious and felt that architects at that time were lacking a sense of mission. I was enthusiastic to show myself succeeding in a fine project. I was highly self-conscious and refused to imitate architectural styles in Europe, the U.S., or Japan. I was thinking of creating China's original style." Could you talk about your mission in architecture?

ZK: Did I really say China's original style? I don't think I used the word style, which is something fixed. I would use the word character. In any case, there are many ways to talk about architecture, but my way is to do a project and show what can be done. What was good about our education at Tsinghua is that we were taught of the importance of doing something before talking about it. We had to prove whether we were right or wrong by doing, not by talking. [Laughs.] But it is true, I was very rebellious when I just returned. I had a lot of anger. I was angry about the superficiality of our culture of architecture. There was so much copying and imitating, while a whole layer of the original, historical architecture was being erased. I wanted to find something of my own. How to express my ideas? How to preserve what was being erased? Architecture is a struggle. I am struggling, but I think I am on the right path.

VB: You really think that you can establish yourself through many years of struggle? Don't

182 Namcha Barwa Visitor Centre, Linzhi County, Tibet, 2008
Photo by Chen Su © ZAO/standardarchitecture

you think that most architects find their way with their very first project and then go back to it again and again, perhaps developing and improving. But careers are made on the success of the first project. Disagree?

ZK: Sure, you define your direction right away. You choose your focus in the very beginning. But nothing is easy or predictable. And here in China, everything is changing so fast.

VB: Are you concerned with your architecture being recognized as regional?

ZK: Well, it is obvious. Such historians as Kenneth Frampton and Alexander Tzonis would say that critical regionalism is not a style, not an individual style. I believe in architecture as local practice. I believe in architecture that reflects its place.

VB: What you are saying is now a shared belief. But it was not so long ago when architecture had little to do with regionalism. Personal styles were celebrated, and architects were invited to bring their unique visions all around the world. I wonder what will happen to you when you start building abroad? Because based on your success in China, your international clients may expect you to build something similar to what you've done here.

183 Niang'ou Boat Terminal, Linzhi County, Tibet, 2013. Photo by Wang Ziling. © ZAO/standardarchitecture

ZK: There are ways to root architecture to its place. Our projects in Tibet are very different from the ones in Beijing. The objective is to find the root, but not be restricted by any form or style. This is where the critical part comes. I don't deny following regional approach. But I don't see myself fixed to any particular region. For us being regional means that we search for the roots of the place. But we are very open and would like to build outside of China. We are a very international practice; at one point we had people from 15 countries here. But before building somewhere else I would prefer to live there for a while.

VB: You are an idealist.

ZK: That is a good thing about architecture. When I travel to a new place, I never try to see the established landmarks. I need to discover the place first, feel its atmosphere, experience the culture, cuisine, people. If I like the place, I will visit it again to get to know it better. I like continuity in places and that is what I want to highlight in my projects. It is this continuity that is becoming the new avant-garde. Perhaps we had too many drastic revolutions in the 20th century. It is time to put back the pieces. And, of course, without nostalgia, without imitating the past.

Is it possible? I think by revisiting history we don't go back; we advance. Researchers find cures for diseases by revisiting old medical books and applying modern knowledge and techniques. Architects can use that as a metaphor. What happened in history does not stay in the past. We are in between, and we are continuously linked with the past to build the future. We can invent the future without forgetting history.

VB: This is what the current revolution is about.

ZK: Absolutely. And don't forget the development of the artificial intelligence. Our world is going to get more personalized, individualized, and ultimately, more humane and emotional. While the machine age was intimidating with its mass production, endless repetition, and coldness of the machine, the new revolution will free us even more. That's the future.

VB: Let's talk about the design process. Where do you derive your inspirations from?

ZK: Really, from places I visit and not so much from architecture itself. I particularly like the anonymous architecture built by people. Because architecture

242

184 Niyang River Visitor Centre, Linzhi County, Tibet, 2008. Photo by Chen Su. © ZAO/standardarchitecture

185 Niyang River Visitor Centre, Linzhi, Tibet, 2008. Photo by Chen Su © ZAO/standardarchitecture

designed by a particular architect tells you how to do things; it is too specific, too personal. But I like to learn from architecture that evolves slowly and shaped by many sources. I like to compare architecture to cooking. Food has been tested by many generations. That's where the cooks derive their inspirations, not from what a famous cook did last week in New York. [Laughs.] And then I get inspirations from literature, music, art. And then there are architects who I greatly admire–Herzog & de Meuron, Rafael Moneo, Peter Zumthor, and Rem Koolhaas–all of whom I came across at GSD. All of them have their strong readings of history, each very distinctive.

VB: It is interesting to examine how architecture in the 1990s and early 2000s seemed to detach itself from history and how such leading formalist architects as Rem Koolhaas came back to architecture's eternal debate with history. His Prada Foundation in Milan and Garage Museum in Moscow came directly out of his fascinating research on preservation that gave architects a new repertoire. Now you would think hard before demolishing something, even if historically insignificant. These repurposed buildings serve as conceptual anchors for new projects. We find beauty now in their solidity and generosity of space. We no longer strive for a strong contrast; we appreciate ambiguities between the old and the new.

ZK: That is exactly right, and a number of our own projects deal with buildings built less than 50 years ago. We need to recognize that history is continuous, and that recent history is also history. What do we consider as heritage? Anything that's avant-garde today may become heritage tomorrow. What's important is to keep raising questions and be critical. We should define our attitude toward what is already built. How do we relate to that with our own work? How do we stay contemporary? How do we stay relevant? How do we form our own identity?

VB: You said, "Architecture is about inventing stories that are inhabitable by people." What do you mean by inventing stories? Don't projects start with a client, a site, a program, and so on?

ZK: I think something was lost in translation. [Laughs.]

VB: It sounds good, "Architecture is about inventing stories that are inhabitable by people."

ZK: Well, it is a good distortion of what I actually said. In a way, architecture is like a novel, every project is. But unlike a novel architecture becomes real. Yes, you have to convince your client, respond to the program, and so on. But let's suppose all that is done. At some point in the future someone will be sitting at your space looking out the window, appreciating a garden or meditating about something. This is going to happen. This is what's exciting to me, not the budget. Of course, all pragmatics need to be addressed and resolved. But every project needs to go beyond that.

VB: Could you explain to me something about this idea behind initiating projects—you said, "We identify our own project, we design it and propose it to society. If it is really needed by society, I will not worry about financial sustainability."

ZK: Sure, some of our hutong projects, such as the Micro Hutong, were initiated by us. What we did was much more than what architects typically do. We raised the money, came up with the business plan, proposed the program, and even rented spaces to people who wanted to do business there. All of this in addition to the actual design. That's what I mean when I say that we initiate projects.

You know, many critics reduce "Reporting from the Front," the 2016 Venice Architecture Biennale by Alexandro Aravena, to raising this issue of problem-solving. But for me it was more about bringing to the architects' attention that it was important to take an active position, not a passive one, by simply waiting for clients to bring work. That's how I understood problem-solving. I have an attitude about finding problems and finding ways to initiate projects. We see problems before they are addressed to us by our clients. We now work more like contemporary artists. They see issues and they initiate projects that address these issues. That's what is so inspiring about artists, not necessarily the work itself, but about having an attitude. Architecture can easily turn into this stern, day-to-day business operation. We can easily forget what was it that first attracted us to architecture.

VB: You didn't.

ZK: I was drawn to architecture because of the creation process itself, working as an artist, responding to the city, culture, to our times. I also believe that architecture is a social project. At the same time, I don't think that architecture as a social project prevents it from being an art project. Just like an art project can also be a social project. But let me ask you a question. What do you think about our architectural identity here in China?

VB: Well, I would like to congratulate you—you have one. It is very strong, and it is easily identifiable. You can't confuse it with anything else. But it also worries me because it has become somewhat formulaic. So many Chinese architects have developed a very similar attitude toward what their architecture should be. Therefore, so many of these projects have become interchangeable. They are rather identifiable collectively.

ZK: This means that our identity is not quite formed yet. It is somewhat forced. I think when Wang Shu was awarded the Pritzker Prize in 2012, so many Chinese architects defined what was it that they needed to focus on—looking for its identity, not personal but collective one. He provided a certain direction. And this direction is quite particular and settled.

VB: There is definitely no variety in the work, not enough. But there is now an army of very good architects and projects, built by the Chinese architects all over the country. The

186 Micro-Yuan'er, Beijing, 2013 © ZAO/standardarchitecture

Chinese Pavilion at this year's Venice Biennale was a revelation for so many people. China is now producing its own architecture. While other countries discuss and speculate, China builds. And frankly, the work may lack variety and risk-taking, but it is much more relevant and compelling than projects brought here by starchitects whose buildings are utterly foreign and grossly out of place, for the most part.

ZK: Yet, the work of so many Chinese architects is becoming very trendy. We have become very playful with identifying what is local and how to articulate it.

VB: There is a strong concern for historical continuity. But what about generational continuity, building upon what was achieved in terms of theoretical inquiries and the idea of architecture as an autonomous project? Architects such as Peter Eisenman and some other intellectuals are brushed away; they have become irrelevant. Architecture is being dumbed down and pretty much about what is in front of us—buildings clad in stone, brick, wood, and so on. Material is just one aspect of architecture, but what is behind it?

ZK: I have to agree with you. The work of these architects is strong, but there is no intellectual rigor behind it.

VB: Rem Koolhaas once pointed out that an architect can't do architecture alone, there is always a team and as a leader you always have to take responsibilities for others. That's why he likes to write because then he is really responsible for what he personally believes in. But you said something interesting, "As an architect, no matter how much support you have, you always feel you are fighting by yourself." Could you elaborate on that?

ZK: First, I fully identify with my office. My office is very well aligned with my mission and sensibilities. When I talked about fighting by myself, meaning the entire office, I referred to our fight for what we believe in and not just serving the needs of a developer or clients in general. That's why we prefer to raise money and identify what could be the next project. But if you are working for a client, there is always resistance. Every client has a mission. As an architect, I have my own mission. The key is to find ways for our missions to overlap. This is a constant struggle; it is too easy to say to the client, "I will give you whatever you like, and I will make it beautiful." You don't need so many years of study for that. We want to do something that is yet unknown. But what we do know is that we reject things that we already know. [Laughs.] For us the process is very scientific, we don't know the result until we discover it.

VB: But wouldn't you agree that certain things in your work repeat? For example, this playful fragmentation into smaller objects and spaces. Your hutong projects, your office here, your art museum in Hangzhou, all share these features.

ZK: All of this is subconscious. This is how I compartmentalize inward-looking spaces, which is very Chinese. And I can assure you that this is a sign of time and I will not stick to it. I will progress to something else.

VB: You will give up something that has become associated with your name so easily?

ZK: I think, as soon as you become recognized by a certain formal language, it is less interesting. I think it is necessary to reinvent yourself constantly.

VB: You think you can continue reinventing yourself formally?

ZK: I want to keep trying. I refuse to acknowledge that something is settled or frozen. I feel something new is emerging and will transform my work. That is my standpoint.

VB: You just said that your mission is not simply about beautifying spaces. How do you see your mission?

ZK: Architecture has its own spiritual power. No one can deny it, no matter what the size is. It is possible to create architecture that is spiritually powerful, that

187 Micro Hutong, Beijing, 2013 © ZAO/standardarchitecture

transmits a very special energy. That's the essence of architecture. This is what will be communicated to many generations to come. The beauty of architecture is that it can touch so many people.

VB: What single words would you use to describe your architecture?

ZK: Spirituality. Will I get there? I strive to achieve subtle, emotional spaces that can have multiple readings.

247

Bibliography

Kenneth Frampton, *Modern Architecture: A Critical History* (Thames & Hudson, 5th edition, 2020)

Nancy Steinhardt, *Chinese Architecture: A History* (Princeton University Press, 2019)

Luis Fernández-Galiano, Editor, *AV Monografias 109/110: China Boom Growth Unlimited* (2004)

Luis Fernández-Galiano, Editor, *AV Monografias 150: Made in China* (2011)

Luis Fernández-Galiano, Editor, *AV Monografias 220: Vector Architects: Cosmopolitan Vernacular* (2019)

Pier Alessio Rizzardi and Hankun Zhang, *The Condition of Chinese Architecture* (TCA Think Tank, 2018)

Li Xiangning, *Contemporary Architecture in China: Towards A Critical Pragmatism* (Images Publishing, 2018)

Li Xiangning, Zhang Xiaochun, *Architecture China: Building a Future Countryside, 16th International Architecture Exhibition La Biennale di Venezia, Pavilion of China* (Images Publishing, Spring 2018)

Li Xiangning. Editor, *Architecture in China: Building for a New Culture* (Images Publishing, Fall 2018)

Ma Weidong, Guest Editor, *A+U: Architects in China, No.064* (A+U Publishing, 2016:06)

Zhi Wenjun, Xu Jie, *Contemporary Architecture in China: 2004-2008* (Tongji University Press, 2008)

Jiang Dai, Editor, *Wang Shu Architecture* (Tongji University Press, 2012)

Wang Shu, *Wang Shu: Imagining the House* (Lars Muller Publishers, 2012)

Felix Burrichter, Editor, *Pin-Up, Issue 26, Interview with Wang Shu and Lu Wenyu by Andrew Ayers,* pp.98-111, *Spring Summer* 2019

Philip Yuan, Vladimir Belogolovsky, *Collaborative Laboratory: Works of Archi-Union and Fab-Union* (Oscar Riera Ojeda Publishers, 2019)

Li Hu, Huang Wenjing, *Towards Openness* (Applied Research + Design, 2018)

Peng Lixiao, Editor, *Urban Environment Design: Atelier Deshaus, 104, 2016/12* (Northern United Publishing & Media Group Limited, 2016)

Peng Lixiao, Editor, *Urban Environment Design: Vector Architects 2008-2017* (Northern United Publishing & Media Group Limited, 2017)

V. Belogolovsky presenting his exhibition "I am Interested in Seeing the Future" curated by Lyu Ningjue March 2018, Fab-Union Space, Shanghai. Photo by Fangfang Tian

BIOGRAPHY
Vladimir Belogolovsky

Vladimir Belogolovsky (b. 1970, Odessa, Ukraine) is an American curator and critic. He graduated from the Cooper Union School of Architecture in 1996. After practicing architecture for 12 years, he founded his New York-based Curatorial Project, a nonprofit, which focuses on curating and designing architectural exhibitions that have appeared the world over and accompanied by his lectures and catalogs. He writes for *Arquitectura Viva* (Madrid) and *SPEECH* (Berlin) and is a columnist on *STIR* and *ArchDaily*. He has interviewed over 400 leading international architects as an ongoing project on issues surrounding individual identities in architecture and has written fifteen books, including *Imagine Buildings Floating Like Clouds!* (Images Publishing, 2022); *Iconic New York* (DOM, 2019); *Conversations with Peter Eisenman* (DOM, 2016); *Conversations with Architects* (DOM, 2015); *Harry Seidler: Lifework* (Rizzoli, 2014); and

Soviet Modernism: 1955-1985 (TATLIN, 2010). Belogolovsky has curated over 50 international exhibitions. Among them *Architects' Voices Series* (World Tour since 2016), world tours on the work of Emilio Ambasz, Harry Seidler, and American tour on Colombian architecture. In 2008, he produced *Chess Game* exhibition for the Russian Pavilion at the 11th Venice Architecture Biennale. He is an honorary professor and corresponding member of the International Academy of Architecture in Moscow (IAAM), and IAAM's official emissary in the United States. The curator has lectured at universities and museums in more than 30 countries. In 2018, at the invitation of Li Xiaodong, Belogolovsky spent the fall semester teaching at Tsinghua University in Beijing as a visiting scholar. His book *China Dialogues* is the result of that four-month-long experience.

"In *China Dialogues* Vladimir Belogolovsky charts a panorama of Chinese architecture through the words of its main players. He draws his 'landscape with figures' with excellent prose, deep understanding, and outspoken wit. The curator makes conversation with a dash of contact sport into an art form, showing once more that interviews are as intelligent as the interviewer."

Luis Fernández-Galiano, Editor-in-chief, *Arquitectura Viva*, Madrid

"Vladimir Belogolovsky's book gathers an inquisitive collection of thoughts from outstanding architects in contemporary China; it is a critical documentation of the author's in-depth conversations about the past, the future, and the current moment of Chinese architecture."

Cui Kai, Honorary President, Chief Architect of China Architecture Design & Research Group (CADG), Beijing

"With refreshing query, engaging themes, and deep insights, Vladimir Belogolovsky's dialogues with China's cutting-edge architects investigate and illustrate a vivid scene of contemporary Chinese architecture."

Li Xiangning, Dean and Professor, Tongji University

"Until the turn of the century, China was generally seen as a country of an ideologically oriented eclectic architecture. However, during the past two decades numerous talented young architects have emerged, projecting new imagery and meanings to today's architecture in general, which is increasingly declining into a shallow commercial aestheticization. Vladimir Belogolovsky shares his deep personal knowledge of current Chinese architecture and the leading individual designers, as well as their thinking and intentions."

Juhani Pallasmaa, Professor Emeritus, Aalto University, Helsinki

"Vladimir Belogolovsky is an important voice in a global architectural realm. His book *China Dialogues* is a pivotal introduction to current architecture in China that did not exist before to such an extent. Well-traveled, the author shares his deep personal knowledge of current Chinese architects' thinking and intentions. Through his judicious editorial choices, this scholarly work synthesizes diverse directions through contrasting examples of very strong authentic and beautiful architecture that explores the deepest strata of China's culture, which is so dear to my heart. The book is full of wonderfully unexpected discoveries of projects with vernacular evocations of unique places. Belogolovsky's dialogues should be the primary text for westerners to understand the ethos of Chinese architecture."

Antoine Predock, Architect and Professor, Albuquerque, New Mexico, Winner of the 2006 AIA Gold Medal